National Park, City Playground

National Park,

City Playground

Mount Rainier in the Twentieth Century

THEODORE CATTON

A Samuel and Althea Stroum Book

UNIVERSITY OF WASHINGTON PRESS

Seattle and London

*This book is published with the assistance of a grant
from the Stroum Book Fund, established through the
generosity of Samuel and Althea Stroum.*

Copyright © 2006 University of Washington Press
Printed in United States of America
Designed by Pamela Canell
12 11 10 09 08 07 06   5 4 3 2 1

University of Washington Press
PO Box 50096, Seattle, WA ,98145
www.washington.edu/uwpress

Library of Congress Cataloging-in-Publication Data
Catton, Theodore.
National park, city playground : Mount Rainier
in the twentieth century / Theodore Catton.
p. cm.
"A Samuel and Althea Stroum book."
Includes bibliographical references and index.
ISBN 0-295-98643-3 / ISBN 13:978-0-295-98643-2
(pbk. : alk. paper)
1. Mount Rainier National Park (Wash.)—History—20th
century.   2. Seattle (Wash.)—History—20th century.
3. Tacoma (Wash.)—History—20th century.   I. Title.
F897.R2C37 2006   979.7′782—dc22   2006016148

This book is printed on New Leaf Ecobook 50,
which is 100 percent recycled, containing 50 percent
post-consumer waste, and is processed chlorine free.
Ecobook 50 is acid free and meets the minimum
requirements of ANSI/NISO Z39-49—1992 (R 1997)
(Permanence of Paper). ♾♾

Contents

Acknowledgments

THIS BOOK IS DEDICATED TO MY PARENTS, BILL AND
Nancy Catton, whose love of Mount Rainier National Park infused my
early childhood in Seattle in the 1960s. They taught my brothers and
me the meaning of "Wonderland" on three full circuits of the Wonderland Trail in 1963, 1967, and 1978. And like so many Seattleites, they
took visiting family and friends to the park innumerable times to drive
park roads, camp in campgrounds, visit museums, and play on lingering summer snowfields at Paradise.

In 1993, while completing my graduate studies at the University of
Washington, I received a two-year assignment by the National Park Service, Pacific Northwest Regional Office, to prepare an administrative
history of Mount Rainier National Park. Most of the primary research
for this book was conducted for that effort, which culminated in a
723–page report published in 1996. Stephanie Toothman, chief of the
Cultural Resources Program, and Gretchen Luxenberg, regional historian, both encouraged me to think beyond the administrative history
to an eventual book that would commemorate the park's centennial in
1999. Seven years past deadline, Stephanie and Gretchen, here it is. In
addition to all the guidance and review of drafts on the history that I
received from Stephanie and Gretchen, I also enjoyed the support of

others in the Cultural Resources Program: Jim Thompson, Kent Bush, Fred York, Cathy Gilbert, Laurin Huffman, and especially my erstwhile office mate and fellow traveler in national park history, David Louter.

Several people on the staff at Mount Rainier National Park generously gave me their time in interviews, phone calls, and chapter reviews from 1993 to 1995. Among them are Gary Ahlstrand, Glenn Baker, William J. Briggle, Gene Casey, Bill Dengler, Robert Dunnagan, Steve Gibbons, Robert Hentges, Rick Kirshner, John Krambrink, Loren Lane, Donna Rahier, Regina Rochefort, Gerry Tays, Dave Uberuaga, Eric Walkinshaw, John Wilcox, and Larry Zelanak. I am also indebted to park archivist Deborah Osterberg, former park superintendents Neal Guse Jr. and John Rutter, and the late park naturalist Floyd W. Schmoe.

Others who gave me insights and shared their own research on Mount Rainier and National Park Service history are Darryll Johnson of the Cooperative Park Studies Unit at the University of Washington; Steve Mark, historian at Crater Lake National Park, Oregon; Frank Norris, historian at the Alaska Regional Office, Anchorage; Robert Bunting, professor of history at Fort Lewis College; Jim Muhn, historian with Morgan, Angel & Associates; and Paul Sadin, former seasonal ranger at Mount Rainier now with Historical Research Associates.

I owe thanks to John Findlay, editor of *Pacific Northwest Quarterly*, and various reviewers for PNQ who provided valuable feedback on portions of the administrative history that I reworked and submitted to that journal. The chapter on the creation of Mount Rainier National Park is a somewhat shortened version of my article of the same title in *PNQ*.

The staff at University of Washington Press was encouraging, patient, and helpful. Michael Ducksworth provided direction when I first began revising the administrative history into a monograph, and Julidta Tarver offered advice and encouragement throughout the long process. Reviewers Ruth Kirk and David Louter gave me valuable comments. Mary Ribesky saw the manuscript through all the stages of production, and Stacey Lynn did a fine job as copy editor.

I benefited from the support of my former colleagues at Historical Research Associates. Ann Emmons and Carla Homstad read and commented on portions of the manuscript. Lisa Mighetto shared her ideas with me about Mount Rainier's place in the identity of the Pacific Northwest.

I am indebted to my partner, Diane Krahe, and my sons, Wally, Ben, and Eli, for their indulgence during the many hours I was away at the computer or the library. My sons accompanied me to Rainier numerous times over the years, so they understand the fascination. Diane, who shares my interest in wilderness history and has her own research project involving Mount Adams, understands too. It was on a hike in our nearby Rattlesnake wilderness area that Diane supplied me with the book's title. She went over every page of the manuscript with a sharp eye and a gentle pen.

While I worked intermittently on my Mount Rainier manuscript, Mom wrote and published her own book on Mount Rainier, *Ups and Downs Around Rainier*, a fictionalized account of our family's Wonderland Trail adventures. That book further inspired this one. Mom also helped me with photo research at the Washington State Historical Society, while Dad sent me a steady trickle of Mount Rainier articles from the *Tacoma News Tribune*. Their interest in this project has surpassed anything I might have imagined when I started on it a decade ago. I am proud and grateful that they have enjoyed Mount Rainier National Park for some fifty-five years and continue to hike its many trails.

National Park, City Playground

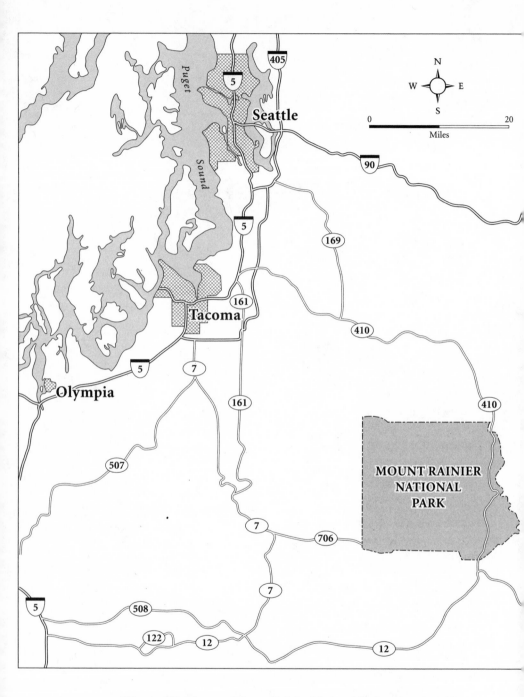

MAP I. Western Washington: Mount Rainier National Park and major cities

CHAPTER I

A Tale of Two Cities

SINCE THE BIRTH OF THE NATIONAL PARK IDEA CITY
dwellers have been the most numerous and enthusiastic supporters of
national parks. In a few instances, certain American cities have formed
strong bonds with nearby national parks: San Francisco with Yosemite,
Denver with Rocky Mountain, Miami with Everglades National Park.
But none of these examples compares to the historic relationship that
the cities of Seattle and Tacoma have had with Mount Rainier. For
the million people who live in the Seattle-Tacoma megalopolis, "The
Mountain" is a very part of their cityscape. Floating on the skyline, it is
an enticing reminder that the national park beckons at the end of their
workweek.

Throughout the twentieth century, the people of Seattle and Tacoma
went to the park in droves, forging a pattern of visitor use that was local,
loyal, and concentrated on summer weekends. Moreover, these Seattle-
and Tacoma-based park users organized themselves. They formed mountain clubs, automobile clubs, good roads associations, national park hotel
companies, transportation companies, camping and recreational equipment cooperatives, downhill ski associations, and mountain guide services. Each organization brought its own agenda to park management.
Insofar as the history of this national park has wider significance for our

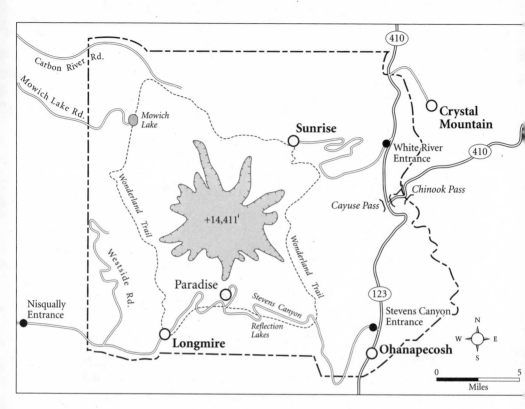

Carbon River Rd.

Mowich Lake Rd.

Mowich
Lake

Wonderland Trail

Westside Rd.

+14,411'

Sunrise

Crystal
Mountain

White River
Entrance

410

Chinook Pass

Cayuse Pass

Wonderland Trail

Paradise

Stevens Canyon

Reflection
Lakes

123

Stevens Canyon
Entrance

N

W   E

S

Nisqually
Entrance

Longmire

Ohanapecosh

0   5
Miles

MAP 2. Mount Rainier National Park with glacier system in center

understanding of the whole national park system, it lies in the changing activities and demands of those city dwellers who have been the park's
principal users. This book tells the story of how the park was established
and administered from 1899 to the present. The book's thesis is that the
development of Mount Rainier National Park has revolved around competing forms of use by the people of Seattle and Tacoma. Park *use*, in
this sense, embraces both recreation and exploitation. It includes the
packaging, sale, and consumption of nature as an aesthetic experience.

Nature appreciation has a long history in the Puget Sound region
that predates both the establishment of Mount Rainier National Park
and the founding of these neighboring cities. When the British explorer
Captain George Vancouver sailed into Puget Sound waters aboard
H.M.S. Discovery in 1792, he beheld a land of "rugged mountains . . .
grand, picturesque" and "innumerable pleasing landscapes." With a

A TALE OF TWO CITIES

navigator's eye for landmarks, he identified and named two of the Pacific Northwest's volcanoes (Mount Rainier and Mount Baker) and barely sighted a third from the masthead (Mount St. Helens). Primarily interested in the possibilities of the region for trade and settlement, Vancouver concentrated in the pages of his journal on descriptions of native inhabitants, climate, soil, and vegetation, noting that the task of scenic description must await "the pen of a skilful panegyrist." Yet Vancouver allowed himself one prescient comment on the region's natural beauty. The land required "only to be enriched by the industry of man with villages, mansions, cottages, and other buildings, to render it the most lovely country that can be imagined," he wrote, "whilst the labour of the inhabitants would be amply rewarded, in the bounties which nature seems ready to bestow on cultivation."[1]

Vancouver was expressing the eighteenth-century ideal of a pastoral middle landscape, a place where civilization shaded into the wild, creating a harmonious whole. In Vancouver's Age of Enlightenment, many philosophers, poets, and landscape painters were giving expression to this pastoral ideal. Their object was to find a proper balance in the world between reason and instinct, art and nature, the city and the country. Indeed, it was fashionable in Vancouver's time to measure the quality of landscapes according to the pastoral ideal. The British explorer brought these ideas with him to the Puget Sound country, or more precisely, he brought his impressions of the Puget Sound country back to Europe. The wilderness around Puget Sound, Vancouver suggested, needed only a dash of cultivation to make it "as enchantingly beautiful as the most elegantly finished pleasure grounds in Europe."[2] In the next century Americans would use that distinctive phrase—pleasuring grounds—to describe their national parks.

What the first settlers of the Puget Sound region thought about Mount Rainier, the Cascade Range, and the Olympic Mountains is something of an enigma. Vancouver looked into the future from his vantage point in 1792 and assumed that European settlement would not only garnish the landscape, but that the settlers themselves would find happiness in the natural beauty of their surroundings. Historians, for their part, have taken a different view of scenic appreciation on the American frontier. They have assumed that settlers were usually among the last people to appreciate scenery. Settlers were too busy felling trees, building homes, breaking sod, and diverting streams to admire the landscape for its aesthetics. The "frontier mind" had a natural disliking for wilderness because it posed real physical dangers and hardships. Insofar as frontiersmen boasted about the local scenic attractions, they were huckstering scenery to attract eastern tourists.[3] In the case of the American settlers who arrived on the shores of Puget Sound in the mid-nineteenth century, it is impossible to say with certainty who was closer to the mark, Vancouver or the historians. If the settlers found psychic value in owning that distant mountain backdrop for their daily toils, they seldom recorded the fact.

The coming of the railroads probably did more than anything to enliven local interest and awaken civic pride in Mount Rainier. In the first place, the transcontinental railroads spurred an intense competition between Seattle and Tacoma as each city sought to become a railroad terminal. Further, the coming of the railroads began a period of economic boom in Washington's history. Beginning with the completion of the Northern Pacific Railroad from the Midwest to Tacoma in 1883, the period was punctuated by the completion of three more transcontinental lines over the next two and a half decades. A branch of the Union Pacific Railroad known as the Oregon Short Line was built to Portland in the mid-1880s. The Great Northern Railroad, terminating in Everett, drove its golden spike at Stevens Pass in 1893. Finally, the Chicago, Milwaukee, and St. Paul (known as the Milwaukee Road) completed the nation's only electrified line from the Midwest to Seattle in 1909.[4] Later these four transcontinental railroad companies—Northern Pacific, Union Pacific, Great Northern, and Milwaukee Road—would figure prominently as potential financiers in the development of Mount Rainier National Park. In the meantime, the railroads created a level of prosperity and leisure in the Puget Sound region that opened many more people's minds to the possibility of experiencing a trip to Mount Rainier.

During the railroad era, residents of the Puget Sound region's two leading cities, Seattle and Tacoma, demonstrated that they were taking pleasure in the natural beauty around them. By the 1880s, many years before the establishment of Mount Rainier National Park, citizens of Seattle and Tacoma laid claim to the mountain as a symbol of the good life in the Pacific Northwest. The beauty of the region's inlets, forests, lakes, and mountains was a source of civic pride, and the image of Mount Rainier floating on the horizon beyond Seattle's Lake Washington or Tacoma's Commencement Bay became the most common symbol of that pride. The best evidence for this may be found in the booster literature of the period.

Boosters were the advertising professionals of their day; they were sensitive to public tastes and attitudes. Booster literature touted the region's scenery not only to lure tourists, but more important, to attract immigrants and capital to the cities. The boosters, of whom there was no shortage in Seattle and Tacoma in the late nineteenth century, were probably making an accurate assessment of contemporary cultural values when they perceived the region's scenery to be a strong selling point.

In describing Mount Rainier, boosters generally implied that the mountain had a tonic effect on the cities' residents even as they viewed it from Seattle or Tacoma. One offering by the Seattle Chamber of Commerce described the city's "magnificent" setting among mountain ranges, all of which were "dwarfed by the stupendous Mt. Rainier." Another pamphlet claimed that the scenery was "truly grand" and contributed "to the pleasure of living in this favored region." Yet another described the eminence of Mount Rainier on the city's skyline: "monarch of American mountains, eternally crowned with snow and ice, radiant in kingly robes of ermine." A souvenir edition of the *Seattle Daily Times* asserted that Puget Sound possessed greater scenic attractions than any place in the country. To drive home the connection between the Puget Sound cities and the mountain scenery, the booster literature frequently used an image of Mount Rainier for a frontispiece.[5]

Seattle's appropriation of the mountain's image reached a climax with the Alaska-Yukon-Pacific Exposition of 1909. The city's boosters intended to demonstrate that Seattle had emerged as one of the great cities of the nation, and the AYP fair featured exhibitions on Alaska and the Orient, underscoring Seattle's importance as a port city. Seattle invested $10 million on the buildings and grounds near Lake Washington, on what would become the University of Washington campus, and advertisements projected an image of a sophisticated "Ivory City" in a land of Eden. As one picture book proclaimed:

On every hand stretch green lawns, shaded walks and glowing flower beds. In every nook and corner the cactus dahlias, rhododendrons and flowering shrubs of the big woods of Washington are massed in profusion. Down Rainier Vista, across the sparkling blue waters of Lake Washington, majestic Mt. Rainier raises her massive head among the clouds, and over all, the blue sky and balmy air of summer on the Puget Sound make of the Alaska-Yukon-Pacific Exposition a veritable fairyland.[6]

Rainier Vista formed the main axis of the fairgrounds, so that the view of Mount Rainier was framed by beautiful buildings down both sides of the promenade and the play of Geyser Fountain in the center foreground. This was the scene around which the whole complex was oriented.

While the 1890s and early 1900s marked the heyday of Seattle's identification with Mount Rainier, Tacomans had been trying to lay claim to the mountain's symbolism for much longer. Indeed, their city took the name Tacoma from the Indian word for "snow peak," which it was said the Indians applied specifically to Mount Rainier. Much of the boosters' efforts to identify their city with Mount Rainier focused on getting the name of the mountain officially changed to Mount Tacoma. Proponents of the name change complained that the mountain's namesake, Peter Rainier, a rear admiral in the British navy at the time of Vancouver's voyage, had no association with the Pacific Northwest. The effort to change the mountain's name dated from as early as 1873, though it reached fever pitch on three subsequent occasions: in 1890 and 1917, when it was twice brought before the United States Geographic Board, and in 1925, when it briefly claimed the attention of Congress. The desire of Tacomans to capitalize on this name association was, of course, the real basis for the feud over the mountain's name, even though the debate focused mainly on the authenticity of the Indian name "Tacoma" and the allegedly unpatriotic and prosaic flavor of the official name "Rainier."[7]

According to testimony before the United States Geographic Board in 1917, the city's founder, one Morton M. McCarver, had decided to change the name of his new town site from Commencement City to Tacoma after the Indian name "Tahoma" for Mount Rainier. McCarver, it was said, had acted on the advice of a visitor who had just read Theodore

Winthrop's *Canoe and Saddle* and was impressed by the references to "Tahoma." McCarver's whole object in founding Tacoma was to select a town site that the Northern Pacific Railroad would choose as its western terminus, and naming his town for the region's most prominent landmark was shrewd. When the Northern Pacific did choose Tacoma, it too saw the advantage of linking the mountain to the city by name association. In 1883, the company announced in its *Northwest Magazine* that the Indian name "Tacoma" would be used in all subsequent publications of the Northern Pacific Railroad. Ironically, the railroad's decision probably did more than anything else to perpetuate the use of "Mount Tacoma" even while it gave opponents their strongest evidence that the name change was a promotional scheme.[8]

The controversy over the mountain's name and the use of the mountain's image as a kind of icon revealed how the two Puget Sound cities were each trying to claim a proprietary interest in Mount Rainier. The two cities were in keen competition not only to become the most visible city in the Pacific Northwest, but also to gain the best railroad connections, capture the most hinterland, and even secure the best access roads to Mount Rainier. Rainier historian Arthur D. Martinson has written that "in hindsight, it seems strange, perhaps silly, that Seattle and Tacoma spent an inordinate amount of time trying to prove which one owned Mount Rainier. By the same token, beneath all the flimflam carried out in the newspapers and other publications, the controversy showed some enduring western characteristics: local pride, developmental patterns and, above all, love of landscape."[9] That the name of the mountain could stir such strong partisan feeling for so many years was proof of the boosters' claims that residents of Seattle and Tacoma genuinely cherished their mountain scenery.

The cities' boosters were right about the local inhabitants in another respect. Residents of Seattle and Tacoma came to view a trip to the mountain as the supreme physical challenge in the region. As late as the 1880s, a trip to the mountain was still almost an expeditionary event, but in the last decade of the nineteenth century it evolved fairly rapidly into a popular mountain-club activity.

Early climbing expeditions fostered local interest in the mountain and even contributed to the national park movement. Many of the pioneer climbers played important roles in the campaign to establish a national park. Among the first four men to reach the summit—Hazard Stevens and Philemon B. Van Trump in August 1870, and Samuel F. Emmons and A. D. Wilson in October 1870—two of them, Van Trump and Emmons, actively supported the national park campaign in the 1890s. Other pioneer climbers who worked on behalf of Mount Rainier's preservation included George B. Bayley, who reached the summit with Van Trump and James Longmire in 1883; John Muir and Edward S. Ingraham, who climbed the mountain in 1888; Ernest C. Smith, Fay Fuller, and Eliza R. Scidmore, who publicized their climbs in the early 1890s with writings, lectures, and lantern slide presentations; and Israel C. Russell and Bailey Willis, members of a geological party, who in 1896 were the first to scale one side of the mountain and descend another.[10]

Mount Rainier climbers formed the Washington Alpine Club in 1891, and its long-lived offspring, The Mountaineers, a few years later. Seattle and Tacoma newspapers followed the climbers' exploits with avid interest. The return of a mountain climbing party was cause for much excitement, as when Ingraham's party of thirteen men and women paraded down the street in Tacoma in 1894, attired in alpine clothing and with alpenstocks in hand, looking "like a band of warriors."[11] According to a newspaper account, the Ingraham party drew a crowd of one hundred or more onlookers and, obviously courting the attention, shouted in unison to the crowd:

> We are here!
> We are here!
> Right from the top
> Of Mount Rainier!

Such antics seem odd a hundred years later, but they were indicative of the unique culture of mountain appreciation forming in the Puget Sound cities. The local mountaineers would play a substantial role in the national park's founding. Some of the individuals in the Ingraham party, for example, shortly engaged in a vigorous debate in the *Tacoma Ledger* over the source and extent of vandalism in the alpine meadows on Mount

Rainier's southern flank and what ought to be done about it. These city dwellers took a proprietary interest in preserving the wilderness quality of Mount Rainier. One idea that continually emerged from such discussions was the need for a police authority at that remote location, something that could be accomplished only by making a national park.

Had the call for a national park come exclusively from this small circle of mountaineers and campers, it would not have gotten far. Others saw commercial possibilities in a national park that was accessed through Seattle or Tacoma. These supporters wanted to promote tourism at Mount Rainier to bring money and renown to their gateway cities. What was needed was a good road to the mountain, and by making a national park, they expected to secure federal support for such a road construction effort. One of the first individuals to promote this idea was local pioneer and guide James Longmire.

Seeing the future in tourism, Longmire found an attractive site by a mineral springs on the southwest side of the mountain on which to develop a resort. In 1884, with the help of some Indian laborers, Longmire cleared a wagon road from Succotash Valley (present-day Ashford, southwest of the mountain and outside of the park) thirteen miles to the springs (present-day Longmire, in the park), where he built a rough cabin. In 1887, he filed a mineral claim of twenty acres, and the following year his son Elcaine built a second cabin outside the mineral claim. By 1889, the Longmire family had constructed two bathhouses and some guest cabins and were advertising their health spa in Tacoma newspapers, and by next season they were operating a rustic two-story hotel.[12]

The entrepreneurial Longmire looked to the cities not only for business but for help in developing Mount Rainier's tourist potential. In 1891, he addressed a joint meeting of the Washington Alpine Club and the Tacoma Academy of Science, proposing the construction of a road from Kernahan's ranch (present-day Ashford) to a meadow named Paradise (at timberline on the south side of the mountain) "so that a buggy might get up there." Tacomans were interested. As one member of the Tacoma Chamber of Commerce remarked to the Board of County Commissioners, "We want to be known the world over as a park city . . . why should we not profit by this—one of our great natural resources?"[13] Although Tacoma businessmen declined to invest in the road, they nevertheless shared Longmire's ideas about the commercial possibilities of nature appreciation.

Tacoma engineer Fred G. Plummer also looked to the city of Tacoma for leadership in getting a road constructed, although he expected the local governments to leverage funds from the state and federal governments. In 1892, Plummer told city leaders that a "good road suitable for carriages" could be built to Paradise for $15,000. Moreover, if the state and federal governments each contributed about $30,000 annually for road development, "a stream of tourist travel could be directed to the mountain inside of three months after work had been begun." Justification for the state and federal funds would be found, of course, in making Mount Rainier a national park.[14]

After Congress passed the Forest Reserve Act of March 3, 1891, national park advocates sought to get a forest reserve established around the base of Mount Rainier. A forest reserve did not have the force of a national park—it could be created or abolished by the will of the president rather than by an act of Congress—yet it could be similar in purpose. A forest reserve was not, as was later often assumed, intended merely for the protection of timber and watersheds. President Benjamin Harrison invoked the Forest Reserve Act to protect forest lands adjoining Yellowstone National Park. Secretary of the Interior John Noble advised the president that reserves could embrace areas of "great interest to our people because of their natural beauty, or remarkable features," and he held further that reserves would protect wildlife and fish "and become resorts for the people seeking instruction and recreation."[15]

In the Seattle office of the U.S. General Land Office, Special Agent Cyrus A. Mosier received instructions to investigate the timber lands surrounding Mount Rainier, canvass the citizens of the region on their attitude toward proclamation of a forest reserve, and report his findings to Washington, D.C. In the course of several trips on horseback to the mountain, Mosier grew ardent about the proposed forest reserve. He bought a "photographic outfit" at his own expense and compiled more than two hundred photographs. His reports to the commissioner of the General Land Office brimmed with flowery description, and in them he framed his own impassioned arguments about what the forest reserve would achieve—and prevent.

> To strip the base of this mountain of the timber, to denude it, to allow the fires to run over the surface and through the undergrowth as will surely "happen" if these lands are entered upon for the timber, will be to tear the frame from this grand painting against the sky and to commit a greater act of vandalism than has ever been committed upon the works of nature on this continent. To preserve this piece of nature unsullied, to keep this forest with its rocks and rills, its shrubs and plants and mosses as they are, making it the home of plants and animals peculiar to the cascades on the western slope in connection with the great mountain peak the flora of whose sides represents the trees and plants of nearly all zones and climes, is to provide a *great public park*, soon to be easily accessible to not only the people who have made their homes permanently upon the sound, but to the people of the whole country.[16]

Mosier proposed the forest reserve to civic organizations in Seattle, Tacoma, Kirkland, Yakima, and other communities in the region. The Seattle Chamber of Commerce attested that the reserve "would meet with the hearty approval of the majority of the people of this State." The Tacoma Commercial Club averred that their city was "particularly interested, being the nearest city to the mountain and the only point from which the mountain is accessible." However, it protested against the use of "Rainier" in the official designation, suggesting "Paradise Park" or "Northwest Park" or "Cascade Park" instead. Secretary of the Interior Noble offered the neutral appellation "Pacific Forest Reserve."[17] President Harrison proclaimed the Pacific Forest Reserve on March 3, 1893. Proponents of a national park hailed this proclamation as an important first step toward their ultimate goal.[18]

By the early 1890s, the people of Seattle and Tacoma had formed a consensus about the desirability of making a national park around Mount Rainier. While the two cities would continue to compete for the most direct access roads to the mountain, they generally worked together for the national park designation. This consensus was built on two interest groups: the mountaineers who wanted to protect and enhance their

Mount Rainier experiences, and the businessmen who wanted to profit from tourism. In this consensus view, the national park designation would bring federal administration, and the federal role would entail two desirable and reinforcing elements: protection of resources and improved public access. It remained for these park proponents to take their message to Congress and across the nation, to find their footing in a national park campaign.[19]

CHAPTER 2

The Campaign to Establish Mount Rainier
National Park

THE CAMPAIGN TO ESTABLISH A NATIONAL PARK AROUND
Mount Rainier was a collaborative effort by Seattle and Tacoma groups
and a handful of national organizations. No single figure stands out as
its leader, nor did any single organization coordinate it. More than a
dozen scientists, many of whom had climbed the mountain, formed one
component of the campaign. They were scattered across the nation, knew
one another professionally, and used the opportunity of professional
meetings to form committees and prepare memorials to Congress setting forth arguments for the national park. Meanwhile, a few dozen
mountaineers, most of whom resided in the Puget Sound area, constituted another component. Their infectious enthusiasm for the mountain, which they communicated in public talks and letters to local
newspapers, helped to persuade Washington's congressional delegation
that the national park was a popular cause. Three young mountaineering organizations, the Sierra Club, the Appalachian Mountain Club, and
the Washington Alpine Club, added their support. Finally, the Northern Pacific Railway had an important and surreptitious effect on park
legislation in the late 1890s.

Bailey Willis, a geologist and mining engineer with the U.S. Geological Survey (USGS), may be credited with initiating the national cam-

paign in 1893. More than a decade earlier, in 1880, Willis had prospected for coal deposits for the Northern Pacific Railway near the northwest flank of Mount Rainier. He had cut a trail from the dense cedar forest on the upper Carbon River up to the gorgeous flower meadows known today as Spray Park, above which looms Rainier's immense, cavitated north face, now known as Willis Wall in his memory. He returned to the mountain whenever the opportunity presented itself. In 1893, at the annual meeting of the Geological Society of America, Willis proposed to his fellow geologists that they initiate an effort to have the area preserved in a national park. The society formed a committee and appointed Willis chairman.[1]

The campaign quickly gained support from many quarters. At a summer meeting, the American Association for the Advancement of Science (AAAS) formed a similar committee. Two months later, the National Geographic Society, meeting in Washington, D.C., appointed a committee on the Mount Rainier National Park proposal, and over the winter of 1893–94 both the Sierra Club and the Appalachian Mountain Club, meeting in San Francisco and Boston respectively, formed similar committees. These five committees combined their efforts in preparing a detailed memorial to Congress setting forth arguments for the national park.[2]

A striking feature of this movement was the strong showing of scientists, particularly geologists. The Geological Society of America committee consisted of three esteemed USGS geologists: Samuel F. Emmons, Bailey Willis, and Dr. David T. Day. Emmons, a protégé of the first director of the Geological Survey, Clarence King, had climbed Rainier in 1870 at the conclusion of the USGS Geological Exploration of the Fortieth Parallel and had written a report on the volcanoes of the Pacific Coast. Willis knew the northwest side of Mount Rainier as well as any man, and he would soon make the first reconnaissance of Mount Rainier's glacier system with Israel C. Russell and George Otis Smith in 1896. The American Association for the Advancement of Science, meanwhile, included two geologists on its committee: Russell, who had recently left the USGS to take a professorship at the University of Michigan, and Major John Wesley Powell, the Geological Survey's current director. USGS support of the national park proposal was crucial, for it gave credibility to the argument that the area around Mount Rainier contained no significant mineral wealth. Other scientists on the AAAS committee included Professor Joseph LeConte, a botanist; Bernhard E. Fernow, chief of the Forestry Bureau; and Clinton Hart Merriam, chief of the Biological Survey. The list of park advocates was a virtual roll call of the politically powerful scientists of the day.

Mountain clubs were a second locus of support. Men and women who had been to the top of Mount Rainier enjoyed great stature in the park movement and provided much of its drive. The two committees that the Sierra Club and the Appalachian Mountain Club contributed to the campaign included four individuals who had climbed Mount Rainier. Philemon B. Van Trump of the Sierra Club had accompanied Hazard Stevens on the first successful ascent of Mount Rainier in 1870. George B. Bayley, another Sierra Club member, had climbed the mountain with Van Trump and James Longmire in 1883. John Muir, founder of the Sierra Club and chairman of the committee on Mount Rainier, had made the ascent with Edward S. Ingraham of Seattle in 1888. The Appalachian Mountain Club committee included Ernest C. Smith, a clergyman from Tacoma who had climbed the mountain with Ingraham in 1888 and two years later had led the party that included Fay Fuller, the first woman to make the ascent. All of these people campaigned for the park by writing articles and giving lectures. Their involvement underscores how much the Mount Rainier National Park idea was rooted in the physical and aesthetic experience of climbing the mountain. The late historian Aubrey L. Haines made this point convincingly in *Mountain Fever: Historic Conquests of Rainier.*

The scientists and mountaineers found support from various local entities: chambers of commerce, university faculties, newspaper editors. Statements of support for the park were idealistic and public spirited, showing no trace of concern that the various values advanced by the park might later conflict with one another. According to proponents, Mount Rainier National Park would serve inspirational, educational, and recreational purposes. It would be of value to science. It would preserve the environmental quality of several large watersheds. It would stimulate tourism. Campaigners argued all of these points in combination. Even at its genesis, Mount Rainier National Park represented different things to different people. There was no preeminent value at the core of the national park idea.

For this campaign, as for other national park campaigns, the rhetoric of preservation suggested otherwise. Preservationists traditionally held that a national park was the "highest use" to which land could be put, in contrast to the "wise use" of multiple resources (or "multiple use," as it later came to be known). These were terms of art that reflected the preservationists' aesthetic appreciation of the sublime in nature, on the one hand, and the conservationists' economic interest in making efficient use of scarce resources on the other. The rhetoric of preservation tended to imply, however misleadingly, that the national park idea had an irreducible core, that preservationists had a common purpose.

Some national park historians have followed this lead. Joseph L. Sax, in his stimulating book *Mountains without Handrails: Reflections on the National Parks* (1980) suggests that the genesis of the national park idea can be found in the nineteenth-century writings of Frederick Law Olmsted. Sax interprets Olmsted's notion of the inspirational quality of scenic landscapes to mean that the central purpose of national parks is to promote "contemplative recreation." For Sax, the idea that contemplative recreation improves the self is the credo of all preservationists. This shared belief is their defining characteristic.[3] Alfred Runte, meanwhile, argues in *National Parks: The American Experience* that the kernel of the national park idea can be found in the American people's "cultural anxiety" in the nineteenth century: the sense of impoverishment they felt when they compared American cultural attainments with European architectural monuments and works of art. This anxiety gave rise to "scenic nationalism" and an effort to showcase the nation's natural wonders in national parks. The parks provided an alternative expression of cultural richness.[4] The problem with both of these interpretations is that they misrepresent preservationists as a homogeneous group with a unified philosophy. The Mount Rainier National Park campaign was rather a heterogeneous group of scientists and mountaineers, national figures and local interests, all with somewhat different ideas about what the park should be. This is an important distinction, because the differences embedded in the park campaign would subsequently widen into disagreements over park administration. The development of Mount

Rainier National Park in the twentieth century would be shaped by conflicts arising from the heterogeneity of values found among its early proponents.

Rainier enthusiasts liked to trace the roots of their national park movement back to Theodore Winthrop's *Canoe and Saddle* (1862). This book, a recollection of an 1853 trip from Puget Sound over the Cascades to the Columbia River by Washington Territory's original sightseer, contains some remarkable passages about Mount Rainier. Campaigners for the park found in Winthrop's aesthetic response to the mountain a worthy, if old-fashioned, expression of their own nature appreciation. "Studying the light and the majesty of Tacoma [Rainier]," Winthrop had written, "there passed from it and entered into my being, to dwell there evermore by the side of many such, a thought and an image of solemn beauty, which I could thenceforth evoke whenever in the world I must have peace or die." Winthrop, like his contemporary Frederick Law Olmsted, was suggesting that scenic appreciation cultivated the mind and improved the soul. Although Winthrop stopped short of advocating a national park—the idea had scarcely been conceived at the time—he did intimate that the mountain possessed public value. "Up to Tacoma, or into some such solitude of nature, imaginative men must go, as Moses went up to Sinai, that the divine afflatus may stir within them," he wrote. Although Winthrop was no doubt atypical of Puget Sound settlers in the 1850s in his response to the mountain, his book gave the national park movement a historical footing.[5]

The romantic notion that such a grand peak presented an irresistible attraction to "imaginative men" also appealed to the veteran climber Philemon B. Van Trump. He referred to the "contagion of mountain-climbing." Rainier had an infectious power that, in his mind, enriched humanity. According to Van Trump, mountaineers possessed the same heroic qualities as explorers: an indifference to danger or physical pain and an indomitable will to conquer the unknown. Meditating on the continuing ill effects of the frostbite he had suffered many years earlier during a night on the summit of Rainier, the pioneer climber declared that the "true mountaineer" could no more regret his experience than any of the "zealous navigators" of the northern seas.[6] Like Winthrop, Van Trump admired Mount Rainier most for what it did to the men and women who tried to scale it. It made them better human beings.

Others in the campaign emphasized the area's inspirational value not only for mountaineers but also for the large numbers of tourists who would be drawn to the lower slopes. The geologist Israel C. Russell asserted in an article for *Scribner's Magazine* that to visit the mountain and its surrounding terrain was to breathe free air, renew one's health, and cultivate "the aesthetic sense that is awakened in every heart by an intimate acquaintance with nature in her finer moods." Similarly, Carl Snyder wrote in *Review of Reviews* that all those who visited the mountain would "gain a new pleasure, a larger artistic sense, and a higher inspiration from the contemplation of the grandeur and beauty" of Mount Rainier. The nature experience would, like a good education, make a positive and lasting impression on each individual. "Its educational advantages would be of unspeakable value," claimed Washington's Senator Watson Squire on the floor of the Senate. It would be good public policy to preserve the mountain's inspirational character in a national park.[7]

The most important early statement of Mount Rainier National Park's worth, aside from the park's establishing act, was the memorial to Congress that Bailey Willis crafted on behalf of the campaign coalition in 1893. The area, the memorial declared, contained "many features of unique interest and wonderful grandeur, which fit it peculiarly to be a national park, forever set aside for the pleasure and instruction of the people." Here was a coupling of scenic and scientific values, of recreational and educational purposes. As might be expected, however, this document emphasized points of scientific interest. It described Rainier's volcanic origins, vast glacier system, and unique assemblage of wildlife and plants. It introduced that arresting image of "an arctic island in a temperate sea" that would become the essence of the park's interpretive story. Willis explained:

> In a bygone age an arctic climate prevailed over the Northwest and glaciers covered the Cascade Range. Arctic animals and arctic plants then lived throughout the region. As the climate became milder and glaciers melted, the creatures of the cold climate were limited in their geographic range to the districts of the shrinking glaciers. On the great peak the glaciers linger

still. They give to it its greatest beauty. They are themselves magnificent, and with them survives a colony of arctic animals and plants which can not exist in the temperate climate of the less lofty mountains. These arctic forms are as effectually isolated as shipwrecked sailors on an island in mid-ocean. There is no refuge for them beyond their haunts on ice-bound cliffs. But even there the birds and animals are no longer safe from the keen sportsman, and the few survivors must soon be exterminated unless protected by the Government in a national park.[8]

The campaign for Mount Rainier National Park also marshaled evidence that the area's scenic and scientific features were superlative examples of their kind. Enthusiasts felt compelled to answer the question, why this mountain and not some other? There were inevitable comparisons with the Alps. All of Switzerland's glaciers, some said, could not match the quantity of ice on Rainier. Nor could Mont Blanc or any of the Alps match the impressiveness of this solitary mountain. How much this rhetoric stemmed from what Runte calls scenic nationalism and how much it owed simply to most educated Americans' familiarity with the glaciers and scenery of Europe is open to debate. In the nineteenth century, preservationists were struggling to develop a language of scenic appreciation that could be used to describe for the benefit of Congress and the American people land values that were not easily quantifiable or comparable with other land values. It was this effort that inspired the phrase "highest use." We should not assume that every comparison between American landforms and the most famous landforms in the world was a reflection of cultural anxiety or scenic nationalism. Mount Rainier was also compared to Mount St. Elias in Alaska, and its glaciers were compared to Alaska's famous Muir Glacier. Until the turn of the century, Rainier was thought to be taller than any peak in the Rockies or the Sierra Nevada; its summit cone was named Columbia's Crest in the belief that it was the highest point in the United States.[9] The purpose of such comparisons was not only to build up pride in American scenery but also to place Mount Rainier on a scale with the world's other scenic wonders. It was a part of the great reconnaissance of the American West.

Still, scenic nationalism clearly played a role in such comparisons.

Descriptions of America's natural wonders and scenic landscapes were often chauvinistic. Directed at tourists, they often amounted to boosterism on a national scale. Years before the western railroads coined the slogan "See America First," the idea had become a common theme in American travel literature. Vermont's Senator George Edmunds, who traveled to Rainier on the Northern Pacific in 1883, wrote in the Portland *Oregonian*:

> I can not help saying that I am thoroughly convinced that no resort in the United States will be so much sought after as this when once people come to know that what men cross the Atlantic to see can be seen in equal splendor, if not surpassed, at home. I have been through the Swiss mountains, and I am compelled to own that incredible as the assertion may appear, there is absolutely no comparison between the finest effects that are exhibited there and what is seen in approaching this grand isolated mountain.[10]

Mountaineer Edward S. Ingraham of Seattle put it bluntly: "It is un-American to visit other shores when our own country contains so many places of interest."[11]

Still another argument for establishing a national park around Mount Rainier was to protect the public's access to it. Park advocates wanted to make sure that the popular high country meadows such as at Paradise were not "captured by private interest." They also wanted to make sure that private interests did not gain control of the approaches. "If the gateways to Mount Rainier and the beautiful natural parks on its sides pass into the ownership of individuals or syndicates," Russell warned, "toll may be charged for breathing the free air." Toll roads and inholdings would detract immeasurably from the feeling of freedom that nature bestowed on the Mount Rainier visitor.[12]

One of the most pressing concerns of the park advocates was vandalism. As the number of recreationists taking the trail up to Paradise increased in the early 1890s, so too did attacks on animal and plant life. There were reports that hunters were wantonly killing mountain goats and bears. Even more disturbing were the accounts of forest fire damage. The actual extent of the damage was disputed; one person stated that two-thirds of Paradise was recently burned over, another found fire-killed trees in only two small areas plus some green trees that had been felled by campers to construct shelters.[13] Regardless, the outlook was not bright as long as there was no supervision of the area. Preservationists noted that the federal government showed no intention of providing anything more than paper protection for the Pacific Forest Reserve, proclaimed by President Benjamin Harrison in 1893, which in any case failed to include the western slope of the mountain.

The issue of vandalism was also significant, because the few dozen enthusiasts from Seattle and Tacoma who journeyed to Paradise in the early 1890s were gaining the remarkable insight that they themselves were the cause of the area's degradation. This revelation did not come without a struggle. There was finger-pointing back and forth between the Seattle and Tacoma mountain clubs. And the fact that they defined the problem as vandalism showed that they wanted to hold certain aberrant individuals responsible. But these distractions notwithstanding, the consensus of the local recreationists was that unrestricted public use of the high mountain meadows would lead to their ruin. There had to be a public authority present to protect the area from pleasure seekers themselves. This was the mountain clubs' primary motivation in calling for the creation of a national park.[14]

The kind of public authority they sought was rudimentary, something merely to discourage vandalism. Ingraham wanted the Pacific Forest Reserve placed under regulations similar to those for Yellowstone National Park. Van Trump proposed that the federal government could post guards in the most heavily used areas during the summer season. The editor of the *Tacoma Daily Ledger* suggested that a few soldiers from Fort Vancouver could be stationed in the Nisqually Valley or sent to patrol the trail to Paradise.[15] As modest as these proposals in the mid-1890s were, they prove that the very people who were frequenting Mount Rainier already saw the need to regulate public use.

This emphasis on recreational use and public order indicated that the local perspective on Mount Rainier National Park was essentially an urban perspective—in contrast, for example, with the local view of Yellowstone, where ranching communities surrounded the park. To the people of Seattle and Tacoma, Rainier was a part of the cities' recreational domain. One Tacoma citizen referred to the mountain as "our joint inheritance." Seattle's superintendent of parks, Edward O. Schwagerl, asserted, "It is not foreign to the mission of the city's park commission to be informed of some of the facts relative to the United States reservation created and designated as the 'Pacific Coast Park Reserve.'" Schwagerl urged the park commission to petition the secretary of the interior to take steps to protect the area from vandalism.[16] The fact that local support was urban and preservationist certainly helped the national park campaign succeed. It is no coincidence that the nation's fifth national park was located so near to one of the West's leading urban areas.

The Rainier campaign included a cluster of arguments that addressed the relationship of the national park to economic development. These arguments involved the likely growth of tourism, the conservation of the water supply for irrigation, and the minimal adverse impact that the park would have on grazing and mining interests. Though economic considerations were not the preservationists' main concern, neither were they ignored. Indeed, the close alliance between local preservationists such as Van Trump and Ingraham and national figures such as John Muir, the National Geographic Society's Gardiner G. Hubbard, and the federal bureau chiefs John Wesley Powell, Clinton Hart Merriam, and Bernhard Fernow would not have been possible had these men thought that the national park would hinder regional economic development.

The campaigners assumed that the national park would be a magnet for tourists. Whether it was primarily the task of the federal government, the western railroads, or local entrepreneurs to develop tourist accommodations in such a park remained under debate, but preservationists agreed that the purpose of a national park was to preserve the scenery for the enjoyment of the people. This was the sharpest distinction between a national park and a national forest. For this reason, preservationists regarded the proclamation of the Pacific Forest Reserve as merely a first step in making Mount Rainier a national park. "The park is without hotels, without roads, almost without trails," wrote one preservationist. "Once in the government's care and made accessible to the traveler . . . its fame will widen with the years."[17] Senator Squire even suggested that tourist business would eventually cover the cost of administering the park. "The outlay of money required for the establishment of the park is very small," he told a skeptical Congress. "Concessions can be leased for hotels, stage routes, and stopping places, the proceeds of which will provide for maintenance of the park."[18] Though they were fairly vague about how it would be accomplished, preservationists made clear that a national park entailed both protection and development.

Squire also contended that Mount Rainier National Park was needed to preserve the mountain forests, which slowed the spring runoff and thereby reduced flooding and summer drought in the lower portions of the watersheds. This was precisely the argument advanced in support of forest reserves. Since the government had already proclaimed the Pacific Forest Reserve, Squire's argument might have been redundant but for the fact that the reserve's boundary failed to take in Rainier's western slope. The proposed national park would correct this problem and protect the upper watersheds of the Puyallup, White, and Nisqually rivers. "This view of the case strongly affects the farming interests of my State," Squire said. "The high mountain and glacial lands are totally unfit for cultivation. The Government alone can protect the rich lower lands from ruin if it acts promptly."[19]

Between 1893 and 1898, Washington's senators and congressmen introduced measures in six consecutive sessions of Congress in attempts to establish a "Washington National Park." The long and bumpy road that this legislation traveled in Congress reveals the apathy and skepticism that confronted preservationists prior to the turn of the century. There was little organized opposition to such a park on the part of grazing or mining interests. Rather, the effort languished for five years primarily because Congress could not be persuaded that it was the responsibility of the federal government to create a national park like Yellowstone in the state of Washington.

On December 12, 1893, Watson C. Squire introduced Senate bill 1250 to establish "Washington National Park." The bill essentially sought to change the Pacific Forest Reserve to a national park. The boundaries described in Squire's bill were no different from the boundaries of the reserve. Like many park advocates in his home state, including Seattle's chamber of commerce, whose memorial he submitted together with the bill, Squire believed that President Benjamin Harrison had proclaimed the Pacific Forest Reserve the previous February with a view to its subsequent conversion to a national park. Squire's bill was referred to the Senate Committee on Public Lands. Three weeks later, on January 4, 1894, Congressman William Doolittle introduced an identical bill in the House (H.R. 4989), which was referred to the House Committee on Public Lands.[20]

Most of the language in Squire's bill came practically verbatim from the Yellowstone Park Act of 1872. Section 1 described boundaries and declared that the area would be "dedicated and set apart as a public park, to be known and designated as the Washington National Park, for the benefit and enjoyment of the people." Section 2 stated that the park would be administered by the secretary of the interior, who would be charged with the "preservation from injury or spoliation of all timber, mineral deposits, natural curiosities or wonders within said park, and their retention in their natural condition." The secretary could, at his discretion, lease small parcels of land as sites for buildings to accommodate visitors. He would also "provide against the wanton destruction of the fish and game found within said park, and against their capture or destruction for the purposes of merchandise or profit." Significantly, Squire's bill did not deviate from the model Yellowstone Park Act on the matter of enforcement, providing only that persons who violated park regulations would be removed for trespass, even though there had been several attempts to amend the Yellowstone law to impose fines for the killing of wildlife in that park. (Congress finally passed such a law for Yellowstone in 1894, but the people who framed the Mount Rainier bill failed to heed the Yellowstone experience.)[21]

On July 10, 1894, seven months after submitting his first bill, Squire introduced a second (S. 2204), which differed from the earlier bill only in its boundary description. The new boundaries followed exactly the recommendations of the joint committee of the Geological Society of America, the American Association for the Advancement of Science, the National Geographic Society, the Sierra Club, and the Appalachian Mountain Club. The new boundaries included the western flank of Mount Rainier but excluded the remainder of the reserve east of the Cascade Crest and south of the Tatoosh Range, together with a narrow strip on the north. The reason for the addition was obvious; the deletions, Squire explained to the Senate, were designed to exclude from the park presumed coal, gold, and mineral deposits. It was at this time that Squire made his one significant speech to the Senate on the Washington National Park. The speech mostly drew upon the joint committee's memorial and elicited no debate.[22]

Neither Squire's bills nor Doolittle's bill was reported back from committee. Doolittle failed to introduce a revised version of his bill, and the discrepancy between the House and Senate versions no doubt hurt the legislation's chances. For some reason, Squire and Doolittle did not resolve this discrepancy when each of them introduced new park bills early in the first session of the 54th Congress, in December 1895. These two bills also died in committee. It is unclear whether the lack of coordination between the two Washington lawmakers was due to oversight or disagreement. In any case, after Doolittle heard from the Committee on Public Lands that his bill would not be approved, he introduced another, H.R. 4058, which drew the boundaries inward on all sides, and reduced the size of the park from approximately twenty-four miles by twenty-six miles to approximately eighteen miles on a side. These were the boundaries described in the Mount Rainier National Park Act as finally enacted.[23]

Doolittle's proposal deserves a close look because it became the blueprint for the eventual Mount Rainier National Park Act. It described the final boundaries, and it included two new provisions. Sections 3 and 4 provided that the Northern Pacific give up grant lands within the national park; in exchange, the railroad could select other sections in any state that the railroad served. These solicitous terms strongly suggest that the railroad company influenced the legislation by one means or another, though NP officials vigorously denied involvement for years afterward.[24]

To the preservationists' disappointment, the new boundaries cut some three hundred square miles of forest land out of the park. What angered many more citizens, however, was the fact that the legislation exchanged the Northern Pacific's land inside the park for public domain timberlands elsewhere (mostly in Oregon, as it turned out, much to the ire of the people of that state). This was too good a deal to have been achieved without bribery, contemporary observers assumed.[25] Certain proponents of the bill were roundly criticized for the provisions covering the Northern Pacific land grant, including Senator John L. Wilson and Congressman James Hamilton Lewis of Washington, who shepherded the legislation through the next four sessions of Congress, then failed in their reelection bids.[26] Whatever the railroad's precise role may have been in seeing the legislation through Congress, the effect was to cast a pall over the final act. The lesson of the Mount Rainier National Park Act appeared to be that in any "pragmatic alliance" between western railroads and preservationists, the railroads would exact considerable tribute for their political support.

On May 11, 1896, H.R. 4058 was reported back from committee with the recommendation that the House pass it with three significant amendments. In Section 2, the maximum term of lease of lands on which to erect visitor accommodations was increased from ten to twenty-five years. Rights of way could be granted for the construction of railways or tramways through the forest reserve and into the park. And most important, a new Section 5 allowed mining in the forest reserve and in the park.[27] These concessions answered, in part, objections that the commissioner of the General Land Office and the secretary of the interior had made to earlier versions of the Washington National Park bill.

These three concessions to development pointed up the fact that national park supporters were now in competition with the support for the new national forests and that the Cleveland administration was definitely more inclined toward the latter type of land management regime. In hindsight, the creation of three new national parks in California in 1890 followed by the passage of the Forest Reserve Act of 1891 appears to mark, as the NPS historian Barry Mackintosh has written, "the fork in the road beyond which national parks and national forests proceed separately."[28] Each new park entailed an act of Congress; each new forest required only a stroke of the president's pen. To contemporaries, however, it was yet unclear how, if at all, national parks and national forests would differ. John Muir, for one, hoped that the forests would be managed in much the same way as the parks. The well-known forester Gifford Pinchot, meanwhile, argued that by placing the new national forests under scientific forestry management, the federal government would obviate the need for national parks. In this context, park proponents considered the concession to mining a small price to pay. It was vital to secure the federal government's recognition of Mount Rainier's extraordinary scenic and scientific interest so that, like Yellowstone, the area would receive a greater degree of protection than a forest reserve would.[29]

Even these concessions were not enough for some members of Congress, who objected to the national park primarily on the basis of expense. Congressman John F. Lacey of Iowa, chairman of the Committee on Public Lands, suggested that the national park designation was redundant because the area had already been withdrawn as a forest reserve. When Doolittle suggested that the people of his state would "make the necessary improvements, for the benefit of all the people of the country" and only wanted assistance from the secretary of the interior in protecting the area from vandals, Congressman Joseph Bailey of Texas reminded legislators of the cost of administering Yellowstone and sarcastically noted, "The difficulty I have is that I have not learned how it is possible to maintain a park by any government without expense." He then obtained Doolittle's assurance that the Washington congressman would not "ask a dollar from the Government in the way of an appropriation." With that, Bailey withdrew his objection and the bill passed.

With the three amendments duly approved by the House, H.R. 4058 came very close to the final form of the Mount Rainier National Park Act. But the bill's progress was slow. On June 10, 1896, the Senate referred the bill to the Committee on Forest Reservations and Protection of Game. Eight months later, on February 17, 1897, the bill was reported back with the recommendation that it be passed without amendment. In March it passed the Senate only to be pocket vetoed by President Grover Cleveland as he left office. Senator John L. Wilson introduced an identical bill (S. 349) in the next session of Congress, but, apparently because no companion bill was introduced in the House, it never returned from committee. On December 7, 1897, Wilson introduced the same bill in the next session of Congress (S. 2552), and one week later Congressman Wesley Jones introduced a Washington National Park bill in the House (H.R. 5024). As this bill became stalled in the Committee on Public Lands, Congressman Lewis introduced the same bill again (H.R. 9146) on March 14, 1898.[30] Finally, near passage, the bill hit one last snag.

The story of the bill's final hurdle comes from Seattle businessman John P. Hartman, who later claimed to have been closely involved in drafting the legislation. This seems unlikely, since Hartman's account begins not with Doolittle but with Wilson and Lewis in 1897. In any case, Wilson and Lewis summoned Hartman to Washington, D.C., to help them overcome the objection of the powerful Speaker of the House, "Uncle Joe" Cannon.

> I reached the National Capitol early in February, and very shortly was ush-
> ered into the presence of Mr. Cannon, piloted by Colonel Lewis. As usual,
> Mr. Cannon was smoking his big, black cigar, ensconced in a swivel chair,
> with his feet on the jamb above the little fireplace where coal was burning
> cheerily in the grate. After preliminaries Mr. Cannon said, addressing me,
> "I have a notion to kill your Bill, and I have the power to do it." Of course,
> I wanted to know the reasons and he said, "It is all right to set these places
> aside but for the fact that in a year or so you will be coming back here seek-
> ing money from the Treasury to improve the place, and make it possible for
> visitors to go there, which things we do not need, and we haven't the money
> therefor, and I think I will kill it." I said to Mr. Cannon, "I promise you, Sir,
> that if this Bill is passed I will not be here asking for money from the Fed-
> eral Treasury to operate the place so long as you shall remain in Congress."
> With that statement, he said, "I will take you at your word and let the mea-
> sure go through, if otherwise it can travel the thorny road."[31]

Shortly after this meeting the bill was reported back and the House passed one minor amendment recommended by Lewis, which gave settlers in the national park the same right as the railroad to claim other public lands in lieu of their lands in the park. In a final amendment, the House dispensed with the politically sensitive but dull "Washington National Park" and named the new national park after the mountain. (Ironically, it was misspelled Mount *Ranier* National Park.) The bill passed both houses of Congress on March 1 and was signed by President McKinley on March 2, 1899.[32]

Despite its flaws, the Mount Rainier National Park Act was an important triumph for the national park idea. Like Yellowstone, Rainier was
established as a national park to preserve the area's scenic and scientific

values. Forests and wildlife were to be preserved in their natural condition. Most of the park lands were carved from a designated national forest, affirming the idea that national parks and national forests were to be placed on a separate administrative footing. As the first national park established after the Forest Reserve Act of 1891 and the Organic Act of 1897, the nation's fifth national park resolved any doubt that the United States government would develop both a national forest system and a national park system, each under a separate body of statutes.

Of the many individuals and organizations who came together in the campaign to establish Mount Rainier National Park, none took any part in the early administration or development of the park. The coalition dissolved as easily as it had formed, leaving for others the task of determining how the national park was to take shape in the new century. Recreational users and commercial interests in Seattle and Tacoma would easily rise to the challenge.

CHAPTER 3

The New Pleasuring Ground (1900–1915)

CHESTER THORNE WAS A BANKER WITH THE COMMON-
wealth Title Trust Company of Tacoma, a Mount Rainier enthusiast,
and president of the Tacoma Automobile Club. In 1907, he addressed a
letter to "The Honorable Secretary of the Interior," James R. Garfield.
"Sir: The Tacoma Automobile Club hereby earnestly and respectfully
request[s] that you do not issue an order absolutely excluding automobiles from the Mount Rainier National Park in the State of Washington."[1] Thorne went on to suggest that the club would support the strictest
regulations on cars (admitted only for set hours of the day, speed limits) as long as they were admitted in some capacity. Thorne recognized
that with the passage of the Mount Rainier National Park Act, the government's initiative to create a "public park ... for the benefit and enjoyment of the people" had passed from Congress to the executive branch.
The act placed the national park under the control of the secretary of
the interior, authorizing him to "take all such measures as shall be necessary to fully carry out the objects and purposes of this Act."[2] In the
first decade and a half of its existence, park users and developers occa-
sionally sought help from their congressional representatives, but more
often, like Chester Thorne, they dealt with the Department of the Interior.

Fundamentally, the secretary of the interior was to ensure that the area remained a public space, both by removing all persons who attempted to homestead there and by exchanging Northern Pacific Railroad grant lands for public domain lands elsewhere. These directives were unambiguous. Further, the secretary was to make regulations for the proper care of the park. "Such regulations," the law ordered, "shall provide for the preservation from injury or spoliation of all timber, mineral deposits, natural curiosities, or wonders . . . and their retention in their natural condition." At his discretion, the secretary could permit the construction of hotels or other visitor accommodations, build roads and trails, and grant rights of way to any railroad company interested in building a line into the park. This was a much more complicated set of directives. Precisely how the secretary should manage this public space would be a matter for interpretation and debate by the secretary, his officials, and the public itself throughout the twentieth century.

Both Congress and the secretary of the interior began with the assumption that the park needed little funding or supervision. Tourists and entrepreneurs entered the new pleasuring ground on their own recognizance. As public use mounted, both the government and park users discovered the need for a stronger park administration.

The most pressing issue involved public access. Seattle and Tacoma residents in particular wanted access to Mount Rainier National Park. Getting to the park was difficult. Getting around inside the park was even more challenging. Residents of the two cities therefore made road and trail development a public issue in the early 1900s.

At the time of Rainier's establishment, a single road went all the way to the mountain. The so-called Mountain Road was built by pioneer James Longmire and a crew of hired laborers in 1893, and went from Kernahan's Ranch to the mineral claim known as Longmire Springs six miles inside the park. As originally constructed, the road consisted of two parallel wheel ruts wending through the dense forest; traffic was restricted to wagons whose axles could clear the dozens of stumps still occupying the centerline. After a few years the larger obstructions were rooted out and the road was open to horse-drawn stages. One stage outfit, the Tacoma Carriage and Baggage Transfer Company, began offering tourists a trip from the city to the national park via an overnight stop in Eatonville.

The relative ease and comfort of railroad travel was not far behind. In 1902, the Puget Sound, Mt. Tacoma, and Eastern Railroad, a Northern Pacific subsidiary, completed a line to Eatonville. In 1904, it extended the line to Ashford, seven miles from the park boundary. Most tourists rode the train to the end of the line, then secured a ride by wagon, carriage, or horseback the remaining distance to Rainier. Some walked. Typically tourists were equipped with little more than a few articles of extra clothing in a luggage bag; a few carried bedrolls.[3]

From 1899 to 1904, the combination of railroad and primitive wagon road brought more than five hundred people each summer to Rainier. Many visitors were content to remain at the Longmire Springs resort, where they could enjoy the mineral baths and admire Rainier from the large forest clearing in front of Longmire's hotel. Most visitors, however, wanted to go higher, ramble in the mountain's famous subalpine meadows, and obtain a closer look at its glaciers. The most popular destination for these adventures was Paradise, a delightful expanse of meadows and irregular clumps of alpine fir located between approximately 5,200 and 5,600 feet elevation on the mountain's southern flank. An alternative destination was Indian Henry's Hunting Ground, a cluster of meadows and tarns at slightly lower elevation on Rainier's southwest slope. Both were about six miles from Longmire, accessed by trails that were built by members of the Longmire family itself.[4]

A smaller number of people used an alternative access route to the northwest corner of the park. Known as the old Bailey Willis Trail, the route began at the Northern Pacific railroad station in Wilkeson and led up the Carbon River. About eight miles inside the park boundary the trail forked, the left branch ascending to Moraine Park above the Carbon Glacier and the right branch heading up to Spray Park and Crater (Mowich) Lake. Tourists camped in both places. In the early 1900s, this trail was passable to foot and horse traffic only, and a trip to the Carbon River high country was considerably more difficult than a trip to Paradise.[5]

There was no shortage of guides available for leading tourists up these various trails. A variety of complaints, inquiries, and recommendations regarding guide services dribbled into the Department of the Interior after 1899. Some of the guides requested licenses, desirous of limiting their competition. One tourist guide, claiming years of experience, wanted to protect his livelihood from "new men who may wish to take holt of this business." Remote from the scene in the nation's capital, Secretary of the Interior Ethan A. Hitchcock was asked to distinguish between legitimate guides and a swarm of interlopers who would defraud the tourists or lead them into danger.[6]

Equally troubling was a report in 1902 from a forest ranger to the forest superintendent of Mount Rainier Forest Reserve alleging that Henry S. Hayes, a resident of Ashford, was collecting a toll from pack trains using the trail between Longmire and Paradise. A private toll violated the spirit of the law in setting aside a public park. Soon afterward, the Department of the Interior informed locals, including the Longmires who had built the trails, that no tolls could be collected in the national park. This, too, pointed to the need for government regulation of public access.[7]

Year by year it became apparent that public access to and within the national park was not developing according to the pattern contemplated in the park's establishing act. The Tacoma and Eastern Railroad, which park campaigners had once proclaimed would "place the park within a delightful two hours' ride from the city,"[8] terminated in Ashford, and the company had no intention of extending its line into the park. The secretary of the interior was authorized to grant railroad rights of way through the forest reserve and into Mount Rainier National Park, but the government had no comers. In addition, although the secretary was authorized to develop "roads and bridle paths" within the national park, funds for road and trail construction were to derive from park "revenues"— principally from the proceeds of licenses and leases associated with tourist services and accommodations—and in the absence of a railroad connection no one was seeking a lease of land on which to build a tourist hotel. Congress had envisioned an orderly development of the national park with the assistance of one or more railroad companies, but the railroad failed to materialize.

Seattle and Tacoma residents demanded the construction of a park road. In 1903, Congress included an item in the Sundry Civil Appropriations Act for Rainier: "To enable the Secretary of War to cause a survey to be made of the most practicable route for a wagon road into said park, and toward the construction of said road . . . ten thousand dollars."[9] It was a modest start, but it marked the first appropriation of public funds for the development of the national park.

The planning, design, and construction of this government road fell to a talented engineer by the name of Eugene Ricksecker. An army engineer since 1889, Ricksecker built roads for horse-drawn vehicles. Neither he nor his superiors in the U.S. Army Corps of Engineers could foresee how quickly Americans would adopt the automobile in the new century, or how profoundly the automobile would affect Mount Rainier National Park. When Ricksecker began his work at Rainier, the automobile was still a novelty throughout most of the West. Few country roads were fit for automobile use, and the few upper-class automobile owners in Washington State in the early 1900s mostly confined their vehicular use to paved city streets. Nevertheless, Ricksecker had the perspicacity to recognize that he was building something quite modern and unusual when the project was assigned to him in 1903: his road would be one of the first scenic drives in the nation.[10]

In the spring of 1903, Ricksecker canvassed local people on various routes into the park and easily settled on the Nisqually River Valley— the route taken by Longmire's Mountain Road—as the best alternative. He gave two reasons for this choice: tourists favored it because a road and trail already existed to Paradise, and climbers favored it because it led to the main climbing route to the summit. Ricksecker then initiated a road survey. He instructed his head surveyor, Oscar A. Piper, to take the road past two outstanding scenic attractions, the Nisqually Glacier terminus and Narada Falls, and as many other points of interest as possible. Piper accomplished the survey between July and November 1903. The route was twenty-four miles long and included two additional points of interest: Christine Falls and a dramatic overlook of the Tatoosh Range from "Gap Point," later renamed Ricksecker Point in honor of the engineer. Instead of taking the direct route up the Paradise Valley as the trail did, the road would ascend the 2,800 vertical feet by a series of "loops," or switchbacks, on the flank of Rampart Ridge.[11]

Ricksecker's aesthetic considerations for the driver controlled nearly every aspect of the road's design. The object of this road, he insisted, was not to convey the driver by the swiftest possible route from point

A to point B, but rather to give the driver a pleasing experience along the way. Ricksecker insisted on a light gradient even though it considerably lengthened the road's ascent. "Steep stretches where teams must walk soon become monotonous and pall upon the senses," he explained. He wanted no more than a 4 percent grade, "the steepest up which teams can trot." Ricksecker also allowed for numerous bends. The road would "follow the graceful curves of natural surface of the ground, as being most pleasing and far less distractive than the regular curves laid with mathematical precision." Instead of taking through cuts, the road would go around each promontory as it ascended the mountainside. Thus, Ricksecker noted, the visitor would be "kept in a keen state of expectancy as to the new pleasures held in store at the next turn."

The engineer kept other aesthetic considerations in view. He specified a generous width of clearing through the forest to ensure adequate infiltration of sunlight so that the road surface would dry out after summer rainstorms and so that the snowpack would melt quickly in the spring. But to diminish the sense of barrenness and artificiality that this swath through the heavy timber might create, he wanted a few large trees left standing. No borrow pits were to remain, and guardrails were to be built of native rubble.

Ricksecker was still building his road when motorists first gained admittance to the park in 1908. That year motorists could drive as far as the Nisqually Glacier—the only glacier in the United States, it was said, that could be reached by car.[12] In 1909 they could get to Narada Falls. But motorists had to wait six more years before they were permitted to drive all the way to the end of the road. The last difficult stretch from Narada Falls into Paradise Valley and then up that valley to the subalpine meadows at Paradise was passable to horse and foot traffic in 1910, but it required widening and better drainage before the government would allow cars over it. Ricksecker died suddenly in 1911 at age fifty-one, his last and greatest work of engineering still in progress.[13]

While Ricksecker was at work on the road to Paradise, Seattle and Tacoma residents were formulating a much more ambitious and comprehensive plan for the development of Mount Rainier National Park. Their leader in this endeavor was Asahel Curtis. Like his more famous brother Edward, Asahel was a professional photographer. Both the

Curtis brothers began their professional lives selling scenic photographs of Rainier, Edward moving on to win fame for his portraiture of American Indians, and Asahel remaining in Seattle to become locally famous for his portraits and picture albums of the Pacific Northwest, and Rainier in particular. Asahel Curtis combined an artist's appreciation for the scenic beauty of Rainier with a businessman's keenness for boosting the park and making it into one of the Pacific Northwest's great attractions. Sometimes a friend of the park administration and other times a burr under its saddle, Curtis was easily the most active and informed citizen supporter during the first fifty years of Mount Rainier National Park's existence.

Prominent in The Mountaineers during its founding years, Curtis might have dominated that organization had the club not already enjoyed the capable leadership of Professor Edmund S. Meany. Instead, Curtis cofounded the Seattle-Tacoma Rainier National Park Committee, an organization dedicated to the "development and exploitation of Mount Rainier National Park."[14] For many years, Curtis straddled the increasingly divergent philosophies of these two organizations. In the 1920s and 1930s, he would represent the business interests of Seattle and Tacoma, demanding further road development in the park when The Mountaineers called for greater circumspection. Eventually, Curtis would part company with The Mountaineers, the National Park Service, and even his fellow members on the Rainier National Park Advisory Board (the former Seattle-Tacoma Rainier National Park Committee) when he sided with timber interests opposing the establishment of Olympic National Park in the mid-1930s. This breach severely compromised the Rainier National Park Advisory Board and effectively ended Curtis's influence on the development of Mount Rainier National Park.

Although his legacy was mixed, Curtis's vision for the park's development was remarkably consistent. His ideas were already discernable in 1908 and 1909, when he organized and led the third annual outing of The Mountaineers. On this outing about seventy-five Mountaineers went up the Carbon River to Moraine Park, from which they made an ascent of Rainier by way of the Winthrop and Emmons glaciers. For Curtis, the expedition had a definite public purpose: to bring publicity to the north side of the mountain. "It is the hope of the club to not only open this region for The Mountaineers trip," Curtis wrote, "but to do as we have done with the Olympic mountains and Mt. Baker, permanently open the north side of the mountain to tourist travel."[15] Even the elaborate preparations for the expedition had a promotional quality, as Curtis reconnoitered the route in 1908 and recommended trail improvements to the acting superintendent, sent a prospectus to the Sierra Club, dangled the club's list of supplies before a couple of prospective packers, and solicited support from the Pierce County Board of Commissioners for trail repairs outside the park boundary. Shortly before the trip, Curtis invited Secretary of the Interior Richard A. Ballinger to join The Mountaineers' camp at Moraine Park while the secretary was visiting the West. "We will be camped for three weeks on the Northern side of the mountain, in a region that has not been visited by many people for years, and it is a region that we feel deserves more attention than it is receiving at the present time in comparison with the Southern side."[16] Curtis wanted to make the national park accessible from all directions so that it would benefit all the people of the state. He wanted The Mountaineers to get behind the effort to induce easterners to take vacations in the West rather than abroad. And with other preservationists, Curtis wanted to spread what John Muir called the "glacier gospel"—the secular faith that nature appreciation humbled and improved the human spirit. "He is a poor mountaineer indeed," Curtis wrote in his account of the outing, "who has not returned to his home the better for the many lessons learned in the solitudes."[17] It was a unique feature of this era that a man like Curtis could express both the glacier gospel of John Muir and a chamber-of-commerce boosterism without the least bit of cant in either case.

In 1910, Curtis helped organize a committee of The Mountaineers to promote better administration of Mount Rainier National Park. The committee sought the appointment of a park superintendent, government licensing of mountain guides, and the construction of a climbers' shelter at Camp Muir. It succeeded in the first two objectives within the year. (It renewed the request for the climbers' shelter in March 1915 in commemoration of Muir, the naturalist and Sierra Club founder, who had died in the previous year. The shelter was built at public expense according to specifications provided by club member Carl F. Gould.)[18]

While The Mountaineers were working on these objectives, Curtis had begun to think more grandly about a system of park roads. In 1911, he received advice from Secretary of the Interior Walter L. Fisher that the full program of road and trail development that he had in mind would require action by Congress, and that he ought to "take it up with the people in the State of Washington who are interested and see what can be done to secure from Congress the necessary legislation and appropriations."[19] Armed with this letter from the secretary, Curtis contacted prominent individuals in the business communities of Seattle and Tacoma, and persuaded them to set aside their civic rivalry and form an intercity committee on Mount Rainier National Park. The committee appointed Curtis as chairman and T. H. Martin, a Tacoma businessman and cofounder of the committee, as secretary. Its member organizations included the Seattle Commercial Club, New Seattle Chamber of Commerce, Tacoma Chamber of Commerce and Commercial Club, Rotary Club of Seattle, and Rotary Club of Tacoma. "An important part of our work," Curtis announced to Secretary Fisher in March 1912, "will be an effort to have Congress authorize the construction of trails and roads and to appropriate funds for that purpose. In this I believe that the united action of Seattle and Tacoma will have much greater weight than their divided action has had in the past." As the work proceeded, Curtis added, the committee would "bring in other parts of the state interested in the park."[20]

The Seattle-Tacoma Rainier National Park Committee proposed a nine-point program of development. It called for surveys of a complete system of roads and trails, improvement of the south-side road and its extension to the eastern boundary of the park, roads from Longmire Springs to Indian Henry's Hunting Grounds and from the Carbon River to Moraine Park and Spray Park, protection of timber in the national forests along the approach roads to the park, a better sanitation system, a climbers' shelter (Camp Muir would be built three years later), a better system of park patrol, and the establishment of a "Bureau of National Parks." The nine-point program was signed by representatives of all the member organizations.[21]

Secretary of the Interior Fisher offered no comment on the advisability of so much road construction in a national park; he simply remarked that the committee's plan was "very comprehensive." It would require funds that Congress had been loath to provide. "The entire question of what is to be done as to the Mount Rainier National Park," he wrote, "depends very largely on the action of Congress in regard to the appropriations, and also the creation of the proposed Bureau of National Parks."[22] But the secretary reiterated his support for both measures, and the committee took the secretary's letter as an endorsement of their plan.

As Curtis and his associates knew, city boosters all over the nation were beginning to pry open federal coffers for road construction money. In December 1912, the Seattle and Tacoma people sent Samuel C. Lancaster to the nation's capital. Lancaster lobbied the state's congressional delegation, then met with President William H. Taft. The president, who had made his own well-publicized visit to Rainier the previous year, personally supported the park's development. He directed Secretary Fisher to prepare a supplemental estimate of $175,000 for the park and to rush it to Congress before the Senate Appropriations Committee ended its current deliberations. Congress approved a mere $10,000 for road surveys beyond Taft's original request for $13,400 for park administration, hardly enough to tackle the comprehensive program of road development suggested by the Seattle-Tacoma Rainier National Park Committee.[23]

Disappointed and impatient to advance their program, members of the Seattle-Tacoma Rainier National Park Committee were more convinced than ever of the need for a Bureau of National Parks, or as supporters now called it, a National Park Service. Lancaster agreed when he returned to the Pacific Northwest practically empty-handed in 1913. National park boosters should not be in a bidding war, he said. Instead, the Seattle-Tacoma group should cooperate with similar bodies in Denver, Salt Lake City, Reno, San Francisco, Oakland, Los Angeles, Phoenix, Santa Fe, Albuquerque, El Paso, Oklahoma City, Cheyenne, Boise, Helena, Portland, and Spokane. Their common agenda would include the establishment of a National Park Service, adequate appropriations for national parks, and a complete study of the See America First movement.[24]

Asahel Curtis and the Seattle-Tacoma Rainier National Park Committee goaded the Department of the Interior to action. It was not enough for the government to build one road into the park and call it quits; Rainier needed to be developed from all sides. With the establishment of the National Park Service in 1916, the Seattle-Tacoma lobby would soon get what it wanted.

After public access, the next most important impetus for a park administration was public safety. The Mount Rainier National Park Act charged the secretary of the interior with certain police powers: he would "cause all persons trespassing" to be removed from the park, and "provide against the wanton destruction of the fish and game."[25] Yet the law did not provide for a police force. The secretary of the interior had to decide where to turn for help: to the U.S. Marshalls, the army, or the new forestry service within his own department. As was the case with road development, local citizens played a key role in shaping the government's action.

As early as 1893, local preservationists called for troops to protect the popular camping ground at Paradise in the newly established Pacific Forest Reserve.[26] They found precedent for such action in the government's stationing of troops in Yellowstone, Yosemite, Sequoia, and General Grant (Kings Canyon) National Parks. These local demands were renewed after 1900, and on December 4, 1901, Senator Addison G. Foster of Washington introduced a bill (S. 270) that would authorize the secretary of the interior to request a detail of troops for Mount Rainier National Park. Senator Foster garnered the support of Secretary of the Interior Ethan A. Hitchcock as well as Secretary of War Elihu Root. The bill was reported favorably by the Committee on Military Affairs and was passed by the Senate, but failed in the House. Another bill providing for a detail of troops to Rainier was introduced in 1910 and once again drew an endorsement by the secretary of the interior, but it too did not pass.[27]

In the meantime, the new forestry service provided protection of Rainier visitors and resources. The Forest Reserve Act of 1897 authorized the secretary of the interior to appoint forest supervisors and rangers to patrol the forest reserves. Under this authority, the commissioner of the General Land Office appointed a forest supervisor to establish headquarters in a town near each forest, and the forest supervisor in turn hired rangers to patrol districts within the forest. Beginning in 1898 or 1899, the forest supervisor of the Mount Rainier Forest Reserve detailed a single ranger to visit Paradise meadows periodically and to keep a watchful eye on campers.[28] This was the first instance of "visitor protection" in Rainier, and must have been among the first such ranger assignments in the nation.

The call for a permanent ranger force in Mount Rainier National Park originated with a single family of professional foresters, O. D. Allen of Ashford, Washington, and his sons Edward and Grenville. In the early 1890s, O. D. Allen, a Yale University botany professor, moved to the Pacific Northwest for the benefit of his health, and established a homestead about two miles up the road from Kernahan's Ranch. Over the next ten years, the Allens made innumerable botanical expeditions to Mount Rainier, producing the first notable scientific collection of Mount Rainier's flora. By the 1900s, the Allen sons possessed what Edward described as "an intimate personal knowledge of all the southern slopes of Mt. Rainier." Though Edward Allen had been in every state west of the Mississippi, nowhere else had he "seen a region so beautiful and more unique." In 1903, Edward and Grenville Allen assumed two of the most influential forestry positions in the region, Grenville as supervisor of the Mount Rainier Forest Reserve and Edward as the General Land Office's forest inspector. Grenville had investigated the unauthorized charging of a toll on the trail to Paradise meadows the previous year when he was a forest ranger, and both men recognized the need for more rangers to patrol the national park.[29]

In March 1903, Forest Inspector Edward Allen made a report to the secretary of the interior urging that the recent appropriation by Congress for improving the park should be used for protection as well as road development. Allen's report was the first official overview of the natural wonders of the new national park. It reiterated Bailey Willis's conception of the park as an arctic island in a temperate zone. "The extent of this truly high mountain territory has preserved conditions such as were widespread immediately after the ice age more perfectly than has any other region in the United States," the report stated, "and there still exist many species of Arctic fauna and flora extinct elsewhere except in the inaccessible North." Forest Inspector Allen recommended specifically that at least two forest rangers be assigned to the park, one in the Paradise-Longmire vicinity and the other in the Spray Park–Carbon River area, "to perform fire and game protection work from July 1 to the coming of heavy snow, usually in November." The secretary of the interior concurred with this recommendation and authorized Forest Supervisor Grenville Allen to assume charge of Mount Rainier National Park and to assign two men to the northern and southern sections of the park beginning that season.[30] This marked the real beginning of ranger protection in Mount Rainier National Park. It is notable that one Allen son recommended it while another implemented it, and that both men were officials of the new forestry service (now the USDA Forest Service).

Grenville Allen served as acting superintendent of Mount Rainier National Park from 1903 to 1910 and was responsible for founding the ranger force. He apparently had in mind from the outset to build a ranger force composed of trustworthy, self-motivated, professional men. The qualities he looked for in these rangers were firmness, discretion, business ability, and of course, woodcraft. It is not known how Allen recruited his rangers, but in some cases he secured their service year after year. Still, as he pointed out to his superiors, the seasonality of the work made it difficult to get competent men. In 1908, with the opening of the park to automobiles and the resulting increase in park revenue, he urged that some of the ranger positions be made permanent. "The organization of an efficient ranger force requires the permanent employment of men who can be depended upon to be thoroughly devoted to their occupation," he wrote. "On the whole, it seems to me that most of the rangers in the park should be employed throughout the year, and I believe that their exertions during the summer would compensate for the periods of enforced idleness during the winter."[31] The following year, the first two permanent ranger positions were created at Mount Rainier National Park.

The rangers performed virtually all of the field work involved in administering the park. Their primary function was patrol. By patrolling the more frequently visited areas of the park, rangers were able to suppress poaching and the more brazen acts of vandalism, such as the cutting of green timber to construct temporary shelters or the making of bonfires using whole trees. Regular patrol also aided in the suppression of forest fires. In late spring and early fall, the rangers turned to road and trail repairs and new trail construction. The principal aim of trail development was to facilitate patrol and thereby improve the protection of park resources. A secondary aim was to open new areas of the park to backcountry users, although Allen was quick to point out that visitor access was a mixed blessing because the very inaccessibility of these areas constituted their best protection against poaching and other destructive activities. Trail development, Allen insisted, had to be accompanied by increases in ranger staffing. Therefore, he limited trail development to the north and south sides of the park. Rangers rerouted and improved the trail to Indian Henry's Hunting Ground, extended the Carbon River trail over to the White River, and improved the trails to Crater (Mowich) Lake and Spray Park. There were existing hunters' trails on the west and east sides, but these remained unimproved.[32]

Increasingly, ranger duties encompassed various aspects of visitor management or "visitor protection" as the rangers preferred to call it. Park rangers sought to protect tourists from harming themselves, and also to prevent them from harming the resources. With some 500 people camping at Paradise each summer, it soon became evident that campers must be given guidelines about how to make camp or else they would unwittingly lay waste to the fragile meadows and small stands of alpine firs that made the place so beautiful. Even the Sierra Club needed to be educated. Club secretary William E. Colby, planning the club's outing to Paradise in 1905, requested permission from the secretary of the interior for his party of 150 to 200 people to "cut half a dozen or so small trees for poles for our large tents and tables." Apparently a similar request had been granted for the club's outing the previous year in Yosemite. Acting Superintendent Allen pointed out to Colby that this would set a ruinous precedent. That summer, Allen ordered the arrest of another camper, Henry Beader of Tacoma, for cutting green timber at Paradise. Although the charges were dropped, Allen thought the arrest had made the necessary impression on the public.[33] These early encounters demonstrated to the superintendent and his rangers that the camping public needed guidelines or it would destroy the "natural conditions" that the park was meant to preserve.

Concerns about campers were soon overshadowed by worries about automobile drivers. The influence of the car culture unfolded rapidly in Mount Rainier National Park, faster than in most national parks due to the proximity of Seattle and Tacoma. In 1908, local automobile clubs prevailed upon park authorities to admit cars. As the initial convoy passed through the entrance gate that summer, it marked the first automobile use of a national park in the United States. By 1910, nearly twice as many people came to Rainier by car as by train and stage. Automobilists outnumbered train passengers even as the outbreak of the First World War discouraged European travel and brought a huge increase of out-of-state tourists to Rainier in 1915. By the late 1920s, the number of automobilists entering Rainier would swell to nearly a quarter of a million annually.[34]

Early concerns about the advent of the automobile focused primarily on safety. How were motor and horse-drawn vehicles to use the same roadway? Indeed, the presence of cars at Rainier highlighted what a menagerie of vehicles now shared the road; the gatekeeper at the park entrance kept a tally of the number of people entering by car, stage, wagon, motorcycle, horseback, bicycle, and foot! With the road's many steep embankments, narrow bridges, and blind curves, the very design features that Ricksecker had intended to please the driver now appeared perilous for such a high-speed vehicle as the motorcar. Acting Superintendent Allen argued against permitting the automobile in 1906, stating that "the presence of these contrivances would be a source of great annoyance and some danger to the public generally." When cars were first admitted in 1908, Allen imposed the strictest regulations for their use. By 1909, however, the acting superintendent had become less begrudging toward the car culture, informing the secretary of the interior that "the owners of automobiles derive a great deal of pleasure from the use of the road," and that the public did not have "any very general objection" to their presence. Teamsters, he added, no longer considered cars dangerous.[35]

The occasional speed demon notwithstanding, most automobile drivers were inclined to observe the park's strict speed limit. One Rainier visitor appealed to his motoring brethren in *Overland Monthly*, "You with your high-power cars may well picture the exhilaration of that ride from Tacoma to the foothills," but upon reaching the park, "the Government road begins and the speed glory must give way to calmer glories of nature." And calming it must have been: as late as 1915, Rainier motorists were held to a creeping six miles per hour on curvy sections and a slightly perkier fifteen miles per hour on straightaways provided that no horse teams were visible. In addition, park regulations required motorists to yield the right of way to horse teams, and when teams approached, the automobile driver was to take a position on the outer edge of the roadway and remain at rest until teamsters were "satisfied regarding the safety of their horses." Accepting these restrictions, the typical motorist handled his vehicle with the utmost respect for horse traffic, or as some observers liked to think, with respect for the national park itself.[36]

Park proponents assumed that private enterprise, not the government, would develop appropriate hotels and tent camps. The Mount Rainier National Park Act authorized the secretary of the interior to lease ground for the erection of tourist accommodations. At the time the legislation was passed, Rainier already had two tourist concerns: the Longmire Springs Hotel and a tent camp at Paradise known as Camp of the Clouds. As time passed, park users demanded further regulation of these concerns by the park authority.

Camp of the Clouds received scant supervision from the Department of the Interior. For the first three summers after the national park was created, John Reese, the proprietor, packed in his supplies and set up camp each July just as he had since 1898. In 1902, at the request of Forest Superintendent D. B. Sheller, Reese obtained a permit for his camp from the secretary of the interior. The permit authorized Reese to occupy two acres on Theosophy Ridge (at Paradise) and to provide tents, bedding, and board to tourists. Intermittently, the permit authorized Reese to graze two milk cows and six horses.[37]

The public generally approved of Camp of the Clouds. Reese's rates were acceptable; it was only the camp's rustic character and poor sanitation that drew the occasional complaint. People wanted nicer accommodations and were willing to pay more for them. Public demand for better sanitation increased in 1911, the first full season that horse-drawn vehicles could take the road all the way to Paradise.[38]

Rainier's other preexisting tourist business was the family-owned

Longmire Springs Hotel. James Longmire, the family patriarch and well-known Washington pioneer, had discovered the mineral springs and natural clearing on his way home from a successful ascent of the mountain with George Bayley and Philemon Van Trump in 1883. With his wife, Virinda, he conceived the idea of developing the springs into a resort. By 1885 he had cleared a trail, built a cabin, and was accommodating a few adventuresome visitors. By 1889, he was advertising "Longmire's Medical Springs" in a Tacoma newspaper, and the next year he opened a hotel with five guest rooms, and began adding barns and other outbuildings to support a growing outfitting business for parties of campers and climbers en route to Paradise. In the 1890s, this old denizen of the mountain supported the movement to create a national park, although he did not live to see it accomplished. He died in 1897.[39]

The Longmire Springs Hotel became a troublesome inholding within the national park. Under the management of James and Virinda Longmire's son Elcaine and his wife, Martha, the hotel and bathhouses occupied an 18–acre mineral claim patented by James in 1892. The parks' supporters mistakenly assumed that the federal government would buy out the Longmires. Instead, the government granted the Tacoma and Eastern Railroad Company a five-year lease on two acres immediately south of the Longmire claim for construction of a rival tourist hotel.

Called the National Park Inn, this second hotel opened for business on July 1, 1906. The long, two-story building contained thirty-six rooms and had a capacity for sixty guests. On the grounds beside the building a number of tents with wood floors, walls, doors, and electric lights could accommodate another seventy-five guests. The National Park Inn's modern physical plant consisted of an electric lighting and refrigerating unit powered by water from the Nisqually River. Built and operated by the Tacoma and Eastern Railroad Company, the hotel provided elegant meals supplied by the commissary of the Chicago, Milwaukee, and Puget Sound Railway Company in Tacoma, and generally passed as a first-class hotel. While sojourners at the Longmire Springs Hotel typically passed the evening around a bonfire on the grounds, guests at the National Park Inn were entertained by musicians before an open fireplace in the social hall.[40]

In retaliation for this government-supported development, Robert

THE NEW PLEASURING GROUND

Longmire, Elcaine's brother, opened a saloon on the family property. Acting Superintendent Allen thought the saloon would be a "public nuisance" and immediately closed it down. Robert appealed to Senator Francis W. Cushman for help, but Cushman was unsympathetic and the saloon remained closed. Virinda Longmire then filed for a 160–acre homestead claim around the 18–acre mineral claim. Acting Superintendent Allen interceded at the General Land Office, and the application was denied. Virinda appealed the decision.[41]

While the case was under appeal, the Longmires enclosed a small portion of the desired homestead claim with a rough fence and pastured some stock there. Again Allen objected, informing the family that it could not graze stock on this tract and that the fence would be destroyed or confiscated by the government. Finally, after the secretary of the interior denied Virinda's appeal in the spring of 1907, Allen directed a ranger to evict Elcaine from the tract in question and burn his cabin. Elcaine apparently tried to forestall this action by encouraging his sister-in-law, Susan Hall, to occupy the cabin with her children during the summer. But the following winter, Ranger H. M. Cunningham found the cabin empty and burned it down. Cunningham reported to Allen:

> I did this at night so as to avoid any possible personal conflict with the Longmires. They—Ben and Elcaine Longmire—were still staying at the Springs on their patented land. I was on good terms with them and they had not said any thing about resisting the removal of the cabin, but I do not think they were staying at the springs so late in the season for any other purpose than to prevent the removal of the cabin. They had removed their effects from the homestead cabin long before.[42]

This ended the Longmires' attempts to expand the property.

If the Longmires had been concerned about losing business to the Tacoma and Eastern Railroad Company's new hotel venture, they soon discovered that the increasing tourist travel to the park was more than the two hotels could accommodate. They built an addition to the hotel, making a total of twelve guest rooms, and erected tents behind it. During the 1908 tourist season the Longmire Springs Hotel registered 925 guests, or nearly one-third of the total park visitation for that year.[43]

Park administrators characterized the Longmire Springs Hotel as a second-class hostelry. Noting that its rates were somewhat lower than those of the neighboring National Park Inn, they considered the hotel an advantage to the public. But they regretted the shabby appearance of the place, which, being on private property, they could do nothing about. The buildings were rough, and the wire fence that ran around the property was strung with signs and advertisements. The little shanty that had served for a short time as a saloon had been turned into a pool hall.[44] There were rumors, year after year, that the Longmires planned either to refurbish or sell the enterprise, but as the place only deteriorated it became more and more of an embarrassment. Finally, in 1916, the family leased the property to some investors, who made the long-awaited improvements the next year. These included a new two-story, seventeen-room hotel, sixteen new cottages in place of the tents, and a new sulphur plunge. In 1920, the Rainier National Park Company bought the lease and entered a twenty-year contract with the family. The original hotel was burned, and the new building was moved across the road, where it became the National Park Inn Annex.[45] The Longmire family would eventually sell their vacant property to the government in 1939.

Tourists increasingly voiced concern about the sanitary conditions in the area. The National Park Inn maintained that the bathhouses and rundown hotel across the road were the source of visitors' complaints. As early as 1909, however, Acting Superintendent Allen complained that the National Park Inn's kitchen disposed of waste in the Nisqually River, and recommended requiring the company to do something else with its garbage. Two years later, Asahel Curtis of Seattle reported on the unsanitary conditions found in the park, noting specifically that "large piles of manure are taken out of the stables at Longmire Springs and scattered over the ground."[46] In the fall of 1911, Superintendent Edward S. Hall had a sewer system installed at Longmire Springs and required both hotels to put in connecting lines.

Rainier's fourth visitor accommodation in this period, a mountain camp at Indian Henry's Hunting Ground called the Wigwam Hotel, was even more unsanitary. Established in 1908, the camp was run by George B. and Susan Longmire Hall. In 1913, Superintendent Ethan Allen supplied the Halls with detailed specifications for improving the

kitchen, dining room, tent floors, and toilets, but received no cooperation from them. Allen was piqued by the Halls' "audacity" in maintaining
that the camp toilets were adequate, describing the same to the secretary of the interior. "These arrangements consist of four poles stuck in
the ground in the semblance of a square, and around these poles are drawn
'gunny' sacks. Inside is a bench." The Halls, unable to comprehend how
the superintendent could become so upset over a little backcountry inel-
egance, claimed that he had a vendetta against them and wanted to drive
them out of business.[47] But Allen's motive was clear; park visitors were
demanding higher standards.

In the spring of 1912, rumors circulated of an outbreak of typhoid
fever in the park. The National Park Inn Company feared that the reports
would depress business and wanted to find the source of the misinfor-
mation. The superintendent knew of only one case of typhoid fever in
the park, though many cases of dysentery had been reported at Longmire and in the tent camps, as well as in all the towns from Ashford to
Eatonville. It seemed that the crowded conditions in the mountain camps
and in the overflow tent accommodations at Longmire were making
a poor public impression. The tent camps and hotels had become, in
the superintendent's words, "entirely inadequate" to accommodate the
increasing number of visitors.[48]

The growth in visitor numbers had other important consequences.
Through strength of numbers, urban park users increasingly opposed
various other park user groups—prospectors, miners, timbermen, stockmen, and hunters—whose economic pursuits seemed increasingly
anomalous in the national park setting. The secretary of the interior
and park officials responded to these demands. By weighing the interests of tourists and nontourists, the park administration was laying the
foundations of national park natural resource policy.

First to be opposed were the prospectors. Section 5 of the Mount
Rainier National Park Act authorized mining and prospecting within
the park, despite specific language in Section 2 requiring retention of
"mineral deposits" in their natural condition. Congress overlooked the
contradiction, and the secretary of the interior waited until after the law
was passed to criticize this feature in his annual report for 1899, but clearly
he recognized it was troublesome.[49]

Under the mining laws, a prospector could locate a mineral claim wherever he could show there was a reasonable prospect of extracting precious metals. The prospector had the right to dig tunnels or holes in the earth, divert water from streams for sluicing, and cut down trees on his claim with which to frame his mine and erect buildings. The mining laws did not give the prospector the right to shoot game; nevertheless, park officials were reluctant to deny permission when the prospector asked to take his gun into the park. The provision for mining and prospecting created a double standard between prospectors and tourists, placing wildlife, trees, water courses, and mineral deposits at the miner's or prospector's disposal.

Prospectors were hard to distinguish from pleasure seekers. "In most cases," Acting Superintendent Allen wrote in 1907, "the claimant makes a summer camping trip, does a few days' nominal assessment work, and returns to his usual vocation." The vast majority of claims consisted of no more than four blazes on trees, the posting of a notice of location, and a filing with the county clerk and recorder. The more persistent prospectors, however, built cabins and cut trails to their claims. They left slash on the ground, making an unsightly mess and creating a fire hazard. Allen suspected that some "prospectors" returned in the fall to hunt the park's game.[50]

Both Allen and Ricksecker, the road engineer, urged Secretary of the Interior James R. Garfield to seek an amendment of the Mount Rainier National Park Act. Probably the two men coordinated their efforts, for they both submitted hard-hitting reports on the issue in the fall of 1907. The desired amendment was inserted in the Sundry Civil Appropriations bill approved by Congress on May 27, 1908.[51] The law prohibited the location of new claims, but existing claims were unaffected. Over time, park officials worked with the General Land Office to have hundreds of claims invalidated, but a few dozen persisted. Legitimate mining operations would continue at a handful of locations in the park for several decades.

Timbermen soon became unwelcome in the park as well. However, it was park users, not government officials, who insisted on barring all commercial timber sales in the park. Consistent with the Mount Rainier National Park Act's listing of "timber" with other natural objects to be protected, early forest management at Rainier focused on the care and management of green, healthy trees. Early park superintendents only dimly acknowledged the ecological relationships between dead and living, old and young, or diseased and healthy trees. A good forest, in their view, was a forest unblemished by burns, insect infestations, or blow-downs.[52] Indeed, to the park's first administrator, Grenville F. Allen, the market value and aesthetics of a forest neatly coincided, and he mistakenly assumed that tourists, too, had a special admiration for stands of big, straight trees. As a result, Allen blundered into a timber sale, proposed by Beall Foster of Tacoma, involving dead and down timber lying within fifty feet of the road for two miles inside the park boundary. Incredibly, Assistant Secretary of the Interior Frank Pierce authorized the timber sale with the simple remark that the department desired "to dispose of all such dead timber within the limits of the park."[53]

The timber sale soon acquired its own momentum. Beall Foster's offer to purchase 200 cords of dead cedar for shingle bolts at $0.85 per cord was superseded by Edward S. Hall's application to purchase 1,000 cords at $1.10 per cord. Hall's bid was then topped by the Big Creek Shingle Company's offer of $1.30 per cord. The department approved a contract with the Big Creek Shingle Company on June 7, 1909. That summer, while the company installed a mill near Ashford and cleared the trees along the Nisqually River to make a suitable landing, Acting Superintendent Allen assigned Ranger William Sethe to mark and scale the timber inside the park. Sethe's estimate came to 5,235 cords, for a total stumpage value of $6,805.50. By the end of 1909, the Big Creek Shingle Company had paid the Department of the Interior $3,600 for stumpage.[54] Thus, before the logging operation in the park was even under way, it had already increased in size more than twenty-five fold.

As the Big Creek Shingle Company moved into the park in the spring of 1910, Rainier enthusiasts in Seattle and Tacoma objected. The Seattle and Tacoma chambers of commerce protested the sale. The Mountaineers sent two club members to investigate and report on the logging operation. The Mountaineers' report charged the new park superintendent, Edward S. Hall (the former bidder on the sale), with collusion in stretching the definition of "dead trees" to include all cedars with dry tops, or practically the whole forest. The Mountaineers' report alleged that the cutting was in violation of the contract, while the contract itself violated the Mount Rainier National Park Act.[55]

Army engineer Eugene Ricksecker decried the sale as well. He described the damage in poignant terms. "This portion of the road passes through the largest body of uniformly large cedars that exist in this part of the country," Ricksecker wrote. So many trees had been removed that a person could now see a thousand feet into the woods where he could formerly see a hundred. The "natural wildness" of this forest, "undisturbed by man," constituted a resource that "should have been jealously guarded."[56]

Secretary of the Interior Richard A. Ballinger responded by dispatching a special inspector to Rainier. Although Special Inspector Edward W. Dixon stopped short of alleging any corruption, he agreed with The Mountaineers' assessment that Hall's definition of dead trees included "practically all the standing cedar in the National Park." Later that summer, Secretary Ballinger visited Rainier himself and was angered by what he found. He wanted the Big Creek Shingle Company to pay a cash settlement and get out of the park immediately. If the department wanted to remove any more dead and down timber, he told his chief clerk, Clement S. Ucker, it would be done by government employees under the superintendent's direct supervision.[57]

While Rainier's administrators erred in thinking that timbermen could operate successfully inside the park, they had no such illusions about stockmen. From the outset, officials opposed livestock grazing within the park. In the 1890s, stockmen in the Yakima Valley had grazed sheep on the east side of Rainier, damaging the flora and provoking the *Seattle Times* to comment that the creation of the park would "effectively keep the sheep herders with their countless flocks out of these wonderful alpine meadows." Fortunately for everyone concerned, stockmen never posed much threat of trespass after 1899. A shift from sheep to cattle raising in the Yakima Valley, together with an improvement in range management on the national forests nearer to home, lessened the attractiveness for stockmen of Rainier's distant and mostly snowbound meadows.[58]

Hunters were another concern. The Mount Rainier National Park Act prohibited "the wanton destruction of fish and game," as well as

"their capture or destruction for the purposes of merchandise or profit."
Park officials construed this language as calling for a ban on most kinds
of hunting. Sport fishing and the killing of predators were two excep-
tions. The hunting ban had at least three purposes: to protect rare species
of scientific interest such as the mountain goat, to help depressed populations of game species recover and spill out of the park into surrounding
areas, and to make all species of wildlife more visible for the pleasure of
tourists.[59]

Sport hunters generally supported the ban, recognizing that the creation of a game refuge was to their benefit. Acting Superintendent Allen
noted the willingness of most visitors to comply with the hunting prohibition. Not all sportsmen respected the law, however. Near the park's
Carbon River section, a few locals kept hunting dogs and were "always
ready, for a small remuneration, to assist the more disreputable sportsmen of Tacoma and Seattle in their hunting expeditions."[60]

Park officials suspected there was more poaching by so-called pot
hunters. This was the name given to low-income farmers and townsmen who went after the game to procure meat for their larders. In western Washington, as in many parts of the country in this period, a
substantial segment of the population rejected the whole idea of state
or federal wildlife management, insisting on the local inhabitant's right
to take wildlife when and where he pleased.[61] The only way to get such
people to comply with the law was by threat of punishment. A park ranger
arrested one such poacher for killing a deer in 1909, and the government secured a conviction and a $100 fine, presumably with some salu-
tary effect. Ranger patrols may have been a deterrent to this type of
hunting, but the rangers knew that a determined poacher could evade
the entire force without difficulty if he took the right precautions.[62]

Some Yakama Indians hunted in the park, believing they had the right
under the Walla Walla Treaty of 1855. In July 1915, Ranger Thomas E.
O'Farrell discovered the remains of a camp at Yakima Park on the northeast side of Rainier. The camp included a shelter and two horse corrals,
all of which were built from timber cut down in the area. Large quan-
tities of bones and other animal remains lay about. O'Farrell reported
to Superintendent DeWitt L. Reaburn that "bands of natives" had been
making annual visits to the park to hunt deer, and did they have treaty

rights? If not, what steps should he take to end the practice? Reaburn forwarded O'Farrell's letter to the secretary of the interior. The department replied that in order to make a determination, it was necessary to know to which tribe the Indians belonged.[63]

Informed that the Indians usually camped at Yakima Park in late summer, O'Farrell sent his two assistant rangers, Leonard Rosso and Arthur White, back there at the end of August. Rosso and White found about thirty Yakama Indians camped in the high meadow with their leader, Sluiskin. Using a Yakama woman interpreter, the rangers told Sluiskin that it was against the law to hunt game in the park. Sluiskin referred the rangers to the Walla Walla Treaty that his nation's chief had signed sixty years earlier in 1855. In Sluiskin's view, the treaty reserved for the Yakama tribe the right to hunt, gather, and fish on all open and unclaimed lands that formerly belonged to the tribe. Rosso and White did not press the issue with Sluiskin, but reported to Reaburn that the Indians claimed rights under the Walla Walla Treaty.[64] Reaburn wired Secretary of the Interior Franklin K. Lane on September 1, 1915: "The Yakima Indians under Chief Sluiskin are now on a hunting expedition in the northeast corner of the park. They refuse to obey the ranger's orders claiming the right to hunt and kill as they please, but say they will slaughter only what is needed."[65] Assistant Secretary Bo Sweeney submitted the matter to the department's solicitor, noting that the treaty's restriction of Indian hunting rights to "open and unclaimed land" probably meant that the treaty right did not extend "within the metes and bounds" of Mount Rainier National Park.[66] But the solicitor's opinion surprised him.

Solicitor Preston C. West argued that the Mount Rainier National Park Act of 1899 did not terminate the Indians' treaty right to hunt game within the boundaries of the park. First, the solicitor argued, the national park did not remove the area from the status of "open and unclaimed land" as it was construed in the treaty. West referred to the long-standing principle in federal Indian law that required the courts to resolve all ambiguities of meaning in Indian treaties according to how they had been understood by the Indians. The Indians who signed the Walla Walla Treaty of 1855, West presumed, recognized "open and unclaimed land" as land that was not settled upon or appropriated by claimants under the general land laws. The treaty's Indian signers did not understand it to mean that their people's hunting right could be curtailed by the establishment of a national park for the public's enjoyment.[67]

Second, the act of 1899 did not specifically address hunting by Indians. With respect to the protection of game, the act of 1899 gave the secretary authority "to provide against the wanton destruction of the fish and game found within said park, and against their capture or destruction for the purposes of merchandise or profit." Looking at the treaty right in the context of 1855, West argued, it did not seem that either party equated the Indian treaty right with these types of hunting. Therefore, West wrote, "the law of 1899 simply stated specifically what was necessarily implied in the treaty." Since the treaty did not give the Indians the right to destroy game wantonly or to hunt game for the market, the act of 1899 had taken nothing away. It followed that the Indians' right to hunt for their subsistence within the park had not been taken away by the law of 1899, either. This did not mean that the Indians' right to hunt could not be regulated, West hastened to add. Since the act of 1899 gave the secretary of the interior broad authority to fulfill the purposes of the park, and the park was created for the public's enjoyment, "the Indians must exercise their privilege in such manner as not to defeat this expressed purpose."

No one in the department followed West's advice to draft park regulations that would be sensitive to Indian hunting rights. The solicitor's opinion was simply ignored. The opinion ran counter to the current trend in game law for increased state jurisdiction over game management, including hunting of game by Indians outside Indian reservations. Shortly after West wrote his opinion, the Washington State Supreme Court decided in *State v. Towessnute* that Yakama Indians outside their reservation were subject to the state game laws. The following year, in June 1916, the U.S. Supreme Court upheld a decision affirming the right of the State of New York to regulate fishing by Seneca Indians on lands that the tribe had ceded to the United States. The Washington State Game Commission brought these facts to the attention of national park and national forest administrators in Washington in October 1916. A further development that bore on the issue of Indian treaty rights in Mount Rainier National Park was the Act of Congress of June 30, 1916,

which accepted the cession by the State of Washington of exclusive jurisdiction over the lands embraced within the park. This act clarified the
authority of park officials to make arrests.[68]

Despite the department's inaction, the initiative to end subsistence
hunting by Indians in the park came from local authorities—seasonal
park rangers, state and county game wardens, newspaper editors—and
not from any general policy that was crystallizing in the National Park
Service (which was newly established in August 1916). On October 28,
1916, Reaburn wired Superintendent of National Parks Robert B.
Marshall that the band of Yakama Indians was back in the park hunting
game. "Shall we arrest them and bring them before the park commissioner," read the telegram, "instructions desired immediately." Marshall
replied affirmatively.[69] Although the decision finally came from park
service officials in Washington, D.C., these officials were responding to
the pressure of events at the local level.

If Reaburn acted immediately on Marshall's instruction, he failed to
catch any Indian violators that season. The following summer, Reaburn
stationed Park Ranger O. W. Curtis in Yakima Park. When word came
from Curtis of the Indians' presence there in early October 1917, Reaburn responded with haste. Starting out from headquarters at Longmire with Ranger John Yorke and former superintendent Edward S. Hall,
now the state game commissioner, he drove his automobile all day on
rough and circuitous roads clockwise around the outside of the park to
the White River, which he reached shortly after dark. Then, leaving two
hours before light the next morning with Yorke, he hiked on foot up to
the Indians' camp. They arrested six Indians in the possession of freshly ·
skinned deer hides, and brought the accused back down to the White
River for a "court" appointment with Hall beside Reaburn's automobile. As the Indians offered no resistance and pleaded guilty to the charge
of illegal hunting, Hall gave them all light fines.[70]

That the new National Park Service (NPS) lacked a definite policy
on subsistence hunting by Indians was further demonstrated by the pro-
longed correspondence that ensued between senior officials of the NPS
and the Office of Indian Affairs over the proper disposition of three confiscated rifles. Assistant Director Horace M. Albright wanted to use
the occasion of returning these items to the Indians to make an official

announcement that the Indians' treaty rights did not extend to the park. Assistant Commissioner of Indian Affairs E. B. Meritt initially opposed an official endorsement of any such thing. Reaburn finally worked out a compromise with the Yakima Reservation's superintendent, Don M. Carr. The warning that these officials issued to the Indians is not in the records, but the arrests evidently had the desired effect. This was the last time until recent years that subsistence hunting by Indians was an issue in Mount Rainier National Park.[71]

The expulsion of Indians from the park demonstrated as well as any action the Department of the Interior's reluctance to innovate policy on how the park should be managed. Rather, department officials took their cue from individuals and organizations based in Seattle and Tacoma. For the most part, these urban-based park users supported measures aimed at protecting their own preferred park experiences, and park regulations in this era reflected the urban users' consensus view of appropriate use of the park. Prohibitions on various forms of resource extraction—mining, logging, and hunting—defined the national park as a place set apart from the surrounding countryside. More subtle was the effort to establish appropriate recreational uses, or behavioral norms, in the park setting. Camping was appropriate, but chopping down or burning live trees was aberrant. Driving automobiles was appropriate; speeding was aberrant. The mineral bath at Longmire Hot Springs was fine, but the saloon had to go. Often as not, inappropriate uses were characterized as aberrant behaviors by a few yahoos; still, park authorities needed to regulate the growing throng of pleasure seekers. Put most simply, the problem of park administration was to enforce public values. With the advent of the National Park Service in 1916, the park administration took more initiative in interpreting what was in the public interest and in making management decisions; nevertheless, Seattle and Tacoma residents would continue to play a central role in defining national park values.

CHAPTER 4

Steve Mather and the Rainier National Park Company (1915–1930)

IN 1915, NATIONAL PARK PROMOTERS ACROSS THE NATION learned that they had a new leader in Stephen T. Mather. A Chicago business tycoon, philanthropist, and longtime member of the Sierra Club, Mather took the reins of national park reform at the invitation of Secretary of the Interior Franklin K. Lane. "Dear Steve," Lane famously wrote to Mather in reply to Mather's complaint about the state of the parks, "if you don't like the way the national parks are being run, come on down to Washington and run them yourself."[1] With no prior experience in government, Mather accepted the challenge. He took an unsalaried position as assistant to the secretary, and immediately revived the campaign for legislation to establish a National Park Service. In a year and a half the bill would be passed; in a little over two years Mather would be appointed the park service's first director.

The advent of the National Park Service began a new era in the history of Mount Rainier National Park. Congress gave the national parks a clear and consistent purpose in the National Park Service Act of 1916. The National Park Service (NPS) developed a strong sense of mission. Stephen T. Mather, who served as first director of the NPS from 1917 to 1929, took a close interest in Rainier's administration and development.

He gave Rainier more personal attention than any subsequent NPS director.

Mather's initiatives at Rainier were emblematic of his efforts throughout the national park system. Mather's vision was to develop the national parks in partnership with closely controlled private capital. In each park, a single "concession" or "regulated monopoly" would provide hotel accommodations and all other visitor services under a renewable, long-term government contract. The government, for its part, would design and build roads and all other elements of national park infrastructure. The Rainier National Park Company, founded in 1916, together with the park service's "master plan" of infrastructure development for Rainier in 1928—the first master plan in the national park system—were both products of Mather's vision and forceful leadership.

The Rainier National Park Company (RNPC) successfully united the leading businessmen of Seattle and Tacoma behind one enterprise. Not all people in the region, however, were pleased by the arrangement. Some critics worried that the NPS and the RNPC were overdeveloping or commercializing the park. Others charged that the RNPC's exclusive franchise was a corruption of the free enterprise system. Still others claimed that it discriminated against the working class, that the concession policy denied low-income groups equal access to the park.

The RNPC had its own difficulties in this era. Despite an eightfold increase in the park's annual visitation from 1915 to 1930, the evolving pattern of visitor use gave company officers little else to cheer about. Visitation was frustratingly concentrated on weekends in July, August, and September. The pattern of visitation made it difficult for the RNPC to keep a resident hotel staff busy during the summer or to make any profit in the "shoulder seasons" of late spring and early fall. The RNPC had to close down and leave its buildings empty for the better part of each year. Worst of all from the company's standpoint, a large proportion of Rainier visitors came from Seattle or Tacoma, drove to the park in their private automobiles, and either returned to the city the same day or car camped. They gave the RNPC little or no business, and the RNPC was almost irrelevant to their park experience. Company officers grew increasingly disillusioned with Rainier's visitor profile. The out-of-state visitor, the railroad traveler, the destination tourist, the high-rolling hotel patron—these types of guests never appeared in as great numbers as company officers desired. Bent on realizing that dream, the RNPC pushed the NPS for various development schemes that would enable the company to tap a larger tourist market.

From the day of his appointment to public office in 1915, Mather dedicated the rest of his life to ensuring the national parks a permanent place in American life. Historian John Ise described Mather as "a man of prodigious and explosive energy, a tireless worker, a born promoter."[2] Robert Sterling Yard, a close associate, eulogized Mather as a natural leader and catalyst for reform: "He was pictured, written up, dined and feted. His appearances were applauded and his words were treasured and quoted. His journeys crisscrossing the country were blazed with newspaper headlines and punctuated with interviews."[3] A hard-bitten idealist, Mather was given to bouts of wrath or depression and finally suffered a crippling stroke in 1929. He died in 1930.

Mather formed his vision for Rainier's development on a tour of the western parks in the summer of 1915. With an entourage of Rainier enthusiasts from Seattle and Tacoma, Mather drove the new park road to Paradise, then took an extended horse trip around the west side of the mountain from Longmire to Carbon River. After this wilderness outing, Mather met with the group of Seattle and Tacoma park supporters formally at the exclusive Rainier Club in Seattle, where, according to his biographer Robert Shankland, he "worked his miracle." He talked the men into forming a Rainier National Park Company and building an inn in Paradise Valley.[4] The inn would provide comfort and style in the heart of scenic splendor; Paradise would be made accessible to everyone.

Not surprisingly, the RNPC maintained a different version of these events in which the original vision of Paradise Inn belonged not to Mather but to the company's first general manager, T. H. Martin. For five years, the story went, Martin had contemplated Rainier through the windows of the Tacoma Building, where he worked as secretary of the Tacoma Commercial Club and Chamber of Commerce. What the city needed, Martin believed, was a first-class hotel at Rainier "in order to entice persons of real vision and financial stature" to visit the Pacific Northwest "and perhaps consider the commercial possibilities in this Great Empire." Martin resigned his post in 1915 to devote his full energies to this plan. According to the company history, the decisive meeting occurred not at the Rainier Club with Mather but in Tacoma on October 3, 1915. There, Martin persuaded a handful of businessmen to bring Seattle and Tacoma financiers together to form a company that would handle all hotels, camps, and transportation in the park. Promptly, the group dispatched Martin to San Francisco to present his proposal to Mather.[5]

The discrepancy between these two stories is significant. It is more than a matter of who deserves credit—the national or local figure, the public official or the capitalist—for conceiving the plan for Rainier's development. Embedded in the park service's fledgling partnership with Seattle and Tacoma capital were two similar but conflicting ideas about the national park's purpose. Martin and the other businessmen who formed the RNPC were interested in profits, but more than that, they were motivated by the prospect of making Rainier into a nationally renowned asset of the Pacific Northwest and a magnet for regional growth. Their vision harked back to the Seattle and Tacoma boosters of the 1890s and early 1900s who sought to identify their respective cities with the mountain's appealing image, to "package" the Pacific Northwest as a place that offered an exceptional quality of life. Mather, for his part, wanted to make the scenic beauty of Rainier accessible to all the people. This would pay dividends of another sort. As Americans became more enamored of the national parks, Congress would deepen its commitment to the national park idea. Mather wanted to make the national park system into one of the nation's most celebrated institutions. Whereas Martin and the RNPC sought to exploit the national park as a "commodity resource," Mather wanted to develop and administer the national park as an "artifact of culture."[6] In 1915 the tension between these two concepts was latent; by midcentury it would emerge as one of the major issues in national park administration.

Mather understood and sympathized with the business community's interest in Rainier. Mather himself frequently promoted the national parks as agents of economic growth. In his annual report for 1925, Mather ruminated that every national park visitor was "a potential settler and investor," and waxed poetic on this theme:

The march of the huge wagon trains along the scarcely discernible trails in the fifties marked the beginning of the settlement of the West. The new people were the settlers and the builders. They carried with them plows, and the seeds from which the granaries of the future were to be filled. Their descendants are the living pioneers of western development. The new West, however, is being built up by later visitors who came to see, and, having seen, brought their families to become citizens of now large prospering communities. Hundreds of thousands in the past few years have pulled stakes in the East and invested in western ranches and fruit farms, in mines, and other industrial enterprises. In all this the national parks, as the scenic lodestones, through their attractions draw these future settlers and investors for their first trip and in this way contribute their vital share in the prosperity of the institutions, scenic resorts, and general business of the country.[7]

Mather's new concession policy was one of his most important reforms. He found a chaotic situation in 1915, not only at Rainier but in all the national parks. Competition between the various tourist concessions within each park was debilitating. The concessioners spent so much effort warding off competitors that they could not give good service to the public. There were too many fly-by-night operators. The messy scene at Longmire, with its ragged line of stables, tent-stores, and advertising signs, was typical. The solution, Mather argued, was to consolidate tourist services in each park under one licensed operator. Each park concession would be a regulated monopoly: *regulated* so that the NPS could ensure that it was providing good service, a *monopoly* so that the operator could be induced to accept low yearly returns on long-term investments. Mather called the concessions "public utilities," a disarming term that suggested their similarity to another kind of regulated monopoly, the municipal utility company.[8]

The label was somewhat disingenuous. Unlike municipally controlled utility companies, the RNPC would be under no profit-sharing plan with its own rate payers, the tourists. Nor would it appeal to tourists for a new bond issue each time it sought to build a new hotel. The company was less accountable to the "public interest," much less the "national interest," than the public utility tag would indicate. Of the RNPC's 142 stockholders in 1919, all but nine lived in Seattle or Tacoma, and all but eight were owners, executives, or general managers of businesses in the region.[9] If these men were public spirited, it was their civic pride in the Puget Sound cities that motivated them to invest in the nearby national park.

The RNPC was incorporated with a capital stock of $200,000 on March 1, 1916. At the first meeting of the board Chester Thorne of Tacoma was elected president and Martin was hired as general manager (at nearly double the salary of the park superintendent.) The RNPC then contracted with the Department of the Interior for the exclusive privilege of providing hotels, inns, camps, and transportation in the park for a period of twenty years beginning on April 24, 1916. Its plan of development, outlined that spring, included new construction of an inn at Paradise as well as two tent camps at Paradise and Nisqually Glacier, and new management of the National Park Inn at Longmire, as well as guide and transportation services.[10]

The centerpiece of the RNPC's development scheme was Paradise Inn. That summer, before the snow had left the Paradise Valley, construction of Paradise Inn began with the installation of a 250-horsepower, hydroelectric power plant on Van Trump Creek at Christine Falls, two miles below the main development site. This was followed by the establishment of a 100-tent camp for the building crew. Due to a lingering snowpack, the RNPC's building contractor, E. C. Cornell, was unable to break ground for the inn until July 20. Despite a short construction season, however, Cornell's crew nearly completed the inn during the summer of 1916. The initial cost, not including furnishings and equipment, came to $91,000.[11]

Designed by Tacoma architect Frederick Heath, the building comprised three main wings, each one featuring steep, gable roofs and a row of dormer windows in the upper story. In the popular style of the period, the building's large timber frame remained exposed on the interior. A guest standing in the cavernous assembly room on the ground floor could look straight up to the ridge pole three stories overhead. Superintendent DeWitt L. Reaburn gave permission to cut dead Alaska cedars from the "silver forest" for the interior decor of the building. This timber, located on the road between Longmire and Paradise, had been fire-killed several years before the establishment of the park and had seasoned to a ghostly light gray or silver hue. The use of this timber was in keeping with the service policy of using native building materials whenever possible. The great, silver logs were the inn's most appealing feature.[12]

Paradise Inn opened for business in 1917 with only thirty-seven available guest rooms and a dining-room capacity for four hundred guests. The RNPC planned to build more guest rooms as demand increased and the company grew. This turned out to be a sound approach, because during the first two seasons of operation the nation was engaged in World War I and travel to the national parks was somewhat depressed. So the company's stockholders bided their time through 1917 and 1918.[13]

Following Paradise Inn's first peacetime season in 1919, the RNPC's stockholders finally had reason to rejoice. The inn had been filled to capacity through most of the season, the RNPC's gross revenues had doubled over the year before, and the company showed a net profit over the year of more than $20,000. The directors were in an ebullient mood when they met in January 1920. They decided to approve the first addition to Paradise Inn, a 104–room wing, which they called the annex. This time the company employed its own labor and used its own trucks to deliver building materials to the site. The annex was completed by the end of 1920.[14]

The completion of the annex ended the first phase of the RNPC's development of the Paradise area. From a commercial standpoint, burgeoning visitor demand in the early 1920s almost immediately justified the RNPC's investment. Each year, Paradise Inn did a thriving business throughout the short season, accounting for more than half of the RNPC's total revenue. Paradise Inn deserved no less praise as an architectural achievement. Considering the heavy snowfall and short tourist season at Paradise and the condition of the road in 1916, building such a grand hotel so high on Rainier was a bold enterprise. An ink engraving of the impressive structure soon graced the RNPC's letterhead and bore the proud caption, "Paradise Inn in Paradise Valley—elevation 5557 ft. Where the flowers and the glaciers meet." The building certainly possessed more grandeur than the two existing hotels at Longmire. It was not in the same class with the log palaces found in certain other national parks—for example, the Old Faithful Inn, the Glacier Park Lodge, or the Many Glacier Hotel—but there is no evidence to suggest that Rainier visitors wanted it to be. Paradise Inn aptly reflected the RNPC's middling position between the undercapitalized park concessions of the pre-1916 era and the railroad-subsidized park concessions of Yellowstone, Glacier, Yosemite, and Grand Canyon national parks.

After construction of Paradise Inn, the RNPC's other main goal was to establish its monopoly over visitor services in the park. With help from the NPS, which informed all existing concessions that their contracts would not be renewed, the transition to a single park concession was accomplished in just over two years.

Some people accused the RNPC of strong-arm tactics in acquiring these interests. After the RNPC purchased John L. Reese's camp equipment and improvements for $8,250 in 1916, past patrons of the camp complained that Reese had been "squeezed out." The RNPC got nowhere when it first tried to purchase George B. Hall's horse barn and livery service at Longmire and tent camp at Indian Henry's Hunting Ground. But when Hall died in April 1917, the RNPC negotiated a deal with the attorney for the Hall estate, acquiring the Hall property for $3,003. The RNPC then closed the Indian Henry's camp. Superintendent Reaburn, noting that the Indian Henry's trail had always been the most popular horse trip out of Longmire, speculated that the RNPC had closed the camp in order "to cripple the business at Longmire Springs, and force the Longmire Springs Hotel Company to sell their property to the Rainier National Park Company."[15]

In the late spring of 1916, Superintendent Reaburn initiated negotiations between the National Park Hotel and Transportation Company and the RNPC on the sale of the former company's buildings, furnishings, and small fleet of touring cars. The National Park Hotel and Transportation Company's president, James Hughes, wanted $42,500. The negotiations stalled, and the National Park Inn continued under the old management for the 1916 and 1917 seasons. In April 1918, Hughes reopened the negotiations with an offer to sell for $37,000. He accepted the RNPC's counteroffer of $30,000 a few weeks later.[16]

The RNPC got lucky with the Longmire Springs Hotel Company, which might have continued under separate management indefinitely since it occupied a private inholding and was not under government contract. In 1916, the Longmire family leased the hotel operation to J. B.

Ternes and E. C. Cornell, who built an annex next to the original Longmire Springs Hotel. In 1919, following lengthy, three-way negotiations between the RNPC, the leaseholders, and the property owners, the RNPC purchased the buildings together with a twenty-year lease on the patented land for $12,000. Ternes became a major shareholder and secretary of the RNPC. The following year, the RNPC moved the new annex across the road to a position adjacent to the National Park Inn, calling it the National Park Inn Annex, and demolished the old Longmire Springs Hotel. Together with the removal of the various tent-stores and outbuildings, this improved the appearance of the Longmire area.[17]

As the 1920s unfolded, the situation at Longmire left both the RNPC and the park administration dissatisfied. It was clear to the RNPC that the National Park Inn would not be very profitable. Ironically, no sooner had the RNPC cleaned up the Longmire area than it became a mere pit stop on the road to Paradise, or at best, an overflow area when Paradise Inn was filled to capacity. Park visitors overwhelmingly preferred to drive to the end of the road and stay in the new inn or campground. The RNPC was disinclined to invest very much in the Longmire area to try to change this pattern. After 1920, the company's sole effort to hold park visitors in the Longmire area was to offer special weekly rates at the National Park Inn in order to attract a different clientele. For the most part, the RNPC wanted to invest where the demand was greatest, at Paradise.[18]

The park service took a different view of the matter. It was concerned about low occupancy at the National Park Inn because there was so much congestion at Paradise: crowded campgrounds, a shortage of parking spaces, traffic jams, park visitors turned away at the inn. There remained one possibility for rehabilitating Longmire as a tourist destination: the attraction of the mineral springs. Superintendent W. H. Peters recommended that the mineral baths be developed for their medicinal properties, that a natatorium be built, and that tennis courts and other outdoor sports facilities be developed. In short, Longmire should be made into a health spa.[19]

In September 1920, the NPS took water samples from eight springs in the national park, two of them in the Longmire area, and sent them to the Bureau of Chemistry's Hygienic Lab in Washington, D.C. This began more than a year of correspondence between top NPS officials in

Washington, experts in the Public Health Service, and the superintendents of Rainier and Hot Springs Reservation, Arkansas. NPS officials concluded that the mineral springs contained no real medicinal value other than the natural benefits that were incidental to a restful and relaxing sojourn in a mountain resort. Nevertheless, it still favored redevelopment of the springs by the RNPC, provided that no false claims were made about the therapeutic powers of the mineral baths.[20]

The RNPC declined to rehabilitate the Longmire Springs mineral baths. In the long run this was probably fortuitous; the park administration would later find the development of mineral baths at Ohanapecosh, in the southeast corner of the park, to be both unsightly and unsanitary, and would have a difficult time closing that establishment. But it also portended the difficulties that would arise when the RNPC and the NPS did not see eye-to-eye on how the park should be developed. The park administration's desire to make Longmire into a health resort was motivated in part by its desire to relieve pressure on the Paradise area. The park service's efforts to move visitor services to lower elevations would become a constant theme in park planning, and would meet with unremitting resistance from the RNPC.

Despite the RNPC's impressive strides, not everyone was happy with the park service's concession policy. The first major challenge to the park service's policy came from a Seattle-based, nonprofit, left-leaning, outdoor club known as the Cooperative Campers of the Pacific Northwest. This group, which made available camping trips to the park for people of modest means, viewed the park service's partnership with private capital as ill-conceived and discriminating against the poor. Park service and RNPC officials decided that the Cooperative Campers were offering services in violation of the RNPC's exclusive contract. The dispute raised legal questions and brought into focus basic issues of fairness in how the park was being developed.

The Cooperative Campers group was founded in 1916. The group's purpose, as stated in its bylaws, was "to encourage the love of simple living in the open air, and to make the wonders of our Mountains accessible, especially through establishing self-supporting but non-profit-making camps for summer vacations."[21] The group required a nominal membership fee of one dollar and invited anyone to join who could satisfy one of the club's officers that he or she could make a "good camper." The group was affiliated with The Mountaineers and Mazamas, but it differed from those clubs in the fact that it organized summer camps rather than outings. The camps ran for nearly two months and members could join the camp for any length of stay while the camp was in operation. They could stay in one camp or hike from camp to camp around the mountain. Members received summer schedules that listed dates and fees for a wide variety of trips. Group sizes were limited to twenty-five people.[22]

The Cooperative Campers operated on a shoestring budget of a few thousand dollars per year. The camp cooks, a packer, and an office secretary in Seattle were the only salaried employees of the organization. Camp managers and leaders of hikes did not receive salaries but could receive fee waivers for their trips. The club's president, elected for a one-year term, served without salary. In its early years, the Cooperative Campers benefited from the energetic leadership of its first president, Anna Louise Strong, a civic activist, writer, and socialist. After Strong's departure in 1919 (she left for the Soviet Union to report on the Russian Revolution), no dominant personality took her place. Major E. S. Ingraham, a pioneer climber of Rainier and longtime leader in the Boy Scouts, remained active in the Cooperative Campers, but did not serve as president.

The cooperative camps were unlike either the mountain clubs, whose members owned and packed in their own equipment, or the RNPC-operated camps, which catered to automobile tourists. Each cooperative camp consisted of four six-person sleeping tents, divided into men's and women's quarters, separated by the cook tent. In addition to tents, food, and eating utensils, the camps were stocked with straw mattresses, blankets, alpenstocks, greasepaint (sunscreen), and other specialty equipment. Camp fees in 1917 were $1.25 per day for shelter, equipment, and meals. Transfer of baggage from camp to camp cost $0.50 to $1.00 depending on the distance between camps. The cooperative camps offered affordable recreation for people of modest means who possessed neither their own equipment nor their own automobile.[23]

By 1917, the Cooperative Campers maintained camps at six locations in the park: Paradise, Ohanapecosh Park, Summerland, Glacier Basin, Mystic Lake, and Seattle Park. It was possible to hike from camp to camp more than halfway around the mountain. Heady with the group's success, Anna Louise Strong predicted that similar cooperatives would develop in other western cities and soon open up "the far recesses of other mountain ranges and other national parks."[24]

The Cooperative Campers' socialist leanings did not escape Mather's notice when he first pondered the matter in December 1917. In addition to organizing the cooperative camps, Anna Louise Strong worked on the staff of a socialist newspaper, *The Seattle Union Record*, and held elective office as a member of the Seattle School Board. That year, she had angered Seattle voters by her strident antiwar position in the newspaper, and was now embroiled in recall proceedings. This was irrelevant as far as the cooperative camps were concerned, but Mather judged that in the present context of war-bred, antisocialist hysteria in the country, the Cooperative Campers might soon self-destruct. When Superintendent Reaburn asked the director whether he should prohibit Strong from conducting cooperative camps in the park during the coming summer, Mather suggested that the matter could await the outcome of the recall proceedings.[25]

Ejected from the Seattle School Board that spring, Strong continued to pour her energy into the Cooperative Campers. In the summer of 1918, the group scaled back its operation and maintained just two camps at Paradise and Summerland. She explained to Reaburn, "The war changes many things and many of our men are gone."[26] The Paradise camp served 155 people and the Summerland camp 67 people, but the average stay of campers at Summerland was more than twice as long, at ten days, so the two camps were comparatively busy. It was the Paradise camp that most troubled Mather since the camp was in direct competition with the RNPC's campground. Fortunately, Strong indicated to Reaburn at the end of the season that the Cooperative Campers intended to discontinue the Paradise camp next season. These campers had expressed a certain amount of dissatisfaction "due to the inevitable comparison with the standards they see about them and also to the fact that people who ride up in autos expect a different type of camp-life from those who walk."[27] Henceforth, the cooperative camps would not compete with car camping but would concentrate on opening up the backcountry.

This new direction might have alleviated the conflict between the Cooperative Campers and the park service, except that Strong now asked for permission to take over the old Wigwam Hotel or tent camp at Indian Henry's, which the RNPC had recently purchased and abandoned. According to Strong, the plan met with the RNPC's approval. Mather and his close assistant, Horace M. Albright, opposed the plan. Mather did not want to place the development of the national park's backcountry in the hands of some local organization of campers; Albright was concerned about the quality of service that the cooperative camps would give to the public.[28]

With Strong's request that the park give her the keys to the ranger cabin at Indian Henry's so that the Cooperative Campers could make use of it that winter, Reaburn's patience snapped. In September 1918, he directed one of his rangers to arrest the Cooperative Campers' packer, George Crockett, for receiving pay for his services in the park without having a concession permit. U.S. Commissioner Edward S. Hall convicted Crockett on the misdemeanor charge and imposed a small fine. Explaining this action to Albright, Reaburn contended that the Cooperative Campers was neither an authorized concession nor an organized outdoor club like The Mountaineers or Mazamas. The Cooperative Campers did not meet the criteria for the latter because it solicited members through printed circulars and newspaper advertisements. Reaburn also reminded Albright that Strong had been recalled from the Seattle School Board for her antiwar statements, and that "her bosom companion, Miss Olivereau, was given a penitentiary sentence of 10 years" for encouraging draft resistance. What really galled the superintendent was Strong's exaggerated claim that the Cooperative Campers were opening up the backcountry. "As a matter of fact she is spending absolutely nothing in the way of developing, but expects the Service to do a lot of things in the way of fixing up and improving conditions for her camp, having no doubt gotten the impression that we should improve her camp as we have done the public camping grounds."[29] Reaburn wanted authorization to prohibit cooperative camps in the coming year.

At this point, the Cooperative Campers virtually disappears from the historical record until 1921. From later statements it is evident that the Cooperative Campers maintained at least one camp in the park each season at Summerland, and probably the N P S chose to tolerate the group as long as it limited its activities to the east side of the park (away from the R N P C's hotels and camps). Moreover, the personal antagonism between Strong and Reaburn ended in the spring of 1919 with Strong's departure for the Soviet Union and Reaburn's request for an indefinite leave from the N P S. Still another factor that may have worked to deter the N P S from taking a stand against the Cooperative Campers in 1919 or 1920 was the concern about the public backlash it could create against the park service. These were the years of the Seattle general strike and the election of a socialist Seattle mayor. There was a movement afoot for establishing municipally run automobile camps not only on the outskirts of cities but in nearby mountain areas, too. In September 1920, Mayor Hugh M. Caldwell of Seattle petitioned the secretary of the interior for permission to maintain a municipal camp in an unfrequented section of Rainier (where it would not compete with the R N P C facilities). Minimal camp fees would be set to cover the cost of operation. Secretary of the Interior John Barton Payne politely refused this request by suggesting that the city of Seattle could establish a municipal camp in the adjacent national forest instead, but subsequently suggested that a camp could be maintained in the northeast section of the park on a cooperative basis.[30] In this context, the N P S may have deliberately muted its earlier opposition to the Cooperative Campers and bided its time.

In 1921, the R N P C opened a new campground facility in the northeast section of the park at the end of the White River Road. T. H. Martin notified the Cooperative Campers in June that the R N P C had an exclusive transportation concession in the park, and that it objected to the plans of the Cooperative Campers to provide its members with transportation between Seattle and the end of the White River Road. The Cooperative Campers intended to charge members $5 to $7, considerably less than the $10 to $12 fares that the R N P C currently projected.[31]

Advised of the situation by Superintendent W. H. Peters, Assistant Director Arno B. Cammerer informed the Cooperative Campers' executive secretary, Norman Huber, that the N P S would not allow the Cooperative Campers to employ its own vehicle in the park. "In order to get the greatest number of people to visit certain sections of the parks that have been opened up," Cammerer explained, "it is necessary for us to install regular service, and in order to make this regular service pay for the benefit of the greatest number we have to insist that no other operators be permitted in competition." Whomever the Cooperative Campers paid to transport campers to the park would be undercutting the RNPC's rates.[32]

But Mather, Albright, and Cammerer found that the Cooperative Campers were not so easily turned aside. The Cooperative Campers purchased their own truck. With the summer season already commenced, Superintendent Peters told his superiors that he saw no alternative but to admit the Cooperative Campers' truck into the park as a private vehicle. After the present summer season, he urged, the NPS would have time to devise a new policy toward the cooperative camps.[33]

That fall, Albright and Cammerer visited Rainier and discussed the Cooperative Campers at length with the superintendent. There was no question that the group was competing with the RNPC: the cooperative camp had received about three times the use that the White River Camp had. The new plan would be to challenge the group's liberal membership policy and treat the group more like an actual camping club than an unauthorized concession, thereby either forcing it into an acceptable mold or running it out of the park. In the coming summer, the park service would require the Cooperative Campers to submit a list of members to the superintendent by June 1. No one would be permitted to use the camp whose name was not on the list, and no more than one hundred people would be permitted overall.[34]

The following spring, Superintendent Peters once again advised his superiors to hedge as the summer season drew near. How could the NPS make the hundred-person limitation stick if it were challenged? The NPS would be on more legally defensible ground, he argued, if it went back to its earlier position that the Cooperative Campers was an unauthorized concession, and simply disallowed the camp altogether. "It is my belief that the Cooperative Campers are operating in direct and hurtful competition to the concessionaire and that when such an organization is allowed at all we are immediately involved in a maze of fine points impossible of solution," he wrote.[35] Peters wanted to restrict the use of the camp to prelisted members but not to cap it off at one hundred, and then to advise the Cooperative Campers at the end of the summer that the camp would not be permitted anymore.

Even with this compromise, however, NPS officials were dragged into a testy correspondence with the Cooperative Campers' new executive secretary, H. W. McKenzie, over the use of the group's truck in the park. The situation was complicated by the fact that Superintendent Peters resigned his post in June, only days before the cooperative camp was to open. The newly appointed superintendent, C. L. Nelson, immediately received explicit instructions from Cammerer to stop the Cooperative Campers' truck at the park entrance, check the campers' names against the membership list, and have the RNPC's vehicles ready, if necessary, to provide the group transportation into the park. At the last moment, Nelson countermanded Cammerer's instructions and directed the White River district ranger to allow the Cooperative Campers' truck to enter the park, and to admit unlisted members along with members who were on the list the NPS had obtained on June 10. In defense of this act of insubordination, Nelson told his superiors that local public sentiment about the Cooperative Campers was divided, and that he did not want to give the organization an issue with which to arouse popular feeling against the park service and the RNPC.[36]

Cammerer sharply reprimanded the new superintendent, stating that his indecisiveness would cost the NPS support when it held a public hearing on this troublesome issue in Seattle in the fall. Cammerer insisted that for the remainder of the season the park staff was to refuse official permission for use of the camp to all unlisted members, and it would keep a record of all violators. This would be used to discredit the Cooperative Campers in the public hearing.[37]

Ironically, the Cooperative Campers group appears not to have survived to attend that hearing, which was finally held on February 19 and 20, 1923, at the Seattle Chamber of Commerce building. If the Cooperative Campers still existed in 1923, it must have moved its operation somewhere outside Rainier. It seems more likely that the group disbanded. The proliferation of free public campgrounds in the national parks and forests, along with municipal camps and public and private organization camps, made the cooperative camps obsolete. When the Playground and Recreation Association of America published a 634-page manual on organized camping in 1924, it did not even mention cooperative camps. It remains unclear whether the low-income people who patronized the cooperative camps found other means of affordable camping as the nation's camping culture evolved, or were forced to turn to other kinds of recreation within the city.[38]

In the meantime, The Mountaineers had joined the attack on the park service's concession policy. With its 1,000–strong membership of mostly Seattle and Tacoma residents, the mountain club further tested the ability of the nearby urban populace to shape park management. The club had a long record of solid support for national parks, so its sharp criticism of the NPS in a broadside titled *The Administration of the National Parks* (1922) came as a disappointment to NPS officials.[39]

The Mountaineers' report accused the NPS of kowtowing to park concessions in general and to the RNPC in particular. The club alleged that profit-driven park concessions were gaining too much influence and treating park superintendents as their own agents in dealing with NPS officialdom. "The resulting tendency is for the development of the parks to proceed disproportionately along lines of commercial profit," the club reported. "The administration of national parks, although based upon high ideals of public service, has not escaped this evil."[40]

The Mountaineers characterized the Cooperative Campers as a "benevolent" organization that had made camping trips possible "to a limited number of persons of congenial tastes and modest means, many of whom would not be able to patronize the regular concessionaire." The club stopped just short of endorsing the cooperative camps, but it insisted that any effort by the NPS to eliminate the camps should be done in a lawful way. It was evident to the club that the park administration was determined to force the Cooperative Campers out of the park, and it found the record of actions taken against this group to be "arbitrary," "insincere," and "petty."[41]

The report by The Mountaineers reserved its most stinging criticism for the NPS prohibition against hired auto stages. The NPS and the RNPC maintained that the park concession had an exclusive privilege of providing transportation services between Seattle or Tacoma and points inside the national park.[42] The controversy over the Cooperative Campers' truck led the NPS to interpret the RNPC's transportation monopoly in the broadest possible way. As a result, the NPS inadvertently thwarted The Mountaineers as well. On a Labor Day weekend outing in 1922, a large party of Mountaineers was inconvenienced and humiliated when park officials made them transfer their whole party and all their gear from hired auto stages to RNPC cars at the park entrance.[43] In the view of the club, the NPS had gone too far in protecting the concession's monopoly, and was fencing the park with so many regulations as to make it difficult for the public to gain access to it.

The RNPC's officers reacted angrily to The Mountaineers' pamphlet and demanded a retraction of some of its statements. Other conservation groups, meanwhile, gave the report mixed reviews. The Mountaineers received letters from the American Civic Association, the National Parks Association, the Mazamas, the Sierra Club, and various other mountain clubs. But The Mountaineers stood by its report. In January 1923, The Mountaineers' president, Edmund S. Meany, received a letter from Cammerer stating that the NPS wanted to hold a public meeting in Seattle at which these various complaints could be discussed.[44]

The meeting, held February 19 and 20, 1923, in the Seattle Chamber of Commerce assembly rooms, was attended by Albright, Nelson, and former Superintendent Roger W. Toll (then superintendent of Rocky Mountain National Park). The representative for The Mountaineers, Irving M. Clark, told the NPS officials that The Mountaineers did not endorse the park service's regulated monopoly policy, but it would not oppose it either. Rather, it sought changes in the policy that would allow more flexibility. Specifically, The Mountaineers wanted the admittance of hired cars, the allowance of cooperative camps "in larger parks where there is ample room for everybody," an end to the requirement that all horse riders hire guides, full disclosure of the concessionaire's yearly profits, better sanitation in the public campgrounds, and overall clarification of the park's rules and regulations.[45]

It is difficult to assess the overall effect of The Mountaineers and the Cooperative Campers on park policy in the early 1920s. The documentary evidence in the park service's files does not support the conclusion that the agitation by these groups brought about specific reforms of park policy. No single example can be cited of a park rule or policy being changed in order to satisfy their demands. Nevertheless, it may have been partly due to the influence of The Mountaineers and the Cooperative Campers that the NPS moved into two areas of visitor service at Rainier in the early 1920s that had formerly belonged to the RNPC. Coming so soon after the successful consolidation of visitor services under a single park concession, these developments would seem to indicate a deliberate scaling back of the park service's partnership with the RNPC in response to the challenges to Mather's concession policy by the Cooperative Campers and The Mountaineers. The first of these services was the nature guide service, or interpretive program, which the RNPC relinquished without complaint as it retained the more lucrative mountain guide service. The second visitor service was campgrounds, which the RNPC found of much greater consequence.

In 1915, most overnight camping at Rainier occurred in so-called hotel camps at Paradise, Longmire, and Indian Henry's Hunting Ground. Campers slept in canvas-walled tents and ate meals prepared by the camp host. Relatively few people had their own camping equipment; those who did were apt to join large, organized outings like those of The Mountaineers. Less than a decade later, more than 90 percent of visitors wanted to camp in public automobile campgrounds.[46] Typically they had their own tents, sleeping bags, and cooking gear (much of it acquired from army surplus outlets after World War I). They required no more than drinking water and toilet facilities to complete their outfit, and after paying a park entrance fee, they expected to camp for free. Most of them came in small parties by private automobile. This was an extraordinarily rapid change in the pattern of visitor use. In this respect Mather's concept of the park concession was outmoded before it was ten years old.

The government's involvement in campground development at Rainier began in 1918 with an $8,000 expenditure for clearing campsites and installing sewer and water systems. Free public camping areas were developed at Longmire, Paradise, and one mile inside the park entrance.[47] Yet the system was still only rudimentary and existed alongside a number of new hotel camps developed by the RNPC. The largest hotel camps were at Longmire and Paradise, where campers could avail themselves of the dining facilities connected with the hotel. The RNPC established additional camps at the park entrance and the Nisqually Glacier overlook. (In this era, the road bridge over the Nisqually River afforded a dramatic view of the Nisqually Glacier terminus; the glacier has since receded out of sight.)

Mather's comments on the RNPC's camps in 1918 reveal a strategy of campground development in transition. "Paradise and Nisqually Glacier Camps with their lunch pavilions and a-la-carte service fill an important need in this park," Mather reported.

> The Paradise Camp is especially popular because here the tourist is at liberty to live under almost any conditions that he may choose. He can live in one of the tents of the camp, using his own bedding and cooking his own meals, or he can rent bedding at a nominal price and eat at the lunch pavilion; or he may bring his own tent equipment and eat at the lunch pavilion or purchase his supplies there and do his own cooking.[48]

The variety of campers' needs seemed to call for a mix of hotel camps and free public campgrounds (not to mention cooperative camps, which Mather omitted from his report). Mather could not have foreseen how quickly the demand for public campgrounds would grow, nor how quickly the hotel camps would become obsolete.

The sanitation problem in Rainier's public campgrounds continued to draw Mather's attention. In 1920 he recommended that the campgrounds should have better facilities for sewage and garbage disposal and that these should be installed by the government. "As a general thing," he commented, "all public utilities of this kind should be owned and operated at a profit by the Government, and should include power plants, telephone systems, and water systems, as well as sewer systems." At Rainier it was too late for the government to build the power plant as this had already been accomplished by the RNPC. In principle, however, Mather wanted the government to take responsibility for basic services that the hotels had provided prior to World War I.[49]

Over the next two years, the public campgrounds began to resemble their modern shape. The park service improved the sewer system at the Paradise and Longmire campgrounds and installed water taps and flush toilets. Park staffers put in camp stoves and tables and established individual campsites within the cleared area. The Longmire campground was equipped with electric lights. Superintendent Nelson assigned a caretaker to each campground, whose duties were to police the grounds and keep the place clean. In 1922, a sanitary engineer from the U.S. Public Health Service pronounced the campgrounds at Rainier as clean as any he had inspected in the national parks. This was all the more impressive considering that the campground at Paradise was one of the busiest in the national park system.[50]

Still the burgeoning demand for campsites outstripped what the N P S and the R N P C could supply. In 1923, Mather secured $25,000 for a new campground at Longmire on the south side of the Nisqually River. Most of the funds were earmarked for a bridge and a loop road, while other improvements included campsite development, water and sewer systems, a community kitchen, and electric lights. The campground was state-of-the-art, oriented to the automobile camper.[51] A smaller public campground was laid out at White River that year, too, complementing the R N P C's White River Camp, which had opened two years before. Yet these improvements fell short of what the national park required. "Travel has grown to such an extent," Mather commented in his annual report on Rainier for 1923, "that the comparatively small midweek crowds desiring camping space could not be comfortably accommodated this year."[52]

Expansion of the public campgrounds continued in 1925. The Paradise and Longmire campgrounds could accommodate about eight hundred people each, the White River campground could accommodate about five hundred, and a new campground at Ipsut Creek, on the Carbon River road, could accommodate about four hundred. In addition, unimproved sites were located on the road to Paradise at Kautz Creek and the Nisqually River, and various points along the White River Road. Together, the unimproved camps could accommodate another seven hundred people. With these developments, it became clear that the government had taken over responsibility for camping facilities in the park. By the mid-1920s, visitors to Rainier had come to expect that the park service would provide free public campgrounds complete with running water, toilets, chopped firewood, and evening campfire programs.[53]

The R N P C's camps declined in popularity as the free public campgrounds became more attractive. Superintendent Owen A. Tomlinson noted in 1925, "Bungalow tents maintained as a part of the Paradise Inn operation are not popular with the visiting public. A great majority of the patrons prefer rooms inside the building and are willing to pay the additional charge for that class of accommodation."[54] For Tomlinson, this underscored the need for additional hotel accommodations at Paradise. In other words, he did not expect the RNPC to stay in the hotel camp business. What had been left to private enterprise in 1915, and considered a partnership enterprise in 1918, was henceforward a government enterprise. This represented a significant evolution in the park service's concession policy.

RNPC officers liked to portray their concession as a victim as well as a beneficiary of its special position in the national park. They insisted that the NPS required the RNPC to make sacrifices for the public interest—by providing services that did not make a profit, for example, or by forgoing promising developments that would offset the company's losses elsewhere. RNPC officers claimed that the public tended to blame the concession for things that were beyond its control in spite of the RNPC's best public relations efforts. "Don't forget that the Park Company is the 'goat' for much criticism based on National Park regulations and restrictions," the RNPC's general manager once told a local magazine reporter.[55] These complaints contained a modicum of truth. But if the RNPC was victimized by anything, it was the sensational spread of the automobile in American society.

Officers of the RNPC were wary of the growing dominance of the automobile at Rainier. As they constantly pointed out to NPS officials, the RNPC made most of its money from patrons who traveled by train, not by car. Whereas railroads brought tourists to national park hotels, automobiles brought tourists to national park campgrounds. It was railroad passengers who boarded the company's auto stages in Tacoma and who stayed at Paradise Inn. Automobile travelers typically came and went without patronizing anything but the RNPC's restrooms.[56]

The RNPC did not want to discourage these growing numbers of car tourists; it merely wanted to get them out of the campgrounds and into the hotels. One promising approach was to attract more business during the "shoulder seasons," especially early summer. Late-melting snow-packs precluded camping at Paradise until about mid-July, but Paradise Inn would attract visitors as soon as the road was plowed. The RNPC badgered the NPS year after year to get the road opened as early in the season as possible. Racing against time, NPS road crews used a tractor, a steam shovel, army surplus TNT, and even hand shovels to get the job done, but to the RNPC it was always too late. Indeed, the RNPC was so anxious to get the visitor season started in June that it operated a saddle horse and baggage sled service from Longmire to get tourists up to Paradise Inn prior to the opening of the road. Unfortunately, the company received many complaints from visitors about the discomforts that this trip entailed.[57]

Soon the park service and the RNPC began to discuss Rainier's potential as a winter playground. Prior to 1923, some 1,200 to 1,400 people snowshoed or skied into the park each winter, many on weekend outings with The Mountaineers. Beginning in that year, the park service kept the road open all year as far as Longmire. The RNPC rented snowshoes, skis, and toboggans, and kept the National Park Inn open "informally." Ten thousand people took this opportunity to visit the park during the first winter season of 1923–24, most of them coming for the day only.

In the winter of 1924–25, the RNPC tried to attract more people to the park by bringing in a team of thirteen Alaskan sled dogs and an Eskimo driver. Tourists paid a fare to ride through the Douglas fir and hemlock forest on the dogsled. This was continued for several years. No one questioned the fact that the dogsled trips were completely out of context at Rainier; rather, they were considered another form of winter sport, along with the popular toboggan runs at Longmire and the ski and snowshoe trips up to Paradise.[58]

From the park service's standpoint, use of the park for winter recreation was a great success. From the RNPC's standpoint, the winter operation was a disappointment because it did not pay for itself, much less earn a profit. The inn could afford to open only during the weekends, and the employees had to be run in and out of the park each Saturday and Sunday on a company bus. While the company lost money each winter, it continued the service anyway, in part for public relations, in part with the hope of developing a larger winter clientele over time.[59]

RAINIER NATIONAL PARK COMPANY

It had become clear that Rainier's real potential as a winter sports center lay in getting people to Paradise. Longmire experienced frequent rain and above-freezing temperatures during the winter, while Paradise's extra elevation assured it of much better snow conditions. With this in mind, the RNPC's T. H. Martin proposed an aerial tramway from the bridge over the Nisqually River up the mountainside to Paradise. It would be purely functional, an alternative to the road during the nine months of the year when the road was closed. Superintendent Tomlinson forwarded this proposal to Mather with the comment that the tramway would make Paradise available for winter use and therefore deserved further study.[60]

The tramway proposal went no further for three and a half years, until January 1928. Then Martin tried to link the tramway development to the construction of a second hotel, Paradise Lodge, at Paradise. "It is our definite plan to maintain the new hotel on an all year basis," Martin wrote, "and to do this it will, of course, be necessary to have some sort of comfortable and practicable method of transportation to Paradise Valley throughout the winter."[61] RNPC President H. A. Rhodes assured Mather that the tramway would not be promoted as a novelty or "Coney Island type of amusement."[62] The RNPC held that the only alternative to a tramway was for the NPS to keep the road open all winter—at an estimated cost of $100,000 per year. Of course, another alternative was to operate the new hotel on a seasonal basis, as with the Paradise Inn, but NPS officials never broached this possibility with the RNPC out of concern that the hotel would not be built. NPS officials did not endorse the RNPC's premise that the expansion of Paradise facilities required that the area have a winter tourist season, but they did not take issue with it either.

The tramway proposal stirred opposition in the park service. Chief Landscape Engineer Tom C. Vint observed that the tramway would mar one of the most spectacular roadside views in the park: the view of the Nisqually Glacier from the Glacier Bridge. Others worried that it would set a bad precedent, opening the door for tramways to be built to the tops of peaks in other national parks. The fact that many such tramways could be found in the Alps was no consolation to them; a review of these European engineering works indicated that they were built without much regard for scenic preservation. Still another concern was that local organizations, including The Mountaineers and the Rainier National Park Advisory Board, might oppose the project.[63]

Mather gave this issue his close attention, consulting not only his own landscape architects, but also the National Commission of Fine Arts in New York City. In August 1928, he tentatively approved the project, explaining to Superintendent Tomlinson that the tramway would not appreciably detract from the landscape nor set a precedent for other park concessions. Merely for winter access, it was not an amusement ride.[64]

The concern that the tramway would mar the landscape was well founded. Working closely with the RNPC's hired engineer, Superintendent Tomlinson was disappointed to learn that the loading station would have to be placed below instead of above the road, where it would be in plain view to anyone approaching the Glacier Bridge from Ricksecker Point.[65]

The concern that the tramway would be precedent setting was also realistic. In 1929, Assistant Director Albright held a conference with the consulting engineer and various other tramway experts on both the Nisqually-Paradise tramway project and a Yosemite Valley–Glacier Point tramway proposal.[66] When the secretary of agriculture went on record against yet another proposed aerial tramway—this one to the summit of Mount Hood in Oregon—NPS officials felt compelled to urge officers of the RNPC to "keep the soft pedal on their project as far as publicity is concerned."[67] This belied Mather's statement that the Nisqually-Paradise tramway would not be precedent setting.

The tramway project fizzled during the summer of 1929. After building its new Paradise Lodge in 1928, the RNPC was short of capital and simply put off the tramway project indefinitely. What Mather's ultimate decision would have been, had the RNPC forged ahead, cannot be known. He was careful to leave himself an out. "No actual opposition to the proposed aerial tramway has developed," he noted in his annual report for 1929, "but all National Park Service officials and all those not connected with the company have expressed themselves as opposed to the location of the cableway in any manner that will interfere with the view of the Nisqually Canyon as one approaches the Glac-

RAINIER NATIONAL PARK COMPANY

ier Bridge from either direction."[68] When Mather wrote this, he knew that the plan involved just such a visual intrusion, even though it was the least intrusive of four routes considered. Thus, a year and a half after his discussions with the RNPC on this issue began, he had not committed himself definitely to anything.

The partnership between the NPS and the RNPC culminated during this era in the most comprehensive planning effort undertaken by the NPS up to that time. The master plan, produced jointly by Mather, Tomlinson, NPS landscape architects, and RNPC officials, purported to include all present and projected development of roads and visitor accommodations throughout the park. A major weakness in it, however, was the RNPC's lack of capital to carry out its part. The NPS tried to help the RNPC to enlist financial support from one or more railroad companies, but the railroads finally offered only token assistance.

The main stimulus for this planning effort was Congress's five-year, multimillion-dollar construction program for national park roads. With this infusion of federal funds, NPS officials now had the opportunity and responsibility to determine which sections of Rainier would be opened up by roads and which sections would be preserved in a primitive condition. As park planners contemplated how the park's network of roads would eventually shape up, the question arose whether the RNPC would provide requisite hotel accommodations at the ends of these new roads. Neither the RNPC nor the NPS wanted to see competition develop from rival concessions in other sections of the park. On the other hand, the RNPC was already stretched to the limit just to complete its facilities at Paradise. Faced with a choice, NPS officials preferred to maintain a single concession and assist the RNPC in growing into a larger operation.

The NPS began by offering the RNPC a better contract. The RNPC's original contract in 1916 was to run for twenty years; however, in 1926 the RNPC was invited to apply for a new one. This contract, which Albright called "the best franchise that has ever been prepared for the National Park Service," included stronger protections against competition and lower government fees (based on a percentage of gross income rather than profit). Most important, the new contract allowed the R N P C to increase its capital stock by mortgaging its properties. This feature was included in the contract by authority of an act of Congress passed on March 7, 1928. The new contract, which ran for another twenty years, was signed on April 2, 1928.[69]

Days after the contract was signed, N P S Chief Landscape Architect Tom C. Vint attended a meeting of the R N P C board of directors in Seattle. R N P C President H. A. Rhodes called for an estimated $960,000 investment over the next five years, considerably more than the company's existing capital stock of $500,000 could allow. Listening to the board discuss the company's new five-year plan for upgrading and expanding its facilities, Vint proposed that the N P S and the R N P C work "hand-in-hand" in fashioning a comprehensive park development plan. Such a plan, though even more ambitious than Rhodes' five-year plan, would actually make it easier for the R N P C to interest large investors, namely the railroads, in its long-range scheme. According to Vint, "the board of directors considered this scheme very favorable and saw its advantage in planning their financial program as well as their construction program."[70] Mather responded even more favorably. The idea of involving the company in a general plan for the entire park, Mather wrote, was "excellent and should be followed out."[71]

Vint returned to the Park Service's new field office in San Francisco and produced a package of drawings and overlays called the "Master Plan for Mount Rainier." The master plan involved the R N P C in three areas: (1) an expansion of the development at Paradise, (2) a new hotel and cabin complex to be built at Yakima Park (Sunrise) after the N P S completed a road up to the site, and (3) another and final development, probably located at Spray Park. Although quite sketchy by later standards, it was the first master plan of its kind in the national park system.[72] Later, a $2.5 million price tag would be attached to these developments—a near tripling of the investment Rhodes had proposed only a few months earlier. The main outlines of the plan were prepared in time for Mather's trip west that July.

At Rainier, Mather rode horseback up to Yakima Park with Tomlinson, Vint, Rhodes, and Asahel Curtis, chairman of the Rainier National Park Advisory Board, to inspect the proposed second development site.

Mount Rainier was the first national park to admit automobiles. A professor at the University of Washington marveled that "an automobile party leaving Seattle or Tacoma in the morning can pitch its evening camp in one of the dense groves of stunted trees at timber-line." Car access and pleasure driving on park roads quickly became distinguishing features of public use at Mount Rainier. (Source: Washington State Historical Society, Special Collections Division, Asahel Curtis photograph.)

A climbing party photographed at Camp of the Clouds. The guide, third from right, holds an ice axe, while the rest of the party is equipped with staffs. (Source: Mount Rainier National Park.)

The Guide Service, a department of the Rainier National Park Company, poses in front of the Guide House, 1927. Summit climbs increased in popularity as word of the guides' professionalism spread. In addition to leading summit trips, the guides led regular trips onto the Nisqually and Paradise glaciers and gave evening lectures and slide shows in the Guide House auditorium. Most of the guides were teachers or college students, and they tried to inform their clients about the natural history of the park as well as lead them safely over the mountain terrain. (Source: Mount Rainier National Park.)

< In the early days campers used the Bailey Willis Trail to reach this meadow on the north side of the mountain. Note the lavish use of timber for tent poles. Park administrators had to educate campers that this kind of woodcraft had ruinous effects on the vegetation at popular camping sites. (Source: Mount Rainier National Park, Tahoma Woods, Asahel Curtis photograph.)

Anna Louise Strong, first president
of the Cooperative Campers of the
Pacific Northwest and a critic of the
National Park Service's concession
policy. (Source: University of
Washington, Suzzallo Library,
Special Collections.)

In 1928, Steve Mather rode horseback up to Yakima Park with Superintendent O. A. Tomlinson, Rainier National Park Company President Henry Rhodes, landscape architect Tom Vint, and park promoter Asahel Curtis. In this staged photograph by Curtis, the men view plans for a new hotel to be developed in the meadow below—portraying the NPS-RNPC partnership in its finest hour. (Source: Washington State Historical Society, Special Collections Division, Asahel Curtis photograph.)

∧ < Wildlife viewing was a popular attraction of the national park. With hunting prohibited in the park, animals such as black bears were more likely to be seen. Roadside encounters such as this one taught black bears to associate humans with food. Decades later, the National Park Service would try assiduously to change both human and black bear behavior. (Source: University of Washington Libraries, Special Collections, O. A. Tomlinson Collection.)

National Park Service planners prepare the Master Plan for Mount Rainier National Park. This plan was the first of its kind, providing a blueprint for the development of all roads, visitor services, and administrative sites. (Source: Steve Mark, Historian, Crater Lake National Park.)

< v Sunrise development area. A major component of the Master Plan, Sunrise was intended to draw visitors to the east side of the park and alleviate crowding at Paradise. Note the rows of housekeeping cabins to the right of the lodge. (Source: Washington State Historical Society, Special Collections, Asahel Curtis photograph.)

Celebration of the automobile and the national park. In the newly graded parking lot at Sunrise, photographer Asahel Curtis composed this fanciful scene suggestive of goddesses and chariots on classical Mount Olympus. (Source: Washington State Historical Society, Special Collections, Asahel Curtis photograph.)

With the RNPC facing hard times in 1931, the NPS allowed development of a golf course to attract wealthy clientele to the Paradise Inn. Park service officials justified it on the grounds that golfing was a form of outdoor recreation and would not detract from the mountain setting. The course lasted through two summers. (Source: Mount Rainier National Park, Tahoma Woods.)

> ∧ The Civilian Conservation Corps. A New Deal program that combined conservation work and unemployment relief, the ccc brought hundreds of young men into the park to improve trails and campgrounds, construct buildings, and perform roadside landscaping. Park officials viewed each ccc enrollee not just as a laborer but also as a new client—a new type of visitor who could find spiritual renewal in nature through the collective ccc experience. (Source: Mount Rainier National Park.)

> A fish warden and pack horses return from stocking a mountain lake with fry. Park managers regarded the lakes and streams as recreational resources, not as distinct biological communities. With assistance from the Bureau of Fisheries, more than a million fry were planted in park waters during the early 1930s. Twenty years later the National Park Service would work to restore native species. (Source: Mount Rainier National Park.)

Company 2941 C.C.C.
Camp Sunshine Point.
Longmire Wash.
#1 Kinsey Photo

Cross-country skier on Mazama Ridge, 1956. Cross-country skiing grew more popular in the 1970s as downhill skiing at Paradise was phased out. (Source: Mount Rainier National Park, Kirk photograph.)

∧ < The Paradise ice caves were a popular attraction. Visitors, including this party of CCC boys, marveled at the blue, green, and pink light filtering into these great rooms under the Paradise Glacier. As the winter's snowpack melted each summer, the RNPC's guide service sped the process along by chopping or blasting openings large enough for people to enter. The ice caves melted during the 1980s. (Source: University of Washington Libraries, Special Collections, O. A. Tomlinson Collection.)

< Skiers at Paradise in 1941, the busiest downhill ski season in the park's history. Americans discovered the European sport of downhill skiing in the 1930s. Among ski enthusiasts, the Paradise area acquired national renown. For a short time, winter sports loomed so large at Mount Rainier that the superintendent described them as the park's most important public use. (Source: Mount Rainier National Park.)

A family pauses at a wayside exhibit, Ricksecker Point, 1960. The Mission 66 development plan extolled this form of interpretation: "The trip around the Mountain will become a continuous experience in seeing, understanding, and appreciating the natural scene. This development, too, will play its part in dispersing use, taking some of the load from Paradise and Sunrise, holding the visitor for a longer period along the road and in roadside developments, and making more of the Park interesting, appealing, and meaningful." (Source: Mount Rainier National Park, J. Boucher photograph.)

Paradise Visitor Center under construction. The modern design met with mixed reactions. The conical roof and round layout were supposed to relate the structure to its mountain setting, but critics complained that it looked like a satellite, pagoda, or flying saucer. At $2 million, this was the most expensive National Park Service building in the nation. (Source: Mount Rainier National Park, R. L. Lake photograph.)

In the 1960s, park managers launched an effort to obliterate unplanned "social trails" that dissected fragile meadows at many popular locales in the park. Soil was shoveled onto the trail, held in place with biodegradable jute matting, and planted with subalpine plants taken from road shoulders in the area. Meadow restoration efforts produced encouraging results and the program steadily expanded. (Source: Mount Rainier National Park, Ells photograph.)

Author and fawn at Van Trump Park, 1969. (Source: William R. Catton Jr. photograph.)

Author's family on the Wonderland Trail, Cowlitz Divide, 1967. (Source: Nancy L. Catton photograph.)

Author's brother en route to Camp Muir in June 1980, one month after the eruption of Mount St. Helens. Note the plume of steam over Mount St. Helens in upper left and the dark stain of ash on the snowfield in foreground. (Source: Stephen L. Catton photograph.)

Wonderland Trail hikers about to descend into morning mist over Berkeley Park, 2002. (Source: Jon Catton photograph.)

Mount Rainier from Spray Park. (Source: Jon Catton photograph.)

Curtis took their photograph: the men seated on a rock outcropping, Vint's maps and drawings spread out across their knees, and in the background, the enormous east face of Rainier rising beyond the bare meadow where the new hotel would be built.[73] It was a perfect image of the partnership between the NPS and the RNPC, symbolizing perhaps the headiest and most promising moment in the partnership's fifty-year history.

Twelve days after leaving Rainier, Mather and Rhodes had another meeting, this time in company with the Northern Pacific's president, Charles Donnelly, in Yellowstone National Park. It appears that this was the first time the RNPC approached the Northern Pacific as a potential investor, and Mather was present to give the railroad executive his most effective sales pitch. According to a memorandum prepared by a Northern Pacific official after this meeting, Mather felt so positive about the Yakima Park site that he thought it would even surpass Paradise in fame and popularity.[74]

The following January 1929, Rhodes gave a fuller presentation of the RNPC's proposal to Northern Pacific officials. This was followed by a conference one month later in Portland involving Donnelly and six other Northern Pacific officials on one side and Rhodes and Martin on the other. Rhodes proposed a $2.5 million investment over five years. Rhodes explained that the RNPC could not obtain that kind of capital from its present stockholders. After "very careful consideration," he believed that the railroads would be "logically interested" not only because of the traffic revenues that would result, but from an investment standpoint, too.[75]

Two months later, Assistant Director Albright wrote to Donnelly in support of the RNPC proposal. Albright described the master plan for Mount Rainier and reviewed the list of other national parks in which railroads had given financial assistance to the park concession. "The time has now arrived," Albright wrote, "when . . . a very large development must go forward in Mount Rainier and it should be undertaken in the same broad gauge way in which such developments had been made in the other parks with financial assistance from the railroads interested in the growth of the tourist business." Albright gave the RNPC's financial plan his "personal endorsement" and hoped the Northern Pacific would consider it favorably.[76]

Donnelly proposed to his counterparts of the Great Northern, Union Pacific, and Milwaukee Road that the four transcontinental railroads serving Washington State should make this a joint venture, each contributing a half million dollars; the RNPC's Seattle and Tacoma stockholders would put up the remaining half million. The Union Pacific's president, C. R. Gray, found this proposal "staggering" but, like Donnelly, did not want to reject it out of hand. Together with H. A. Scandrett, president of the Milwaukee Road, he suggested that the companies send a representative to the park to look it over. The Great Northern's president, Ralph Budd, agreed but insisted on sending his own representative.[77]

After investigating the park concession and the proposed development sites in July 1929, both railroad representatives filed favorable reports. The Northern Pacific's man thought the proposed Spray Park development would exceed visitor demand, but considered the prospects for new hotels at Paradise and Yakima Park to be excellent. The Great Northern's investigator was even more positive, suggesting that the expanded development of the park could make it the central tourist attraction of the Pacific Northwest.[78]

The decisive meeting of the four executives occurred in Chicago on January 6, 1930, when they reached unanimous agreement to decline the RNPC's offer. Why the four railroad presidents did not accept the advice of their own investigators is not entirely clear. In reply to Albright's further entreaties that March, the railroad executives insisted that they did not want to make the investment because it would be precedent setting. The analogy between Rainier and other national parks in which the railroads were involved was not fair, they said, because Rainier was not accessed directly by rail. Unlike Yellowstone, Glacier, Grand Canyon, Zion, and Bryce Canyon, they noted, Rainier had an alternative source of capital in the nearby cities of Seattle and Tacoma.[79]

Although the railroad executives made no mention of the economic crisis following the stock market crash in October 1929, this may have weighed in their decision as well. When Albright tried once more to enlist their help in 1931, asking the railroads for $200,000 to assist with the Yakima Park development only, Donnelly replied that the present economic conditions made it impossible. In February 1932, in the very depths of the Depression, the RNPC finally got the four railroads to buy a paltry $2,000 of company stock each.[80] After entertaining such high hopes for the railroads in 1928–29, this turned out to be all the investment that officials of the RNPC and NPS would ever see.

CHAPTER 5

Through Depression and War (1930–1945)

STEVE MATHER AND THE SEATTLE AND TACOMA BUSI-
nessmen who backed the Rainier National Park Company in the 1920s
shared similar visions for Mount Rainier National Park. They expected
the park to attract visitors from across the nation, to function as a national
park in that sense. The park's popularity exceeded their expectations,
but the throngs of easterners, midwesterners, and southerners failed
to materialize. Instead, the swelling numbers of people who came to
Mount Rainier in the 1920s largely hailed from the surrounding region.
Most came on weekends to use the park as a city playground.

The Great Depression etched this pattern more deeply into the character of the park. Although hard times depressed tourism as people spent
less money on nonessentials, the Depression also had an opposite effect
as widespread unemployment and underemployment gave people more
leisure time. During the hardest years, Americans purchased fewer automobiles and less gasoline and deferred recreational travel. But by 1934
they were buying these commodities as avidly as they had in the previous decade. The national trends were reflected in the annual visitation
numbers for Mount Rainier, which fell by more than a third from 1931
to 1933, recovered in 1934 and 1935, and grew by leaps and bounds from
1935 to 1941. Indeed, by 1940 the park was accommodating more than

twice the numbers seen in any one year during the 1920s, and, as in the 1920s, these visitors were predominantly local.[1]

The Depression influenced visitors' lodging preferences at Rainier more than it affected total park patronage. The RNPC's occupancy rates dropped sharply during the years 1931 to 1933 and remained depressed throughout the era, while campground use increased. This too reflected national trends. As automobile historian Warren James Belasco has written, "Tourists economized on operating expenses, mainly room and board, in order to keep cars running. Expenditures for hotels, restaurants, vacation clothing, and travel supplies fell from $872 million in 1929 to $444 million in 1933."[2] Belasco documents the growth of the autocamp and motel industry at the expense of hotels during the 1930s. The rise of the motel in American life changed visitor demand at Rainier. Tourists who could ill-afford a room in the Paradise Inn wanted to stay in small "housekeeping cabins," not the tent cabins of yesteryear. The RNPC built hundreds of housekeeping cabins at Paradise and Sunrise to meet the new demand.

While the Depression no doubt reinforced the developing pattern of predominantly local or regional use of Mount Rainier National Park, both the Depression and World War II set the stage for a burst of federal activity and national use of the park that neither Mather nor Seattle and Tacoma investors could have anticipated. Beginning in 1933, the NPS became deeply involved with various federal relief programs. Civilian Conservation Corps (CCC) camps were built at eight locations within the park, and at different times the Civil Works Administration (CWA) and Works Progress Administration (WPA), each had two camps and a multitude of projects in the park, while the Public Works Administration (PWA) oversaw an extended program of road and bridge construction involving still more work crews and camps. During World War II, the park accommodated the military in various ways. As federal activity in the park increased, Seattle's and Tacoma's capital investment in the park diminished. After the war, businessmen in both cities would push for development no less aggressively than they had in the Mather era, but they would find new political forums for their demands. For these reasons, the Depression and World War II were watershed events in Mount Rainier National Park's evolution in the twentieth century.

The Rainier visitor in the 1930s had greater options for exploring the park than earlier travelers had. More often than not the visitor arrived in a private auto. While a majority still made Paradise their destination, a growing number opted to visit the new Sunrise development on the east side of the park. With the completion of a state highway over Chinook Pass in 1931, eastern Washington residents acquired direct access to Rainier and joined the throngs of weekend recreationists coming from Seattle and Tacoma. Still others made their way to the less-traveled northwest and southeast corners of the park via improved roads to Mowich Lake and Ohanapecosh, respectively.[3]

At Paradise, the visitor might partake in one of the RNPC's popular horse trips. The Skyline Trail, a five-mile loop trail that took in the heights above Paradise meadows, remained the most popular horse trail in the park. RNPC trail guides led parties on the half-day ride mornings and afternoons. Much of this route lay over melting snowfields until late summer. One can only imagine what the horse traffic did to the delicate subalpine meadows; the park service would not assess or monitor these impacts until many years later. The RNPC's wranglers also led trips to the Reflection Lakes and the foot of the Tatoosh Range, while the concession's guide service offered regular foot trips to Nisqually Glacier, Paradise Glacier, and Pinnacle Peak. The NPS encouraged tourists to get out on the glaciers as long as they were with experienced guides.[4]

Many tourists hiked unaccompanied to the fire lookout on Anvil Rock or the rock shelters at Camp Muir. Superintendent Owen A. Tomlinson remarked that Camp Muir was "used extensively by amateur climbers and others who hike about aimlessly and improperly equipped for hiking or climbing at that altitude."[5] When a visiting official recommended that the NPS install a telephone line to Camp Muir for visitor safety, Tomlinson noted that "undoubtedly if the telephone was placed in Camp Muir, hundreds of casual hikers who reach that point would keep a telephone line more than busy with idle and unnecessary gossip."[6] Such comments suggest why the NPS favored guided walks in the Paradise area. Glacier crevasses, sheer cliffs, and exposure to high altitude weather presented a multitude of hazards to visitors.

The Paradise ice caves were another popular attraction. It was a unique experience to look up at the blue, green, and pink light filtering into these great rooms under the Paradise Glacier. Due to the rapid melting of this glacier, the caves changed from year to year. As the winter snowpack melted off each summer, the RNPC's guide service sped the process by chopping or blasting out openings in the ice large enough for people to enter. Normally this occurred toward the end of the summer, but in 1932 the RNPC requested permission to dynamite a hole in the ice in July so that this popular attraction could be made available earlier. After some philosophizing about the problem of "forcing nature," Assistant Director Cammerer approved the request. As Tomlinson pointed out, the ice caves were a good source of revenue to the company's guide department, and with business ailing, "the pressure is greater than ever for hastening the opening of the Paradise Ice Caves."[7]

The lingering snowpack around the Paradise area held its own attractions. "Nature coasting" was a popular and much-photographed activity. Nature coasters donned lumbermen's "tin pants," which were trousers made of some kind of resilient material and soaked in paraffin for waterproofing. A popular postcard image of Rainier in this era depicted a line of nature coasters—usually young women—seated on a steep snowfield one behind the other in stairstep fashion.

A stream of tourists drove up the new road to Sunrise when it opened on July 15, 1931. Each succeeding weekend brought more people, and on three weekends during August the travel to Sunrise exceeded that to Paradise.[8] Superintendent Tomlinson was jubilant, confidently predicting that travel to Sunrise would nearly double travel to Paradise now that the state road over Chinook Pass was completed. That did not happen, however. The pattern of visitor use soon stabilized the other way, with Paradise receiving about two times as many visitors as Sunrise.

The Sunrise development confirmed the park's growing orientation to the automobilist. The most popular attraction in the entire new development was the Sunrise Point parking area and overlook. As the new road gained the crest of Sunrise Ridge, it made a broad, 180-degree turn that provided the automobilist with a panoramic view. A large parking bay inside the turn and pedestrian bays around its perimeter completed this site's functional design. Hundreds of cars packed into the Sunrise Point parking area each day. At the end of its first season of use, Tomlinson wrote approvingly, "Perhaps the fact that this vantage point is on the main highway where the visitor may, from the comfortable seat of his automobile, enjoy all the thrills of the mountain climber, had something to do with its popularity."[9] The park administration was satisfied to have most park visitors driving up only for the pleasure of the road and its scenic views.

There were opportunities for nature study and recreation at Sunrise. The NPS improved the trail system around Yakima Park to accommodate the new crowds of people. The most popular walk was the Rim Trail. Within a modest eight hundred feet of the parking area and ranger station, the visitor could gain an unobstructed view of the massive Emmons Glacier, from the summit of Mount Rainier to its terminus in the White River Valley below. Other trails followed easy grades up the slope behind the plaza and turned east or west near the crest of Sourdough Mountain, yielding occasional grand views to the north as well as a constant view of Mount Rainier to the southwest. In that era of better air quality, it was possible on a clear day to see northward all the way to the Selkirk Range in British Columbia. Beginning in 1931, a ranger-naturalist was stationed at Sunrise to answer questions, give lectures, and lead nature walks. Longer hikes to Burroughs Mountain and Berkeley Park were also available to the visitor at this time.[10] Visitors also found a variety of guided trips and amenities provided by the RNPC at Sunrise. Regular half-day horse trips could be purchased for $3.00. Small and plain "housekeeping cabins" could be rented for $1.50 to $2.50 per day. In the Sunrise Lodge, which first opened in 1931, the visitor could rent bathtub, shower, and laundry facilities; purchase groceries; and enjoy cafeteria-style dining.[11]

Although the vast majority of Rainier visitors never ventured more than a few miles from the Paradise and Sunrise areas, a growing number reserved their greatest enthusiasm for the backcountry. Increasingly, these "wilderness" enthusiasts distinguished between wild country that was accessible by car and true "wilderness" that was accessible only by foot or horseback. Organizations such as The Wilderness Society, founded in 1935, and older mountain clubs such as The Mountaineers, argued forcefully that road development threatened to overwhelm the nation's few remaining areas of wilderness. The Mountaineers prevailed on the NPS to set aside the northern section of Rainier as an undeveloped, roadless, "wilderness area" in 1928, anticipating a much wider protest in the 1930s against too much road building in the national parks and national forests.[12]

Evolving ideas about wilderness were a factor in stimulating more backcountry use. Physical improvements to the trail system were another. In the 1920s, hiking the entire Wonderland Trail around the mountain took from twelve to fourteen days. In the 1930s the trip was accomplished in about eight to ten days. With the completion of the road to Sunrise, backpackers could deposit a food cache at the ranger station for resupply as they came around the mountain, thereby lightening their loads.[13]

The NPS encouraged greater use of the backcountry. Park naturalists urged visitors to get out onto the hiking trails. As early as 1921, the superintendent had recommended the establishment of four or five "hotel camps" at intervals on the Wonderland Trail to facilitate this trip. Although that plan never materialized, the NPS developed a system of free public shelters instead. With the help of the Civilian Conservation Corps, the number of backcountry shelters proliferated. By the mid-1930s there were perhaps a dozen trail shelters in the backcountry, making it possible to spend each night in a shelter while hiking around the mountain.[14]

Ironically, Mount Rainier's growing popularity in the 1930s bore little resemblance to the vision of a mountain resort shared by Seattle- and Tacoma-based investors in the 1920s. Indeed, the Depression wrought havoc for the RNPC. During the worst years of the Depression the concession's gross revenue shriveled to about one quarter of what it had been in 1929. In six out of ten years during the 1930s the company lost money. In the spring of 1933, the company's indebtedness was so severe that it was barely able to scrounge together enough capital to open for business. The Depression was all the more stunning to company officials because the preceding decade had been so full of promise. For the whole 1920–29 period, the RNPC averaged an annual gross revenue of $437,000 with a net profit of approximately 17 percent. Stockholders were told that the company's business would quadruple when all the approach roads to the park were completed.[15] As it turned out, the 1920s were the RNPC's heyday. The company would suffer further financial reverses during the war years and again in the early 1950s. It would never approach the level of business that its founders had anticipated. After grossing more than a half million dollars in 1925, it would not pass that mark again until the late 1950s. The Depression delivered a blow from which the company never recovered.

Mather's partnership of public and private investment, the heart and soul of his concession policy, also suffered irreparable damage from the Depression. Already hard-pressed by the end of the 1920s, the partnership was practically superseded by the medley of federal relief programs that came into existence under the New Deal. Businessmen of Seattle and Tacoma who served on the board of directors of the RNPC saw their influence ebb rapidly as NPS officials concerned themselves less with private capital and more with federal administrators in Washington who held the purse strings of the Public Works Administration (PWA), Civil Works Administration (CWA), Emergency Relief Administration (ERA), Civilian Conservation Corps (CCC), and other New Deal agencies.

But the company's problems went deeper than its loss of revenue and influence. It was already committed to a five-year plan of redevelopment. The economy crumbled at the very time that the RNPC was stretching its financial resources to modernize its accommodations at Paradise and invest in a major new development at Sunrise.[16] After borrowing heavily to pay for new lodges and cabins at Paradise and Sunrise, the RNPC was $375,000 in debt. The company tried to increase its stock but could find no new subscribers as the business climate deteriorated. Desperate for cash, the company tried to borrow $350,000 through an issue of $500 notes that would mature at 6 percent in five years. Altogether, the RNPC raised a mere $30,000 in notes. In 1933, the RNPC appealed to Secretary of the Interior Harold Ickes for a loan from the Reconstruction Finance Corporation (RFC), but since a large part of the money was needed to retire the company's debts, the RFC could not help.[17]

In those first and worst years of the Depression, the company faced dramatic loss of revenue. Brand new housekeeping cabins stood empty through the summer; a newly redecorated and refurnished Paradise Inn experienced room vacancies on weekends in July; waitresses and busboys stood around with nothing to do in the inn's elegant dining room. The RNPC's account books were awash in red ink: a $69,000 loss in

1931, $91,000 in 1932, $73,000 in 1933. Superintendent Tomlinson could do little more than offer encouragement and praise of the "progressive attitude" and "fine spirit of cooperation" displayed by company officials "during a time of serious business depression."[18]

The company looked for ways to cut operating expenses. Transportation service between Seattle, Tacoma, and Portland and the park was turned over to the North Coast Transportation Company in 1931. The company proposed to sell its hydroelectric plant on the Paradise River to the government. This proposal took the form of a bill, which Washington's Senator Wesley Jones introduced in the Senate on December 14, 1931. At the annual meeting of the board of directors in January 1932, it was suggested that the Seattle and Tacoma chambers of commerce be requested to lobby for the bill through their representatives in Washington, D.C. Albright also supported the proposal. Yet the bill failed to pass.[19]

In August 1932, the RNPC's General Manager Paul Sceva and President Alexander Baillie wrote to the secretary of the interior to request a waiver of the $2,000 annual franchise fee. "We rather feel we are partners of the Government in maintaining these facilities for the comfort and convenience of visitors," Baillie wrote. "I am not using idle words when I say that if this charge is not eliminated from our contract it will be impossible to raise money from the public to create increased facilities." This request was politely refused. Assistant Secretary Joseph M. Dixon reminded Baillie that the RNPC had been allowed a smaller franchise fee than the Curry Company of Yosemite when the RNPC's new contract was negotiated in 1928.[20]

Company officials lowered their sights for the new development at Sunrise. Even after they scaled back the original plan for a large, deluxe hotel, they opened the more modest Sunrise Lodge in July 1931 with some $50,000 of interior finishing yet to be completed. The new building contained a cafeteria-style food service, baths, supply store, post office, and employee quarters, but no guest rooms. Uphill from the lodge were 215 housekeeping cabins.

To attract business to this new development, the RNPC began marketing the Sunrise development as a dude ranch. The company brochure stated, "Memories of the Old West are revived and experienced in the

Sunrise Dude Ranch where real western riders entertain and lead you on many interesting trips." Yakima Park was billed as a former cattle range abounding in "romantic legends." The Mount Rainier Mining Company's idle works in Glacier Basin were styled the "Ghost Gold Mine" and were the destination of moonlit horseback rides. A small box canyon called Devil's Hole was claimed to have been a hideout for rustlers, where two bad men were said to have defended themselves against an attack by a large posse of local townsmen.[21] This kind of exploitation of the national park was not in keeping with the purpose of the park concession, but under the circumstances, park officials did not object to it. Indeed, the design theme of the new administrative buildings at Sunrise, which commemorated the Indian past in Yakima Park by the use of a dubious frontier-blockhouse architectural style, only contributed to the hype.

An important thrust of the RNPC's new marketing effort at Sunrise was its offering of a weekly rate that included cabin, meals, and a horse, all in one package. The aim, once again, was to attract easterners to Rainier. The RNPC also coordinated its publicity and sales efforts with the transcontinental railroads, offering all-expense fares that included two and three days' worth of accommodations at Rainier in the cost of a railroad ticket. These tickets could be purchased at any railroad office or travel agency in the United States and Canada. Beginning in 1932, RNPC officials persuaded the Seattle, Tacoma, and Yakima chambers of commerce to help pay the cost of the company's promotional literature.[22]

On the south side of the mountain, the company adjusted its rates and schedules to appeal to a local clientele. During the 1933 season the guide service at Paradise was greatly curtailed, the photograph business was not opened, and most guest services were concentrated at the Paradise Lodge, the inn being used only for overflow guests on weekends. These drastic measures lasted just one season, and succeeded in trimming the company's losses from what they had been the year before despite the fact that park visitation fell to its lowest point during the whole Depression.

In perhaps its most pathetic attempt to draw more business, the RNPC opened a nine-hole golf course at Paradise on August 1, 1931. This short-lived venture was approved by the director of the NPS, Horace Albright, who agreed with President H. A. Rhodes of the RNPC that a golf course might entice local people to stay at the Paradise Inn during the week. Albright wrote in a memorandum to his staff, "Golf is a country game not a city one. It can be justified in parks easier than tennis. Anyway, I want to try out the thing and as the Rainier Company needs revenue more than any other Company I am disposed to let them try the experiment." He put his chief landscape architect Tom Vint in charge of its design.[23]

If the company's Seattle- and Tacoma-based investors needed any further evidence of their diminished influence in the park, they found it in the park service's commitment to various New Deal relief programs. Rainier hosted hundreds of unemployed men in relief camps during the Depression. In the desperate winter of 1933–34, the Civil Works Administration (CWA) employed several hundred men and paid for their room and board at Longmire, Ohanapecosh, and Carbon River. From 1938 to 1940, the Works Progress Administration (WPA) had two camps in Rainier at Longmire and Ohanapecosh. Between 1933 and 1940, the Civilian Conservation Corps had camps at Tahoma Creek, Narada Falls, Ipsut Creek, St. Andrews Creek, White River, Ohanapecosh, and Sunshine Point, with as many as two hundred men in each camp company. Altogether, these relief camps held as many as a thousand men. Despite the adverse conditions that brought the men there, many of the camps' occupants were enjoying their first or most memorable national park experience.[24] The myriad projects that they accomplished—campground improvements, minor road and trail improvements, landscape rehabilitation, and construction of buildings, shelters, picnic areas, plant beds, scenic turnouts, and sundry other items—changed the look and feel of the national park.

The establishment of the Emergency Conservation Work (ECW) program, more commonly known as the CCC, presented park administrators with two new challenges. One objective, plainly, was to accomplish valuable conservation work. The other objective was to provide emergency relief for CCC enrollees. These were distinct, albeit compatible objectives. Park officials viewed each CCC enrollee not just as a source of labor but as a new client, a new type of visitor who could find spiritual renewal in nature through the collective c c c experience. As Superintendent Tomlinson explained to the c c c camp superintendents, the fundamental values that guided national park management in normal times would be "effective in their entirety during the Emergency Conservation Work, with the additional requirement of training and character building of the young men enrolled as a part of the nationwide employment relief plan."[25] As a former military officer, Tomlinson welcomed the chance for the park to serve as a place for "man building."

Getting the c c c started proved to be a mammoth task. President Franklin D. Roosevelt's announced goal was to have a quarter million men enrolled in the c c c by July 1933. n p s director Horace Albright, serving out his last months in government service, represented the Interior Department on the c c c's organizing council that spring as the administration formulated how this goal was to be accomplished. It soon became obvious that conservation agencies like the National Park Service and the U.S. Forest Service were too small to build and run the camps as originally envisioned; only the U.S. Army could handle that. Therefore, the division of responsibility between government agencies was made as follows: the army would process the enrollees and form them into companies with army commanders, dispatch the companies to their respective camps, build the camps, and maintain discipline in the camps; the conservation agencies such as the n p s and the U.S. Forest Service would select all c c c camp locations, furnish the camps with tools and vehicles, employ the enrollees in useful conservation work, and supervise their efforts.[26]

Meanwhile, the Labor Department was given the special task of enrolling supervisory personnel in the c c c. These would be older men with experience in forest work or a building trade who would serve as camp leaders and crew foremen for the young enrollees. The law required that they be recruited from the local area and that they receive a higher rate of pay than the other enrollees, so that the c c c would not take away local jobs or further depress the wage scale. In what must be one of the gems of the New Deal's vast array of organizational handles, these supervisory personnel were given the title of "local experienced men," or l e m s.[27]

Superintendent Tomlinson worked with army officers from Fort

Lewis, Washington, in planning when and where c c c camps would be built in Mount Rainier National Park, and by mid-July they had more than a thousand men deployed in the park in five c c c camps. Most of the men were performing trail work and roadside cleanup while their camp buildings were still under construction. Before the camps were even occupied, Tomlinson was informed that all funds authorized for new construction at Rainier had been impounded and pooled with funds set aside for the c c c. This was in addition to a 25 percent cut in regular maintenance and operation allotments and a 15 percent cut in the allotment for personnel. Of course, Tomlinson could see that federal expenditures in the park would soon increase under the c c c, but this did not lessen the sting of seeing the park's own operating budget reduced so sharply. The purpose of the impoundment of funds was to ensure that the e c w program would be assimilated quickly into the bureaucratic power structure.[28]

Park officials played a significant role in providing a positive experience for the c c c enrollees. Their involvement with the c c c went far beyond what the division of responsibilities between the n p s and the army required of them. On paper, the park administration's responsibility was to design suitable work projects for the c c c; the army, meanwhile, was to set up and supply the camps, organize the c c c companies and transport them to the park, and maintain discipline in the camps. But park officials did much more than assign jobs. Superintendent Tomlinson worked closely with Brigadier General Joseph C. Castner, commanding officer at Fort Lewis, Washington, in planning the placement of camps. Landscape architect E. A. Davidson and engineer R. D. Waterhouse provided instruction to c c c superintendents and foremen, some of whom were former n p s colleagues. Park rangers and naturalists had considerable contact with the c c c enrollees during their leisure time in the park, leading them on fishing, hiking, and climbing trips. "The men have excellent opportunity for recreation on account of the friendliness of park officials," a c c c inspector reported. Even the park's interpretive program catered to the needs of the c c c enrollees. "Park officials also lecture on forestry," the inspector wrote, "and will show movies from time to time on forestry work." In November 1933, an appreciative park staff treated the last departing c c c company to an elaborate turkey dinner at Longmire. In his annual report for 1933, Tomlinson stated that the ccc enrollees had received much useful training in conservation work and citizenship, and he credited his own ranger staff with helping to keep the young men healthy and happy. It was partly through the many ranger-led activities that the ccc enrollees came to a "full appreciation of what their Government was doing for them."[29]

The thousands of ccc enrollees who passed a summer or two at Mount Rainier came from diverse backgrounds. Enrollees had to be eighteen to twenty-five years old, single, unemployed, physically fit, and from a family on relief. Usually enrollees were assigned to companies with men who came from the same city or county. African Americans were considerably underrepresented in the ccc, and in most cases they formed separate companies. Native Americans likewise formed separate units, which were employed on Indian reservations and administered by a separate branch called the ccc–Indian Division. Ideally, a ccc company was assigned to a camp within about two hundred miles of where it was formed, so that the young men could go home to their families every other weekend. However, since most of the enrollees came from the East and most of the national forests and parks were in the West, a large number of ccc companies were put on trains and sent westward. As a result, ccc companies that were assigned to camps in Mount Rainier National Park tended to be either from nearby counties in Washington State or from distant states in the East or deep South.[30]

Tourists were curious about the ccc. President Roosevelt's "Tree Army" received substantial media coverage, and tourists were eager to see these vaunted young men in action. RNPC buses made the Narada Falls camp a regular stop for tourists en route to Paradise. Hundreds of auto tourists stopped at Narada Falls each day as well. The waterfall itself drew many onlookers, of course, but it was the camp superintendent's feeling that most people were chiefly interested in seeing what a ccc camp looked like. "Owing to the fact that this camp is under constant observation by the public in general," wrote the camp superintendent, "a special attempt has been made by this camp to present a smart appearance."[31]

So popular was the ccc during the New Deal that its conservation work has become almost legendary. According to tradition, most of the pre–World War II rustic-style administrative buildings that are seen in the national parks and forests today were designed and built by the ccc. In fact, the government rustic style was already established. "The New Deal," architectural historian Phoebe Cutler has written, "did not innovate so much as it mass-produced."[32] Moreover, ccc crews were mainly assigned to low-skilled jobs. Buildings, roads, bridges, and other edifices that are commonly associated with the ccc era were built by government contractors. Indeed, the Public Works Administration (pwa) was at least as responsible as the ccc for the florescence of government rustic in the 1930s. Nevertheless, the ccc's actual accomplishments were extensive and varied. Quarterly reports on the ccc quantified each camp's accomplishments in terms of man-days spent on each project. The number of projects, large and small, multiplied with each passing enrollment period. Statistics for the whole park mounted so quickly as to become mind numbing. Never before or since had the park administration had so much unskilled labor at its command.

If building construction made up a relatively small proportion of the total man-days expended by the ccc at Rainier, these rustic structures are nevertheless the ccc's most enduring legacy. The fine log cabins, the well-crafted stone comfort stations and trailside exhibit shelters, the carefully laid flagstone paths, the many stone guardrails—these features are as ubiquitous as they are unpretentious. They have become a familiar part of the national park experience for millions of Americans. As one nps architectural historian has contended, "Park design includes numerous subtle and sometimes subconscious cues to the visitor. These features contribute to the sense of place of a national park."[33] The ccc— and the particular way in which the nps used the ccc—made a significant contribution to that special quality that makes national parks such a distinctive part of the American landscape.

Winter recreational use of Rainier burgeoned during the 1930s as Americans discovered the European sport of downhill skiing. The first American ski school, with European ski experts providing instruction, opened in New Hampshire in 1929. Three years later, winter sports received a big boost when the third winter Olympics were held in Lake Placid, New York. Two years after that, in 1934, the first rope tow in the

United States was installed at Woodstock, Vermont. It was powered by the rear wheel of a jacked-up Model T Ford. Despite some early technical difficulties with this contraption, the idea quickly spread to the West. By the mid-1930s, there were new, rope-tow-equipped ski hills from Wilmot Hills, Wisconsin, to Jackson Hole, Wyoming, to Stevens Pass, Washington.[34]

Downhill racing events began to draw spectators and the national media. The First National Downhill Championship was held at Mount Moosilauke, New Hampshire, in 1933. The First U.S. National Downhill and Slalom Championships were held at Rainier's Paradise in 1935. It was at this event that the American team for the fourth winter Olympics was selected. In 1937, the first Harriman Cup race was held at the Union Pacific Railroad's new ski resort at Sun Valley, Idaho.[35]

Personalities also contributed to the growing popularity of downhill skiing. Alpine skiing techniques were introduced to American skiers by a flock of prominent German and Austrian skiers who fled Nazi Germany in the mid to late 1930s. Austrian champion Otto Schniebs attracted ski disciples at Dartmouth. Hannes Schneider, another Austrian, taught skiing in Conway, New Hampshire. Friedl Pfeiffer went to Sun Valley, Sepp Ruschp to Stowe, Luggi Foeger to Yosemite, and Otto Lang to Rainier.[36]

Among ski enthusiasts, the Paradise area acquired national renown. In April 1934, the *Seattle Post-Intelligencer* sponsored an event at Paradise that definitely put Rainier on the map of national ski competition. The first annual Silver Skis race featured a five-mile course from Camp Muir to Paradise Valley—an elevation drop of approximately 5,000 feet. The route was thought to be one of the most challenging in ski competition. Sixty contestants made the arduous trek from the end of the road up the slope of Rainier, then came racing down before a large crowd of spectators. Six months after the race, in December 1934, the National Ski Association voted to use the lower part of the Silver Skis course for the site of its national championship downhill and slalom ski races, to be held the next spring.[37]

This contest attracted more than the usual amount of interest because it also served as the occasion for the Olympic ski team tryouts. The downhill racecourse started at Sugar Loaf at 8,500 feet elevation and descended past Panorama Point into Edith Creek Basin, near the Paradise Inn. The course had an overall pitch of 33 percent. The slalom course was laid out on the uphill side of Alta Vista, a prominence above the Paradise Lodge. Sportscasters from the Columbia Broadcasting System provided live coverage for radio listeners throughout the United States, while three wire services described the event for newspapers. Moving-picture photographers documented the contest for newsreels. An estimated 7,500 spectators drove approximately 2,000 automobiles into the park and hiked up to Paradise to get a view. Superintendent Tomlinson had the road plowed a mile above Narada Falls to provide extra parking space. It was the busiest weekend in the park's history up to that time.[38]

Winter use presented park officials with a dilemma. Ever since Stephen Mather had singled out Rainier as one national park with the potential to become a significant winter playground, the park administration had striven to encourage more and more winter use. Tomlinson was sensitive to local ski clubs' demands for better access to Paradise Valley; in his view, the large expense of snow removal was the only significant factor weighing against it. He had his maintenance crew plow the road as far as Narada Falls during the winter of 1935–36, and kept the road open to Paradise in the winter of 1936–37. Meanwhile, he listened sympathetically to the request of the RNPC's manager, Paul Sceva, that the government build an aerial tram from Narada Falls to Paradise for winter visitors, promising to take the matter up with his superiors.[39]

But Tomlinson also admitted that heavy winter use of the park was creating severe administrative challenges. Problems of winter use ranged from the cost of snow removal to inadequate parking and lodging facilities, treatment of ski injuries, avalanche danger, and public pressure for permanent ski lift and aerial tram fixtures that would mar the landscape during the summer season. Moreover, these difficulties were not limited to the Paradise area. Thousands of skiers began driving to the Cayuse Pass area, on the eastern edge of the park, for a day's worth of recreation. Local ski clubs and civic groups from Enumclaw to Seattle started calling for ski facilities at Sunrise, too.[40]

Although Tomlinson did not necessarily share their views, some NPS officials even began to question whether downhill skiing was an appropriate activity in a national park. The skiers' growing emphasis on speed, technique, athletic competition, and urban amenities led some park officials to view downhill skiers as an unwelcome user group. This was perhaps the most controversial aspect of the problem. It called for a subjective judgment on the kind of experience that downhill skiers typically had in the park. Doubts about the appropriateness of this sport in a national park setting were crucial because they strengthened public debate over seemingly more objective winter-use issues, such as snow removal costs and ski lift development.

Rainier's landscape architect, Ernest A. Davidson, argued that the growing popularity of the park as a downhill ski area was insidious. Skiers were pushing for developments that would be injurious to the national park's broader purpose of providing for the public's enjoyment of nature. He tried to define the problem objectively this way:

> There is a point where a fine healthy outdoor sport begins to degenerate. This point is reached when the majority of its so-called devotees are more interested in the various side-lines of the sport than they are in the sport itself; when the sport becomes the social thing-to-do, rather than the athletic thing to be done; when the results of participation become physically useless or harmful, rather than physically beneficial. At Mt. Rainier this point is dangerously near.[41]

Davidson suggested that the NPS should not plow the road above Narada Falls or provide any rope tow or other mechanical lift at Paradise. Then those skiers who wanted a physical challenge would rightly come to the national park, while those who wanted only the thrill of the downhill runs would go elsewhere.

By the winter of 1937–38, Paradise was the leading ski resort in the Pacific Northwest. The NPS permitted the installation of a rope tow at Paradise during the winter of 1937–38. Powered by an eight-cylinder Ford engine, the rope tow could haul 250 skiers per hour from the guide house to the saddle of Alta Vista. Enterprising skiers extended the length of the downhill run all the way to Narada Falls, where they caught a company shuttle bus back up to the foot of the rope tow. Floodlights were installed to allow night skiing, and the Paradise Inn rented out rooms through the winter season.[42]

THROUGH DEPRESSION AND WAR

The park administration balked at other proposed developments. Superintendent Tomlinson tried unavailingly to persuade officials of the Washington State Highway Department to close the state road up to Cayuse Pass during the winter, arguing that there was too much avalanche danger. The superintendent urged The Mountaineers not to advertise an organized ski outing to the Tipsoo Lakes country, above Cayuse Pass, suggesting that once the area was discovered the NPS would be hard-pressed to develop shelters and sanitary facilities for the winter crowds.[43] When an estimated 34,000 people used the Cayuse Pass area for skiing during the winter of 1937–38, Tomlinson tried to get the Enumclaw Ski Club to provide a ski patrol, but refused to commit any of his own staff to this area. For several seasons in a row, the NPS withstood pressure from the Pacific Northwest Ski Association and various local ski clubs to build a modern ski lift from Paradise to Panorama Point. The NPS permitted the annual Silver Skis competition to take place in 1936 and 1938 through 1941, but with a minimum of fanfare. The NPS refused all requests to hold additional contests at Paradise, asserting that the fireworks displays and carnival-like atmosphere normally associated with these meets were not appropriate in a national park.[44]

By the end of this period, park officials were wondering whether the effort to develop a winter season in Rainier had been too successful. Winter use grew faster than anyone anticipated, outpacing the growth in visitor use overall. Winter use—defined for statistical purposes as the number of people who entered the park during the six-month period of November through April—accounted for 5 percent of the park's total visitation in 1923 (November 1922 through April 1923) and climbed to 30 percent by 1941. The most rapid growth came at the end of the 1930s. Despite park officials' growing misgivings, however, the NPS made two significant concessions to skiers, which were apparent confirmation of Rainier's status as a major ski area in the Pacific Northwest. In 1938, NPS director Arno B. Cammerer approved plans for a large dormitory building at Paradise, to be constructed from CCC, PWA, and regular appropriation funds. Known as the Ski Lodge, the building was designed with four main compartments, each with lobby, toilet, shower, and dormitory area, to accommodate eighty people. The hope was that low-income families, semi-charitable groups, and college and high school students could be accommodated for about 75 cents per person per night.[45] The Ski Lodge was finally completed in December 1941, the same month that the United States entered World War II. As the war years brought a hiatus to winter use of Rainier, the future use of this building was unclear.

The second significant concession to ski groups was NPS director Newton B. Drury's decision, approved by the secretary of the interior on December 12, 1940, to permit the installation of a demountable, T-bar type of ski lift. The T-bar represented an intermediate-sized lift: more intrusive than a rope tow but less so than a chairlift. The plan was to extend the lift well beyond Alta Vista to the foot of Panorama Point. The Pacific Northwest Ski Association had been calling for a chairlift for the past three years. In June 1941, the RNPC announced that it was not prepared financially to build such a lift, but this only postponed the issue until after World War II.[46]

Following the American entry into World War II in December 1941, President Roosevelt called upon the park service to join in the national war effort, marking the second time in ten years that the park service had to respond to a national emergency. Just as it had during the Great Depression, the NPS had to adjust its priorities and change the way it did business while protecting the core of its mission. It was necessary to recognize the extraordinary nature of the times without losing sight of the fact that, as the keeper of the nation's wonderlands, the agency bore an exceptional responsibility to the future. As Drury explained, national parks symbolized the very values that the nation was fighting for and it would not do to sacrifice those values in the cause of victory. The NPS had to ensure that the national parks would be preserved for the people's enjoyment after the war. Even more than the Depression, the war effort diminished what little influence local investment capital still retained in the national park.

Mount Rainier National Park, like the NPS at large, faced an immediate reduction in force as personnel went into the armed services and Congress slashed national park appropriations. The new superintendent at Rainier, John C. Preston, oversaw three draft registrations at designated stations between July 1941 and April 1942. Robert K. Weldon, district ranger at Paradise, was the first permanent staff member inducted into the army; many seasonal staff members volunteered at the end of the 1942 tourist season. The loss of personnel was compounded by the rapid dismantling of public works programs, including the ccc. Construction contracts for the Stevens Canyon Road were terminated in the fall of 1942.[47]

Wartime cuts in staff and budget paralleled a drop in visitation as gasoline rationing and shortages of automobile parts discouraged travel. The reduction in travel to Rainier mainly occurred in 1943 and 1944, when official restrictions on travel were most severe. The number of visitors in 1943, for example, was only a fourth of what it had been in the peak travel year of 1940; winter use declined to practically nil as the park service ceased plowing the road beyond Longmire.[48]

The national call to arms brought renewed demands by mining, grazing, and lumbering interests to open the park to resource exploitation. These demands were often cloaked in patriotism, couched as if the nation's vital interests were at stake when in fact the motivation was profit and the plans for resource exploitation did not really promise to have any measurable effect on the war effort. In responding to these pressures, NPS officials had to make sure that the public, in its patriotic zeal, did not lose sight of national park values. Between 1942 and 1944, the park administration deflected threats to the park by mining, grazing, and lumbering interests.

NPS officials went out of their way to make national parks available for recreational use by the U.S. Armed Services. Busloads of soldiers who were stationed at Fort Lewis, Washington, received free trips to Rainier while the men anxiously awaited deployment overseas. Director Drury praised Rainier (along with Yosemite, Sequoia, Mount McKinley, and Olympic national parks) for its role in serving thousands of military personnel. He observed that this alone was "significant justification of the national-park concept," as untold numbers of soldiers were "being given opportunities they never had before, and may never have again, to see the inspiring beauty and historical significance of this land of ours."[49]

Rainier's unique contribution to the war effort was its use as a training ground for ski troops. The mountain attracted the military for the same basic reason that it attracted scientists and tourists: it stood out as an "arctic island in a temperate sea." The vertical zones that made the fauna and flora of Mount Rainier so diverse and beautiful also made the area a good place to find terrain and weather conditions that could simulate fighting conditions in the European Alps and the European winter. Snow and inclement weather were abundant, and if army officers found the weather at Paradise too mild for their purposes, they only had to march their soldiers higher up the mountain to test cold-weather clothing and equipment under the most severe conditions. Men tested sleeping bags and snowsuits on the summit of Mount Rainier. They did sentry duty at night wearing a kind of sleeping bag with legs and feet. One party of ski troops made a circuit around the mountain carrying rifles and eighty-five-pound packs.[50]

The army found Rainier an attractive ground for mountain infantry exercises because of its location near Fort Lewis, too. Established as an army training camp in World War I, Fort Lewis survived the army's lean years in the 1920s and 1930s to become one of the major army installations on the West Coast in World War II. In the 1930s, the commanding officer of Fort Lewis had cooperated with Superintendent Tomlinson on the administration of the ccc. Still, despite the U.S. Army's longtime presence nearby, the use of Mount Rainier for mountain infantry exercises developed fairly suddenly. On a November day in 1940, a platoon of the 41st Infantry Division, calling itself the Military Ski Patrol, arrived at Paradise for a "preliminary instruction exercise," accompanied by public relations officers and a photographer from the *Seattle Post-Intelligencer*. The four-hour visit heralded a full winter of ski training and maneuvers by a second "Military Ski Patrol"—twenty-four soldiers of the 15th Infantry Regiment, 3rd Infantry Division, also based at Fort Lewis. These soldiers were quartered in government housing at Longmire.[51]

The two military ski patrols from Fort Lewis were of an experimental nature; this was the first time in the history of the U.S. Army that soldiering and skiing were combined. With the possibility growing that the army would be called to fight in central Europe, army officials began to contemplate the need for specialized mountain units. The idea was given a special impetus by the impressive performance of Finnish ski troops against the Soviet Army during the winter of 1939–40. Photographs of Finnish soldiers on skis gained wide circulation in the American press. Following exploratory discussions with the presidents of the National Ski Association and the National Ski Patrol during the summer of 1940, the U.S Army initiated military ski exercises with small groups of volunteers at Mount Rainier; Lake Placid and Old Forge, New York; Camp McCoy, Wisconsin; and Fort Richardson, Alaska.[52]

The first regiment of ski troops, the 87th Mountain Infantry, was formed at Fort Lewis the following November. Army units in all parts of the country sent their crack skiers to the new regiment. The U.S. Forest Service and the NPS contributed more than a score of rangers. Meanwhile, the War Department entered an agreement with the National Ski Patrol, a civilian organization, to recruit experienced skiers for the special unit. New England ski clubs and Ivy League ski teams provided numerous volunteers. Many European exiles and immigrants joined the 87th Mountain, prompting one writer to call it a virtual foreign legion.[53]

The 1,000-man regiment wintered at Fort Lewis during the winter of 1941–42 and sent contingents to train at Paradise under a cooperative agreement with the NPS. In a noteworthy compromise, ski troops claimed full use of the rope tow above Paradise Inn on weekdays and yielded the ground to park visitors on weekends. The army rented and occupied the Paradise Lodge and Tatoosh Club facilities of the RNPC.[54] In the spring of 1942, the 87th Mountain transferred to the army's new Camp Hale, located on the Continental Divide in Colorado, where it formed part of the 10th Mountain Infantry Division. The 87th Mountain saw combat in the Italian Alps in 1945.[55]

Through fifteen years of economic depression and war, the administration of Mount Rainier National Park evolved into something quite different from the partnership of public and private investment that Stephen Mather had nurtured in the 1920s. The NPS formed new partnerships with myriad other federal agencies from the CCC to the army, and activities occurred at Mount Rainier chiefly because it was a federal area, a *national* park. Yet the nearby cities of Seattle and Tacoma continued to supply most of the park's visitors and to shape recreational demand, as with the growing interest in winter use. With the return of peace and prosperity, the two Puget Sound cities would profoundly influence the park in new ways.

CHAPTER 6

The Contentious Years (1945–1965)

ON JUNE 22, 1945, PRESIDENT HARRY S. TRUMAN ENTERED Mount Rainier National Park at the wheel of a purple convertible. Accompanied by Washington Governor Mon C. Wallgren and an entourage of reporters, photographers, Secret Service agents, and state patrolmen, the president led the motorcade to Paradise, where he "frolicked in the snow and threw snowballs," dined in the Paradise Inn, and played the piano in the inn's cavernous lobby. After this presidential display of national park patronage—a fine show of confidence in the new postwar era—Truman met with Superintendent Preston for about thirty minutes and asked "many questions about the National Park Service and Mount Rainier in particular."[1] Whether anything substantive came out of the meeting is doubtful, but Truman appears to have been the first politician to use Rainier as a backdrop and the national park as a symbol of what the federal government could do for Washington State. In the years to come, numerous Washington State senators and congressmen would follow his example.

A year later, Truman's secretary of the interior, Julius A. Krug, traveled to Washington State to listen to residents' demands for new overnight accommodations and ski facilities at Paradise. Meeting with local business leaders in Seattle on June 17, 1946, Krug acknowledged the need for more development and pledged all assistance that the Department of the Interior could provide. He emphasized, however, that the government was faced with spending cuts, and he expressed hope that private industry would put forward the necessary investment capital. The money, Krug argued, should come from local banks and railroads and airlines that served the Pacific Northwest and benefited most directly from tourism. Krug's meetings with local business leaders were reminiscent of Mather's pitch to Seattle and Tacoma capitalists thirty years earlier. Accompanied by NPS director Newton B. Drury and Superintendent Preston, the secretary sought to initiate a new partnership between the park service and private capital in Mount Rainier National Park.[2]

The park—indeed the whole national park system—stood at a critical juncture after World War II. The public was poised to enjoy more vacations and leisure travel than ever before. Use of national parks would increase dramatically in the coming two decades, imposing heavy burdens on an aging infrastructure. As politicians, bureaucrats, and citizen activists clashed over the proper course of redevelopment at Rainier, three basic ingredients of park planning would mix in a witch's brew. First, the ailing concession had to be put on a new footing. Second, downhill skiers must be accommodated at Paradise or encouraged to take their sport elsewhere. Third, the park's old problem of poor visitor circulation— the tendency for visitors to concentrate and experience congestion at Paradise and Sunrise—needed correction. It took twenty contentious years to find workable solutions to these three interlocking problems, considerably longer than anyone might have imagined in those heady days at the end of World War II.

By 1945, the relationship between the NPS and the RNPC had passed through two distinct phases. From its inception in 1915 until the onset of the Great Depression, the partnership functioned basically according to plan; the locally owned RNPC was a model company in Stephen Mather's national park concession policy. During the Depression, the RNPC cut operating expenses and services and accepted a more modest role in developing the park. The NPS, for its part, tapped into an array of new federal programs for construction projects, demonstrating more independence from local business interests. When these alternative sources of funds vanished during World War II, the stage was set for a third phase in the partnership. Now the NPS looked once more to the private sector for investment capital, while local business leaders looked to the government for a renewal of public funding. The result was an uneasy compromise, a policy of government *ownership* coupled with private *operation* of all guest facilities.[3]

The challenges facing the RNPC and the NPS after World War II were so acute and yet so typical of the whole national park system that Director Drury profiled the concession problem at Rainier by way of illustration in his annual report on the national parks for 1947. After a decade and a half of economic depression and war, the company was financially weak and in low standing with its investors. Its inns and lodges were old and in an alarming state of disrepair. Some of the buildings could only be described as firetraps and were not well suited to the day-use visitor who composed a growing proportion of all park visitors. The company hesitated to invest in the rehabilitation or replacement of these buildings when its contract with the NPS was nearly due to expire, giving the RNPC little security for its investment. Finally, the company was burdened by rising operating costs after the war, especially for labor. Assistant Secretary of the Interior Girard C. Davidson told the House Committee on Public Lands that the problem of the concession in Mount Rainier National Park was perhaps "the No. 1 problem of the Park Service."[4]

The RNPC's twenty-year concession contract was one of several national park concession contracts that were soon to expire. These contracts dated from the late 1920s, when the NPS had had the foresight to renew, years before their expiration dates, the several twenty-year contracts that had originated under Mather's new concession policy in 1916. The uncertainties brought about by the Depression and World War II prevented a repetition of this smooth procedure in the early 1940s. Now with this second generation of contracts beginning to lapse, NPS Director Drury found himself in a pickle.

The RNPC's contract was to expire on December 31, 1947. RNPC president Paul H. Sceva, a feisty little bulldog of a man, announced the company's desired terms for renewal in June 1946. He wanted the park service to build new facilities that the company would operate under lease. He wanted the park service to purchase the company's buildings,

THE CONTENTIOUS YEARS

and the company would invest the proceeds in new transportation equipment. Finally, he wanted the park service to recognize that the new arrangement would be experimental and subject to fair adjustment, especially with regard to winter operations. Sceva avoided the term "concession" altogether, calling his plan an "operating lease."[5]

Drury observed that the operating lease idea would probably amount to a government subsidy—a doubtful proposition when only a small percentage of Rainier visitors actually stayed in the lodges.[6] Pacific northwesterners generally had no such qualms about federal aid, however. Skiers observed that nearly every ski area in Washington and Oregon was located on federal land; therefore, they argued, it was incumbent on federal land managers to plan and provide for ski resorts in the region. Boosters in the Puget Sound cities' chambers of commerce argued that Portland had its Timberline Lodge at Mount Hood, so the park service should provide the same kind of facility at Mount Rainier. The WPA had built Timberline Lodge in the 1930s, and the Forest Service leased the development to a private operator for a modest annual fee with no expectation of recovering the government's investment. The RNPC's investors and their supporters pointed out again and again that the government had invited Puget Sound area businessmen to form the company and build the park's hotels in the first place; now the government had an obligation to assume the equity in those aging structures. With these arguments circulating in the local press and in public meetings, it was the rare Pacific Northwest resident who quarreled with the idea of a government subsidy for visitor facilities at Rainier.

The NPS needed congressional authorization to acquire the RNPC's buildings. On February 28, 1947, Representative Thor C. Tollefson of Tacoma introduced a bill providing for the acquisition of the RNPC's buildings and the construction of new buildings by the government. Sceva was determined to secure the park service's and the Department of the Interior's support for the measure. A month after the bill was introduced, Sceva wrote to Drury complaining that Superintendent Preston was making public statements that the NPS was neutral toward this bill. Drury responded by ordering Owen Tomlinson, the former park superintendent who was now regional director of the park service's Western Region, to instruct Preston that the park service, as a general policy, was in favor of government ownership of concession buildings.[7] Later, when asked by the House Committee on Public Lands to comment on the bill, the Department of the Interior gave a favorable report. Assistant Secretary Oscar L. Chapman informed the committee that experience had shown that public accommodations could not be built and operated by private capital at a profit in Mount Rainier National Park, and further, that it was the park service's duty to provide public accommodations.[8]

On September 15, 1947, a subcommittee of the House Committee on Public Lands held a hearing on the Tollefson bill at Paradise Lodge. The subcommittee's composition was indicative of new regional and party alignments in Congress; of the nine members of the subcommittee who were present, seven were Republicans and hailed from western states. Congressmen Tollefson and Russell V. Mack of Washington were also present. The central issue of the hearing was whether or not the government should purchase the buildings, thereby granting what amounted to a subsidy of overnight accommodations. Sceva testified at length on the company's financial hardships. He was followed by Fred H. McNeil of the National Ski Association, Art Ganson of the Seattle Chamber of Commerce, Elmun R. Fetterolf of the Tacoma Chamber of Commerce, and Leo Gallagher of The Mountaineers, all of whom supported Tollefson's bill. The hearings closed with the testimony of Assistant Secretary C. Girard Davidson, who reaffirmed the department's support for the bill while cautioning that the purchase would be a mere stopgap measure pending a much greater congressional appropriation to build new facilities.

Davidson also alluded to a review of national park concession policy by an advisory group to the secretary of the interior. This important servicewide review was currently under way. Asked why the park service had not yet assessed the value of the concession's buildings, Davidson explained that the secretary was awaiting the recommendations by the concessions advisory group. Apparently the existence of this group was a revelation to most members of the subcommittee. Tollefson would later assert that the subcommittee's anticipation of the advisory group's report influenced its decision to table the bill.[9] This was understandable, for it was likely that the bill would in some way set a precedent, and it seemed prudent to await the secretary's own policy review before addressing a particular situation such as Rainier's. In any case, the concessions advisory group's findings were crucial for the RNPC and Rainier.

Secretary Krug went entirely outside the government for advice on park concessions. The group of five comprised a certified public accountant, a representative of the hotel industry, a member of the American Automobile Association, a representative of the traveling public, and a member of the National Parks Association. The group's report was nearly a year and a half in the making, and was finally submitted to the secretary on February 19, 1948. Ironically, the fact that the secretary requested this review caused some speculation that there would be a fundamental reverse of policy, that Mather's basic concept of the single concession or regulated monopoly in each park would be rejected in favor of free enterprise. Far from recommending that, the concessions advisory group reaffirmed the basic idea that free enterprise would despoil the national parks. Indeed, NPS officials construed the report as a ringing endorsement of existing policy. This tended to mask the fact that the concessions advisory group did recommend a few significant changes. Most notably, it recommended that the government should acquire and maintain concession buildings in all national parks where they had been built by private capital. On the pivotal issue raised by Drury—whether government ownership and maintenance of concession buildings should amount to a subsidy—the concessions advisory group suggested that the government could indeed subsidize the concession. This finding was crucial, for it implied that visitor facilities did not have to be economically sound to be justified on the basis of public need; the free market relationship between supply and demand did not apply to national parks. Therefore, in providing for public use of national parks, the NPS could not only enlist the help of private enterprise; it could assist private enterprise in its endeavors, too. This actually strengthened the hand of investment capital in the emerging development plan for Mount Rainier National Park, for it enlarged the meaning of public demand. The fact that Secretary Krug adopted the concession advisory group's recommendations as policy later that year was good news to the RNPC and the company's backers in Seattle and Tacoma.[10]

By the time Secretary Krug enunciated his new policy for national park concessions, the RNPC's twenty-year contract had already expired. If the RNPC had been alone in this circumstance, the company might have been in a weak bargaining position. But many other concession contracts had expired during the past two years, too. All had been replaced with interim one-year contracts. Conferring and testifying jointly with other concessioners at congressional hearings, Sceva approached the contract negotiations as if the NPS, not the RNPC, had everything to lose. Not satisfied with the secretary's statement of policy, he and other concessioners were emboldened to demand more. In particular, they desired more security from their long-term contracts. They argued that the NPS should return to its earlier practice of negotiating new contracts several years in advance of the expiration dates of its current contracts, and they demanded the right of first refusal when the NPS offered new or additional concession contracts in each park.[11] Concessioners presented these and other demands to the Subcommittee on Public Lands during capitol hearings in May and June 1948. Sceva went to Washington with prepared testimony, although the subcommittee did not call him as a witness. In Sceva's place, Tollefson testified on the difficulties faced by investment capital at Rainier. Other witnesses included a representative of the Union Pacific Railroad Company's interests in Grand Canyon, Zion, and Bryce Canyon national parks, a representative of the Western Conference of National Park Concessionaires, the president and general manager of the Lassen National Park Company, and NPS Director Drury. The concessioners expressed frustration and even threatened to shut down their operations unless NPS concession policy was modified in their behalf.[12]

Despite the tenor of the hearings, neither Krug nor Drury was willing to yield much ground to the RNPC. They still hoped that new investors could be found, either for the company itself or for a new franchise that would buy out the RNPC. In the meantime, the RNPC must be induced to make preparations for the following year. On May 28, 1948, in the very midst of the hearings, the NPS offered the RNPC a one-year contract for 1949. It called for the company to make various repairs and improvements to its buildings, including installation of sprinklers in Paradise Inn, to bring the buildings up to code. The sprinkler system had been under discussion for two years.

This proposal was still on the table when Secretary Krug announced, on July 26, 1948, that all national park concessions must comply with the department's labor initiative instituting a forty-hour workweek. The secretary's order met with strong protest from concessioners, who had traditionally employed a forty-eight-hour workweek. The shorter workweek would require a longer payroll. Sceva, together with other concessioners, complained that the room and board for these additional employees would impinge too much on operating costs. Sceva calculated that the forty-hour workweek would cost the RNPC $10,000 per year. Discouraged by the department's labor ruling and its insistence on a sprinkler system for Paradise Inn, the RNPC's board of directors voted to reject the one-year contract offer. On August 25, 1948, Sceva sent Drury a counterproposal calling for an interim five-year contract. The longer term, Sceva insisted, was necessary to protect the company's investment in sprinklers. Drury rejected this proposal on September 10, indicating that the department would soon issue a new type of concessioner contract for the RNPC's consideration. Not waiting for this, Sceva wrote to the secretary of the interior on September 30, 1948, announcing that the board of directors had voted not to renew its contract after the current one expired on December 31, 1948.[13]

Relations between the RNPC and the NPS had reached a low point when a meeting took place in the fall that had disturbing implications for the park service. In late November, Acting Superintendent Harthon L. Bill informed Drury that a number of organizations involved in Washington's tourist industry had come together to reconstitute the Rainier National Park Advisory Board. This body had been an important agent in the allocation of federal funds for road construction during the 1920s. Finding its influence much diminished during the Depression and the New Deal, it had gone out of existence in 1936. Now it was back, called into being by the excitement over the Tollefson bill and recent press reports that the RNPC might be forced out of business. Precisely what role Sceva played in its restoration is unclear; he informed the acting superintendent that he had attended the first meeting of the new advisory board in an "unofficial capacity."[14]

On the surface this seemed like a throwback to an earlier era. Like the first Rainier National Park Advisory Board, the new board was animated by a desire to secure federal aid for the development of Mount

Rainier National Park. But the first advisory board had focused on roads, while the new board concerned itself with overnight accommodations. Roads were a public enterprise almost anywhere they were built, whereas lodging facilities were not. Road construction contractors did not have a vested interest in commercializing the park; the tourist industry did. Giving federal assistance to the concessioner carried the risk of binding the park administration too closely to these commercial interests. Park development could then be pushed too far.

On December 31, 1948, Secretary Krug sent another one-year contract proposal to the RNPC. Sceva replied on January 4, 1949, that the RNPC would accept no less than a two-year contract. Further, the contract must preserve the present labor agreement of a forty-eight-hour workweek, and any infringement of the agreement would enable the RNPC to terminate its contract on thirty days' notice. Krug answered on January 17 that the controversial labor ruling would not take effect until January 1, 1950; therefore, if the RNPC would accept a one-year contract, the labor issue could be set aside for the time being. The company accepted an interim contract on these terms. Both men expressed hope that Congress would act on the Tollefson bill in the coming year.

Tollefson reintroduced his bill two days later; however, by July its prospects for passage during the current session of Congress grew dim. Opponents of the measure claimed that it was only "bailing the Rainier National Park Company out of a losing business," and that the RNPC had used poor judgment in the first place when it built the inn at such a high elevation on the mountain. There followed another round of posturing by Sceva and Krug. The RNPC accepted another one-year contract with the proviso that it did not have to provide service during the winter. Hastily, the park made alternative arrangements for a winter season centered at Tipsoo Lake instead of Paradise.[15]

Meanwhile, efforts continued on behalf of the park facilities legislation. Sceva obtained the support of Senator Warren G. Magnuson of Washington and the freshman congressman from Everett, Henry M. Jackson, as well as the new secretary of the interior, Oscar L. Chapman. After the House passed the bill in the summer of 1950, Drury expressed hope that Senate approval would follow quickly and "end the agony" during the current session.[16]

In its final version, a section of the bill was eliminated that would authorize the secretary to repair, reconstruct, and build new facilities. The bill's purpose was narrowed to purchasing the RNPC's buildings. President Truman signed the measure into law on September 21, 1950. A year and a half later the government bought the RNPC's buildings for $300,000 (equal to roughly one-third of the company's total investment of $884,000 exclusive of automotive equipment). The RNPC would continue in existence for another eighteen years, eventually conveying all assets and liabilities to Fred Harvey, Inc., in October 1968.[17]

Both the House and Senate committee reports emphasized that government *ownership* of the facilities at Rainier would not prohibit private *operation* of the same. Belying the act's importance for national park policy, the House report went further, insisting that the circumstances at Rainier were peculiar and that the bill was "not intended to set a precedent or pattern for Government acquisition of concessions in any other national park or monument." But this pronouncement was followed by the contradictory statement that the bill was "in accord with the 1948 report of the Concessions' Advisory Group to the Secretary of the Interior."[18] The 1948 report clearly advocated a policy of government acquisition of concession facilities throughout the national park system. The pattern at Rainier would soon be repeated in other national parks. In reality, the act constituted an important turning point in the relations between private capital and the park service.[19]

Skiers presented NPS officials with another quandary. Park officials wanted to make Mount Rainier's winter scenery available to the public. Not all of Rainier's winter visitors came for the ski slopes; a significant minority came to enjoy other forms of winter recreation, such as snowshoeing, cross-country skiing, or a quiet stay at the National Park Inn during the off-season. Nor were the thrill-seeking downhill skiers oblivious to the scenery. Nonetheless, most NPS officials agreed that downhill skiing stretched the limits of appropriate recreational use of the national parks, and they were uncomfortable with the increasingly crowded conditions on and around the ski slopes. These judgments about downhill skiing were difficult to explain. They gave rise to a series of arcane statements of winter use policy by NPS Director Cammerer in office orders of April 7, 1936, and January 27, 1940, and by Director Drury in office orders of August 13, 1945, and March 21, 1946.[20]

Drury's first statement of policy, issued one day before V-J Day and the end of hostilities in World War II, paralleled Cammerer's statement in its affirmation of the park service's long-standing commitment to encourage winter use of the parks. But it adopted a somewhat more conservative stand toward ski installations such as runs, tows, jumps, and warming facilities. Tows and jumps, for example, had to be completely removable at the end of the winter season, and warming facilities would be strictly oriented to day use. The park service would not allow highly competitive events or "winter carnivals" aimed at drawing large crowds of spectators, as these would tend to detract from the experience for families and other groups who sought recreation. Drury wanted to appeal to the amateur ski enthusiast who was drawn as much by the park environment as by the sport itself. Regional Director Tomlinson made the same distinction when he advised Superintendent Preston not to equate ski clubs with mountaineer clubs. "We know that the majority of ski organizations are interested only in skiing as a sport," he wrote, "as distinguished from the general enjoyment of the park values where skiing is incidental to the broader use of such park values."[21] The NPS wanted to develop winter use sites for the casual skier while encouraging competitive and resort skiers to go elsewhere.

If the state of Washington had had more ski areas in 1945, local skiers might have found the policy acceptable. Unfortunately, Paradise remained the foremost ski area in the region in the minds of most Pacific Northwest skiers. Newer ski areas at Snoqualmie Pass, Stevens Pass, and Mount Baker still lacked basic facilities, and that was the full extent of ski development for an estimated 150,000 skiers in the state.[22]

Washington skiers began to develop their own agenda even before the end of World War II. As early as the spring of 1944, the Federation of Western Outdoor Clubs (FWOC) an offshoot of the National Ski Association, began goading the park service and the forest service to produce postwar recreation planning studies for each state. The FWOC wanted national parks to play an important role in the development of ski areas. In the first months following the end of World War II, the FWOC, the Pacific Northwest Ski Association, various local ski clubs, and even The Mountaineers criticized the new winter use policy announced by Drury. These groups wanted overnight accommodations, and they thought the prohibition against "highly competitive" events too restrictive.[23]

When Drury issued a revised statement of N P S winter use policy on March 21, 1946, he sought to placate skiers while quietly reducing their influence. The statement began by explicitly retracting Drury's earlier opposition to holding competitive events in national parks. Rather, the statement could now be read as embracing the downhill ski fraternity. "It is recognized that important recreational benefits are available during the winter months in areas of the National Park System having a heavy fall of snow and where the climate is otherwise not too severe," Drury wrote. "It is further recognized that, if made available under proper controls, the use of our areas for healthful out-of-door recreation during the winter months is a very desirable way to make the scenic and other natural values of the System available for the benefit and enjoyment of the people." Another modification of his earlier statement was subtle but significant: Drury deleted a provision that would allow ski clubs to operate their own ski tows under special permit, reserving this privilege instead for the park concession.[24]

Pacific Northwest skiers discovered their political influence during the winter of 1945–46. In October 1945, Superintendent Preston announced that the Paradise area would be closed through another winter, as the N P S was still operating on a wartime budget. Several community, high school, and university ski clubs were alerted to the prospect of yet another winter without access to the state's leading ski area. The sports editor of the *Seattle Post-Intelligencer*, Royal Brougham, who had been instrumental in promoting the Silver Skis event in Paradise in the 1930s, lobbied Senator Warren Magnuson to secure road maintenance funds for the park. Magnuson succeeded in getting a special supplemental appropriation of $11,500 for snow removal (Mount Rainier was the only park so favored), but it did not clear Congress until January. In the meantime, Governor Mon C. Wallgren pledged the assistance of his State Department of Highways. This calculated move received good press coverage while the governor's later retraction of the offer, on the advice of his attorney general, went unnoticed. Park service maintenance crews went to work on the road in midwinter and had it open on March 3, in time for the spring ski season.[25] Magnuson and Wallgren, both seasoned Washington politicians, had found that intervening in the administration of Mount Rainier National Park earned them the public's gratitude. Ski clubs, for their part, learned that their special interest in Rainier carried weight with politicians.

Chambers of commerce were quick to find common ground with the ski clubs. Both groups wanted a larger commitment to visitor accommodations at Paradise. Preston noted in his annual report for 1947, "Ever since the end of the war there has been a concerted effort, led by ski clubs, chambers of commerce, sporting good stores and other organizations and individuals, to have accommodations at Paradise available through the winter season."[26] As previously noted, leaders in the tourist industry reestablished the Rainier National Park Advisory Board in 1948. The purpose of the new advisory board was to bring together representatives of the Pacific Northwest Trade Association, the State Hotel Association, the State Restaurant Association, the Washington Automobile Club, and other organizations interested in the development of Rainier. Although the advisory board's resurrection was short-lived, NPS officials viewed it warily as one more sign of a growing lobby for commercial exploitation of Mount Rainier National Park.[27]

The prodevelopment lobby succeeded in its effort to influence park planning. Secretary of the Interior Julius A. Krug met with Governor Wallgren and various Seattle and Tacoma business leaders to discuss postwar use and development of the park. The business community wanted all-year overnight accommodations at Paradise. They envisioned a new, government-built hotel together with a chairlift, similar to the Timberline Lodge and ski area on Mount Hood. Krug pledged his support for an all-year development of some kind at Paradise, setting in motion new development plans by the NPS.[28]

Chief Landscape Architect Thomas C. Vint outlined what would be required. He offered two working assumptions: first, that the aged structures at Paradise would be replaced by a single new structure designed to endure heavy snow loads, and second, that the new building would be built by the federal government. Specifically, Vint proposed construction of a $2 million structure designed for efficient, practical hotel accommodations as well as day use. It would have approximately a hundred guest rooms, six large dormitory rooms, accommodations for sixty to eighty employees, dining room, cafeteria, kitchen, lobby, lounge, gift shop, store, and other public facilities all under a single roof.[29]

As the NPS utilized Vint's working plan to negotiate a new concession contract with the RNPC, it became evident that the commitment to all-year facilities at Paradise had placed the NPS in an awkward position. Not only were such facilities unfeasible without government subsidy, but the NPS would be unable to ensure the safety of visitors along avalanche-prone sections of the road. So concerned were the park service's engineers that they began to look again at the alternative of a tramway. Vint bluntly advised the director in May 1948 that Secretary Krug's commitment to keeping the road open year-round was "almost in the 'stunt' class." Vint insisted that the whole premise of all-year operations was a grievous mistake. "I cannot recommend the tramway—nor can I recommend the road as a means of access during the winter season for reasons of public safety," he informed Drury.[30]

Faced with such sharp dissension, Drury did what any seasoned administrator would do: he formed a committee. Chaired by park landscape architect Harold G. Fowler, the winter use committee was tasked to investigate alternative sites for downhill skiing. It looked at Tipsoo Lake and the Tatoosh Range within the park, and White Pass and Corral Pass outside the park. It compared these sites and Paradise with the four other existing Washington ski areas located at Stevens Pass, Snoqualmie Pass, Ski Acres (a mile east of Snoqualmie Pass), and Mount Baker. The committee acknowledged the need for at least one major ski area in the state, and it confirmed that Paradise was the best location of any within the park. To develop Paradise as a major ski area, the committee wrote, it would be necessary to build a new approach road to avoid the avalanche danger in Paradise Valley. Other requirements of a major ski area would include overnight lodging and meal service, underground parking for 100 cars, outdoor parking for 1,000 cars, and a permanent chairlift.[31]

The winter use committee did not endorse this type of development. It merely stated what would be needed if the NPS were required by lawmakers or the secretary of the interior to develop Paradise as a winter sports area. Indeed, in contrast to Vint's principled protests, the committee's analysis was starkly matter-of-fact. Perhaps this cold presentation was calculated to stir the blood of administrators higher up in the organization. Perhaps, on the other hand, the committee could be faulted for forfeiting this vital opportunity to criticize the whole concept of downhill ski developments in the national park.

If Drury thought the public's demand for overnight winter accommodations might simply go away, he was mistaken. Soon the Seattle and Tacoma newspapers reported a speech by Washington's Congressman Thor Tollefson, delivered on the floor of the U.S. House of Representatives, deploring the lack of ski facilities at Mount Rainier National Park and blistering the NPS for allowing the park to languish under a "lack of policy."[32] He implied that it was Congress's job to make that policy. Nothing illustrated so well the new politics of Mount Rainier National Park administration. In 1946, Washington politicians had extracted a special congressional appropriation for snow removal at Rainier; in 1950, they had obtained a law providing for the federal government to purchase the RNPC's aging hotel buildings. Now they focused on getting a congressional appropriation to build a new overnight lodge and chairlift at Paradise. As long as public opinion favored such development, they seemed deaf to the park service's warnings that it was anathema to the national park idea.

Local merchants led the resurgence of public interest in Rainier development during 1953 and 1954. In the fall of 1953, a group known as Greater Tacoma began calling meetings on the subject of reopening Paradise for winter use. The meetings brought together business leaders, resort owners, ski clubs, and others who wished to lobby Washington's senators and congressmen. Another group called Roads to Paradise Resort Association organized for the same purpose. Meanwhile, in the town of Eatonville, a group of citizens launched what they called "Operation Bootstrap," an effort to assemble data on the cost of snow removal between Longmire and Paradise, which they thought would strengthen their case for getting the road reopened for winter use.[33]

Governor Arthur Langlie addressed the subject of Rainier development in a letter to Secretary of the Interior Douglas McKay on October 16, 1953. Langlie observed that the park was the state's outstanding tourist attraction and alleged that park use was severely restricted by NPS policies. If the park were adapted for use by skiers, Langlie argued, it would be usable for more than three months out of the year and would once again attract capital investment. Paradise had greater potential for ski development than Sun Valley, but skiers would not use the area unless it had some kind of permanent, uphill transportation. Langlie favored a chairlift or tramway to 10,000 feet elevation for both winter and summer use.[34]

Secretary McKay's reply to the governor, drafted by the NPS, acknowledged that Paradise was the most promising area in the park for winter use, but did not indicate what type of uphill transportation was favored. NPS Director Conrad L. Wirth proposed to save that information for a follow-up letter, when it would be stated that ski lift facilities would be limited to demountable T-bar tows. Sending a copy to Regional Director Lawrence C. Merriam, Wirth confided: "The important point at this stage is that we are approaching a commitment, all things being considered, for winter sports development in Paradise Valley. I definitely want to avoid the impact of chairlifts and aerial tramways and the related pressures that would come for summer operation of them."[35] Wirth was already staking out what he hoped to be a defensible middle ground.

But as correspondence between the governor and the secretary continued through the winter of 1953–54, their positions became increasingly polarized. In December, Langlie formed a Mount Rainier National Park Development Study Committee. The committee was composed of some of the most rabidly prodevelopment men in the state: Elmun R. Fetterolf, former chairman of the Rainier National Park Advisory Board; Joseph C. Gregory, an official of the Automobile Club of Washington and editor of *Washington Motorist;* Roger A. Freeman, advisor to the governor and a chief exponent of the proposed aerial tramway.[36] That same month, Wirth received a briefing on the park service's Mount Rainier winter use studies from Regional Director Merriam. Merriam's report underscored the physical difficulties of developing Paradise for winter use. Even if a new winter access road were built and the cost of a new hotel were surmounted, Merriam cautioned, there would still remain the problem of Paradise's stormy weather, which would probably prevent Paradise from ever becoming an economically successful major ski area.[37]

In February 1954, Joseph C. Gregory announced in the *Washington Motorist* that the Automobile Club of Washington was launching a campaign for full development of Mount Rainier National Park. The club claimed to have polled its 43,000 members and found a mandate to "change the thinking of the N P S." According to the club's poll, an overwhelming majority of members favored construction of a complete, all-year resort at Paradise. After devoting the whole February issue of the *Washington Motorist* to Rainier, Gregory maintained a drumbeat of criticism of the N P S in subsequent issues. In his most strident articles, Gregory demanded a modern hotel at Paradise with swimming pool, tennis courts, and spacious green lawns.[38]

The National Parks Association (N P A) responded by defending the status quo and blistering the Automobile Club in two editorials in the spring and summer issues of *National Parks Magazine*. "Mount Rainier National Park Needs Your Help At Once," wrote the N P A's executive secretary, Fred M. Packard, in a newsletter to all N P A members. The Automobile Club of Washington was agitating for a "permanent steel chairlift" on the flank of Mount Rainier. Packard urged members to write immediately to Secretary McKay and insist that chairlifts were out of place in a national park.[39]

Wirth held a series of public meetings in Seattle and Portland in August 1954. He met privately with the governor's committee, received its report, and conferred with the Automobile Club's board of trustees. He exchanged ideas with The Mountaineers, the Mazamas, the ski clubs, the Federation of Western Outdoor Clubs, and local chambers of commerce. His visit to the Pacific Northwest was not only a fact-finding mission but also an effort to rally public opinion against the chairlift scheme. The N P S did not want "a Coney Island at Mount Rainier," Wirth told his audiences.[40] A little more than a month after returning to Washington, D.C., Wirth submitted a twenty-nine-page report on the proposed development to Secretary McKay.

There can be no question that Wirth's report was the product of his own careful thought on the subject. While the middle fourteen pages of the report came directly from Regional Director Merriam, Wirth front-loaded the report with so much of his own material that the report became his own statement. Moreover, he attached such a strongly worded letter that McKay could not mistake its import. The issues were so close to the heart of the national park idea, Wirth explained, that the idea itself was on the line. "Whatever the money considerations may be, I am sure—just as sure as I can be of anything in this world—that [the national park idea] must endure as one of the basic American philosophies," Wirth wrote. "The national park concept is one of the important natural assets. If we destroy that concept we alter a point of view that I believe is basic to our American philosophy and way of life."[41] Back him up, Wirth was telling his boss, or the secretary would have to appoint a new park service director.

Secretary McKay delayed his decision nearly three months, but finally supported Wirth. In a letter to Governor Langlie, the secretary carefully laid stress on the developments that were programmed or presently under way. For the present, Paradise was again open for winter use, with the concessioner operating rope tows and a food service at the Paradise Lodge. The NPS would build a new approach road to reduce the avalanche hazard, and it would recondition Paradise Inn and develop a new campground below Paradise Lodge to accommodate more summer use. McKay concluded with the decisive statement that the department would give no further consideration to a chairlift or tramway in Mount Rainier National Park.[42]

Wirth had won the crucial battle. All experts agreed that without a chairlift, Paradise could not become a major ski resort. In contrast to so many other public use issues, the park service had time on its side in this case. With the growth of other ski areas in the region, pressure for this type of use at Rainier would ease. Wirth's endorsement of a demountable type of ski lift merely reiterated what his two predecessors, Cammerer and Drury, had each maintained: if the concessioner wanted to put forth the effort and expense to dismantle the contraption at the end of each ski season, the NPS would authorize its installation. The only new items in the development plan were the alternate approach road and the additional campground. From the standpoint of scenic preservation, the new road was certainly preferable to the construction of snowsheds or tunnels along the existing road.

Nevertheless, some conservationists interpreted the secretary's announcement as a setback for national park principles. It seemed to them that the secretary had approved the development of a ski resort at Rainier. The proposed T-bar appeared to be a capitulation to the ski clubs and a grave compromise of national park standards. One local conservationist, Polly Dyer of The Mountaineers, suggested to Superintendent Preston Macy that the T-bar at Paradise, like the notorious Echo Park Dam in Dinosaur National Monument, belied a fatal lack of commitment to wilderness preservation by the government.[43]

The National Parks Association was torn by the secretary's announcement. Some NPA officers thought the director had acted courageously. But Devereux Butcher, editor of *National Parks Magazine*, thought that Wirth had given up too much. He proposed to rebuke him publicly in a signed editorial. The NPA's president, Sigurd F. Olson, and its vice president, Charles G. Woodbury, both tried to persuade Butcher not to print the editorial, arguing that it would cause a breach between the NPA and the NPS. Butcher printed his editorial anyway in the January-March issue of the magazine. Others in the NPA wrote letters of support to the park service director. The NPA's executive secretary, Fred M. Packard, worried that Secretary McKay would decide that he had gained nothing for his cooperation with the park service, sack the director, and reverse his decision on the chairlift.[44]

Wirth did not lose his job, but the souring of relations between the NPS and conservation groups carried a price. The chairlift controversy set the stage for a subsequent battle over Wirth's Mission 66 plan to move overnight accommodations from Paradise to a lower elevation. In that battle, regrettably, conservation groups like the NPA and The Mountaineers gave the park service precious little support. Conservationists failed to understand the range of administrative concerns surrounding these issues, and reacted myopically to such developments as the T-bar and the new road to Paradise as if they were signs of a new wave of park development.[45] In this instance, their aloofness from the park service hurt their own cause.

By the mid-1950s, it had become abundantly clear that the controversies surrounding Mount Rainier National Park administration reflected, to a large extent, the cumulative effect of some fifteen years of scrimping by the park service. The budget austerity imposed on the national parks during World War II was never fully rescinded after 1945 as Congress focused on paying down the war debt while maintaining a high level of defense spending. It took several years—indeed, another war—for the American public to realize the effect of defense mobilization on the national parks. With the Korean War barely concluded, the president of The Mountaineers wrote to the director of the Bureau of the Budget in December 1953:

> Our investigations of the matter show that the Parks are being placed on a stand-by basis in this time of national emergency. We feel that this is a false economy which will be more burdonsome in the years to come. Besides, the attendance in these parks, even though we have the emergency, have been increasing at an alarming rate. Over 100% in the last fourteen years.[46]

Other conservationists made similar points in the national media, helping to create broad public awareness of the state of the parks. For example, Bernard DeVoto's scathing article in *Harper's Monthly*, "Let's Close Our National Parks," described the decaying infrastructure and demoralizing working conditions in the national parks, and an article in *Reader's Digest* by Charles Stevenson, titled "The Shocking Truth About Our National Parks," warned prospective visitors of the unsanitary, even slum-like, conditions that were typical of the hotels and campgrounds.

Director Conrad L. Wirth conceived of an ambitious, well-publicized, spending program to rehabilitate the national parks. Wirth's idea was to submit a comprehensive, ten-year plan for the renovation of the national park system, thereby obviating the need to go to Congress and the Bureau of the Budget for development funds in two- and three-year driblets. The program would begin in 1956 and end in 1966, coinciding with the fiftieth anniversary of the founding of the park service. He called it "Mission 66." Wirth persuaded President Dwight Eisenhower and the key committees in Congress to support Mission 66 because it would rectify nearly fifteen years of neglect resulting from budget cutbacks during World War II and the Korean War. It would restore the parks to a condition that would satisfy the growing millions of Americans who used them each year.[47]

Mount Rainier National Park featured prominently in the early planning effort. In February 1955, Wirth created a seven-member Mission 66 committee and a seven-member steering committee composed of the supervisors of the people on the main committee. Former Mount Rainier park naturalist Howard Stagner sat on the Mission 66 committee, and Thomas C. Vint, the principal author of Rainier's original 1928 master plan, sat on the steering committee. Wirth wanted the report on Mission 66 drafted and ready to submit to President Eisenhower and Congress within a year. In the course of that year, the Mission 66 committee devoted more study to Mount Rainier than to any other national park.[48] The Mission 66 development plan for Rainier was the first one out of the gate after Eisenhower approved the program.

Ironically, when Wirth unveiled his plan for Rainier on March 15, 1956, the park was plunged into controversy again. The twin objectives of Mission 66 were to upgrade and expand facilities for the rising tide of "day-use visitors" going to the parks, and to revamp visitor circulation to alleviate crowding. At Rainier these objectives translated into one overall solution: move all overnight guest and administrative facilities to lower elevations, if not altogether out of the park. Following the recent controversies over the chairlift and government acquisition of the RNPC buildings, the plan appeared to be counter to everything that business interests and state politicians had advocated during the past decade. Ignoring the fact that Mission 66 promised to lavish $10 million on new development in the park, business leaders joined state politicians in denouncing the plan. Elsewhere in the nation Mission 66 was well received by the public; in Washington State it met with opposition and rancor.[49]

Wirth expected that the plan would be controversial. Paul Sceva, the irascible president of the RNPC, reacted so strongly to the plan that Wirth asked him not to share the information with anyone until the plan was made public. Sceva denounced Wirth's request as a "gag order" and fumed about it six months later to a committee of Congress. Sceva also criticized the park service for neglecting to seek the RNPC's input sooner in view of the company's forty years of experience as the park concession.[50] Wirth retorted that Sceva had acted irresponsibly by leaking confidential information to selected prodevelopment groups. Moreover, the park service had been on record since 1945 regarding its desire to move overnight accommodations to lower elevations, and the RNPC had explained its position on that concept exhaustively in the course of its contract negotiations.

The plan put forward two new development sites at lower elevations, one on the south side and one on the east side. On the south side, the plan proposed a new development on Skate Creek, just outside the boundary of the park south of the Nisqually River. The site would be accessed by a new state road between Ashford and Packwood (Skate Creek Road) and a short connecting road to Longmire. On the east side, the favored development site was located a short distance off the Mather Memorial Parkway at Crystal Creek, just inside the northeast corner of the park. With some clearing of trees it would afford a fine view of the mountain, and it was convenient to Sunrise, Tipsoo Lake, and the proposed Corral Pass ski area northeast of the park.[51]

NPS planners believed that the milder climate at these lower elevations would induce private capital to invest in new overnight accommodations. Ironically, they compared their vision for Rainier to the situation in Great Smoky Mountains National Park. There, virtually all visitor services were furnished by the community of Gatlinburg, Tennessee—a place that would become so overrun by the tourist industry in the 1960s and 1970s that it would stand as the most notorious example of a national park gateway town anywhere in the United States.

The plan struck developers as odd and inconsistent. Contrary to the secretary of the interior's concession policy of 1950 calling for government ownership of visitor facilities, the NPS now seemed to be going back to Mather's idea of seeking private investment. The Mission 66 plan declared: "It is a long-standing National Park policy—a policy in which Congress has repeatedly manifested its concurrence—that the construction and operation of concessions are proper functions of private enterprise."[52] This was disingenuous in view of the recent act of Congress authorizing the government to purchase the RNPC's buildings.

Neither the Skate Creek site nor the Crystal Creek site was ever developed. Washington State business leaders and politicians rejected the very concept of moving overnight accommodations to lower elevations in or outside the park. This crucial part of the Mission 66 plan for Mount Rainier was eliminated, and the park service was forced to go back to the drawing board and explain how it would redevelop the Paradise area for overnight use.

Washington State's two senators, Warren Magnuson and Henry M. Jackson, played key roles in amending the Mission 66 plan for Mount Rainier. In March 1956, they wrote a joint letter to Senator James Murray, chairman of the Committee on Interior and Insular Affairs, questioning the wisdom of the development plan and requesting a hearing. In two hearings, the first held on Capitol Hill and the second in Tacoma, Magnuson and Jackson grilled Wirth on the purpose of moving overnight accommodations to lower elevations. At the second hearing, David Brower of the Sierra Club defended the park service's work, explaining that the number of visitors drawn to Paradise and Sunrise was known to exceed the "carrying capacity" of these fragile areas. This yet unfamiliar concept sailed over the senators' heads. At the conclusion of the hearings, they directed the park service to make a further study of suitable overnight accommodations at Paradise, regardless of whether they were built with private or public funds.[53]

The NPS duly submitted its report in March 1957. The building design for a new Paradise hotel was so odd and incongruous as to be impossible to consider seriously. Taking into account snow loads, NPS architects proposed a ten-story building that would house all government and hotel operations at Paradise. The first three floors would be used for parking, the fourth floor would be on a level with the average depth of snow in winter and would contain the lobby and dining room. The six floors above this would contain 270 guest rooms, 60 employee dorm rooms, and an employee dining room. The estimated cost for the building was $5 million. Upon receiving this report, Senator Jackson wrote to Wirth, "I am pleased that the report is labeled 'preliminary,' because, frankly, it strikes me that some more feasible plan could be devised than for a 10-story hotel that will lose more than $318,000 a year."[54]

Senator Magnuson, working with House conferees on the House appropriations bill, inserted an item in the Senate report directing the park service "to complete its studies and make recommendations as to how private enterprise might be encouraged to do the job." Acting on this directive, Senator Jackson invited Laurance S. Rockefeller of Jackson Hole Preserve, Inc., to conduct a feasibility study on the park service's behalf.[55] Three months later, on October 15, 1957, Wirth agreed to fund such a study by Jackson Hole Preserve, Inc.

Representatives of Jackson Hole Preserve, Inc., made several visits to the park in different seasons, interviewed numerous businessmen, civic leaders, and conservationists in the Pacific Northwest, and issued a report some fifteen months later in January 1959. The authors of the report confirmed Wirth's view that given the harsh climatic conditions, no overnight facilities could be operated at Paradise on a profitable basis taking into account depreciation of the buildings. If, however, the park service was to construct new overnight facilities at Rainier, the authors found that Paradise was the best location. Further, they believed that day-use services and overnight lodging should be coordinated in one facility and operated by a single concession.[56]

As might be expected from such an equivocal finding, the report by Jackson Hole Preserve, Inc., was interpreted in opposing ways. To Acting Secretary of the Interior Roger Ernst, the report supported the park service's contention that a lodge at high elevation at Rainier was not economically feasible. Jackson Hole Preserve, Inc., had provided no compelling reasons for building a lodge at government expense, Ernst stated, and absent any legislation by Congress, the NPS had no intention of undertaking such a project.[57]

Washington's congressional delegation, meanwhile, argued that Jackson Hole Preserve, Inc., had endorsed the idea of a government-subsidized hotel development. Senators Magnuson and Jackson and Congressman Tollefson introduced joint resolutions to authorize the construction of a hotel at Rainier. After these measures failed in 1960, they reintroduced them the following year. Tollefson claimed that 85 percent of Washington residents and nearly every newspaper in the state favored overnight accommodations at Paradise. According to Tollefson, Jackson Hole Preserve, Inc., endorsed this view.[58]

When Secretary of the Interior Stewart L. Udall requested a report by the NPS director on the House and Senate joint resolutions, Wirth stood firm. He reiterated what he had said (and what David Brower had described more pointedly) in the congressional hearings, that the development of overnight accommodations at Paradise would jeopardize park values by bringing too many people into a fragile area. "It is not simply a matter of finding space for a hotel, but of finding adequate space needed for a facility which in itself becomes a magnet in holding people in the area beyond the time devoted to scenic enjoyment and recreational pursuits." Wirth also revealed the price tag, which his architects now estimated would run to $12 million.[59]

Secretary of the Interior Udall reported unfavorably on the joint resolutions, but he was too politically astute to leave the matter there. He initiated a joint study with the Department of Agriculture to examine the feasibility of developing a ski area and "first-class mountain inn" on national forest land just outside the northeast corner of the park. Udall's information director announced the study at a closed meeting in Seattle attended by Magnuson, Jackson, and a dozen public officials and businessmen from Seattle, Tacoma, and Olympia. Business representatives insisted the site was flawed. Located deep in the forest, hotel guests would find nothing to do there. They said the study was a trial balloon to see if the public would let go of the Paradise site. A reporter for the *Tacoma News Tribune* interpreted the announcement another way. "It appears it is Crystal Creek or nothing," the reporter wrote, "all locked up, signed, sealed and delivered."[60]

Washington State politicians had no intention of letting go of the matter. In November 1961, Governor Albert D. Rosellini appointed a six-member citizens' advisory group to study the problem of overnight accommodations at Rainier. In January, Rosellini suggested that the NPS reconsider the development of a chairlift at Paradise. Even more ominously, he appointed Clayton D. Anderson to the directorship of Washington's Department of Parks and Recreation. Anderson, a former horse wrangler at Paradise, was already on record against the Mission 66 plan to move campgrounds at Paradise and Sunrise to lower elevations. Out of the fractious debate emerged a political deal: the Department of the Interior and the Washington Department of Commerce and Economic Development would each contribute $10,000 toward yet another study of Rainier development sites.[61]

The governor and the Department of the Interior took more than a year to agree on a consultant for the study. Finally the contract was awarded to Harris, Kerr, Forster & Company, and two members of the firm, Henry Maschal and Richard Raymond, visited the park in May and June 1963. They considered each site from the standpoint of summer and winter use, local natural features, climate, and historical development. Their findings were emphatic. "We do not recommend the construction of any hotel type accommodations within Mount Rainier National Park," the report stated.[62]

Washington State officials were dismayed by the conclusion. At the closed-door briefing on the report held at the Hilton Inn in Tacoma on August 7, 1963, one state official wanted to know why Harris, Kerr, Forster & Company offered a complete reversal of the report by Jackson Hole Preserve, Inc. Maschal replied that the earlier study had looked at the feasibility of overnight accommodations based on the assumption that the government would provide $9 million. They had made no such assumption. Moreover, the park service's insistence that day use was the wave of the future had finally made an impression. "The very limited areas available for development are and will in the future be increasingly needed for day use facilities and accommodations and for overnight camping," the report stated.[63]

Conservation groups applauded the study's findings. The Mountaineers averred that the purposes of the national park were best served if its significant features were preserved for recreational, educational, and inspirational enjoyment. Overnight accommodations, the club magazine stated, should be moved to less fragile areas of the park. The National Parks Association now favored elimination of overnight accommodations at Paradise at the end of the Paradise Inn's useful life.[64]

Most important, Senator Jackson now decided that Paradise should be developed for day use only. He requested his own tour of the park in June 1963, about the same time that Maschal and Raymond were conducting their study. Afterward, Superintendent John Rutter and the RNPC's Paul Sceva each described in detail the senator's day in the park, his musings and thoughts as far as they could determine. Their two accounts differed widely; the wily politician managed to convince Rutter that he was opposed to overnight accommodations at Paradise at the same time that he gave Sceva assurances that a day-use visitor center would not preclude such development. In any case, Jackson obtained Magnuson's help in securing a $465,900 down payment on the day-use facility for the 1964 fiscal year. The visitor center included restaurant, museum, information center, ski rental shop, and warming hut. Construction of the building began in 1964 and was completed in 1966. As expected, its eventual cost far exceeded the original allocation. Indeed, the NPS had to abandon its plans for a new visitor center at Sunrise. At $2 million, it was the most expensive building in the national park system.[65]

Public reaction to the new facility was decidedly mixed. The building's modern design pleased some and disappointed others. Designed by the two architectural firms of Wimberly, Whisenand, Allison and Tong of Honolulu and McGuire and Muri of Tacoma, the building's round layout and conical roof were supposed to relate the structure to its mountain setting. Other visual design features included the "swooping, bough-like shape of the beams, the branching 'tree' columns, the 'switchback trail' ramps, and the sloped 'cliffs' of the stone base."[66] To many people's way of thinking, however, the building did not harmonize with the landscape in the least. People complained that it looked like a satellite, pagoda, or flying saucer. Its weird, extraterrestrial effect was compounded when Paradise was shrouded in fog, as was often the case. When snow still blanketed the ground, people joked that it looked like the Seattle Space Needle—up to its neck in snow. A legend grew that the Honolulu-based architectural firm had designed the building for a site in the Hawaiian Islands, only to dump it on Rainier instead. This was not true, however.[67]

Construction of the visitor center ended twenty years of vociferous debate about how the park should be redeveloped. These were pivotal years in the park's first century. The NPS succeeded in blocking construction of a chairlift and high-rise hotel—developments that would have tragically marred the scene and set a dangerous precedent for other national parks. The NPS was thwarted, however, in its effort to relieve pressure on Paradise. Local interests prevented it. The famous subalpine meadows, popular with Seattle and Tacoma residents since the 1890s, would continue to be at the hub of visitor activity into the 1990s.

Mission 66 planners favored innovation and new construction, not rehabilitation. Ironically—and not altogether surprisingly—the culmination of Mission 66 in Mount Rainier National Park coincided with a growing movement nationwide to preserve historic buildings rather than tear them down to make room for new development. It was a sign of the times that the most newsworthy event during construction of the Paradise Visitor Center was neither the groundbreaking nor the grand opening, but rather the burning of Paradise Lodge on June 3, 1965, to provide space for more parking. Local residents reacted as though the park service had destroyed a piece of their heritage. Hastily, park officials sought to reassure the public that Paradise Inn would remain standing; the obliterated building was only the more modest and recent of the two hotels at Paradise.[68]

Paradise Inn might have gone the way of Paradise Lodge, but changing public perceptions about historic buildings prevented it. Responding to the upsweep of interest in protecting the nation's physical heritage, Congress passed the National Historic Preservation Act of 1966. Among other provisions, the act established a National Register of Historic Places and charged all federal agencies with taking inventory of government-owned properties that were potentially eligible for listing on the register.

Once again, the aging structures at Paradise placed Rainier at the center of a vigorous debate, albeit an internal debate out of the public eye. Soon after the park service had initiated an inventory of the park's historic resources, certain questions arose. Should buildings erected after the creation of the national park be nominated to the National Register of Historic Places? Should the park service take a hand in commemorating its own handiwork? Since the park service had been designated by Congress to administer the National Register of Historic Places, should it be chary of a conflict of interest in nominating its own properties? Should the park service's mission to preserve natural conditions in the park override consideration of historic values?

The preliminary inventory suggested that a number of old buildings provided evidence of past government stewardship of the park and warranted further study "to determine their significance." By 1973, fourteen structures had been identified as potentially eligible for listing on the National Register of Historic Places, but only one building—the Longmire cabin that predated the park—was classified as a historic structure.[69] This classification belied the park service's bias against treating its own administrative presence in the national park as an artifact of American history. Most park officials—especially those who had risen through the ranger ranks or whose educational background lay in the natural sciences—preferred to think of the park as a completely natural landscape.[70]

Two cultural resource surveys of Rainier in the mid-1970s brought this disagreement to a head. The first inventory, by Robert L. Carper of the agency's own Denver Service Center (DSC), recommended a total of ninety-two structures for historic classification. After consultation with the superintendent, the regional office pared the list down to twenty-one.[71] The second inventory, by DSC historian James Mote, recommended that none of these buildings should be nominated to the National Register of Historic Places; only the Longmire cabin met the national register criteria for listing. When regional historian Vernon Tancil objected that Mote was taking too narrow a view of historic resources, Mote replied, "I resist what seems to be a trend within the Park Service to confuse Park Service physical growth with events of historical significance." To preserve an early ranger station or the first park inn, Mote said, would be "unwarranted self-memorialization."[72] The philosophical argument between Tancil and Mote soon involved the chief of the historic preservation division at the DSC, the chief of the cultural resources division in Washington, D.C., and Regional Director Russell E. Dickenson. With the historians unable to reach agreement, Dickenson ordered yet another historic resource study by a third DSC historian, Erwin N. Thompson.[73]

Thompson's study was intended to combine and supersede the studies by Carper and Mote. His report provided an inventory of historic resources and a narrative history. Agreeing with Tancil, he devoted a substantial portion of the study to government and concessioner buildings and park administrative history. By the time he completed the study in 1979, the Longmire cabin had been entered on the National Register and the Paradise Inn was in the process of being listed. Thompson recommended a total of eighty-seven other structures, including ranger stations, ranger residences, patrol cabins, service buildings, trail shelters, fire lookouts, bridges, and entrance arches.[74]

After Thompson completed his study, there was no longer any doubt that Mount Rainier National Park would be recognized and managed as a cultural area as well as a natural area. Resource managers still had to address complicated issues about the scope of historic preservation in the park, particularly where the protection of historic resources conflicted most visibly with the restoration of natural processes. And as the National Register of Historic Places evolved, more structures and then whole districts in Mount Rainier National Park were listed and afforded protection. At the end of the twentieth century, the entire network of roads and development areas in Mount Rainier National Park was classified as one whole cultural landscape—an outstanding example, historians said, of national park design.[75]

Historic preservation carried a price. Rehabilitation of the Paradise Inn (and other old structures) was a costly endeavor. Making the RNPC perform year-to-year upkeep, much less major rehabilitation, on a building that it no longer owned was not easy. The park service tried to weave various rehabilitation projects into the concession's five-year contract from 1953 to 1958 and its consecutive one-year contracts from 1959 to 1965, but the results were disappointing. In 1965, the NPS once more granted the RNPC a five-year contract, eliminating the requirement for rehabilitation and maintenance and instead charging an annual fee based on a percentage of gross revenue, which the NPS then used to perform rehabilitation and maintenance itself. All of this gave the park administration a large stake in seeing the Paradise Inn do a good business; otherwise its preservation would put an enormous strain on the park budget. Thus, the decision to recognize Paradise Inn's historical significance and preserve the building ended all discussion of moving overnight accommodations to lower elevations. The inn endured as a charming reminder of the park's early years, thereby undermining the most important objective of Mission 66 in Mount Rainier National Park.

Another aim of the Mission 66 plan for Mount Rainier was crowd dispersal, usually phrased more delicately as "distributing the visitor load." Road construction was central to the plan, with the main projects listed as completion of the Stevens Canyon Road, construction of a new winter access road to Paradise, and improvement of the Westside and Mowich Lake roads.

In the view of Mission 66 planners, new roads would disperse visitors—especially day-use visitors—more widely around the park. Most day-use visitors were mobile, dependent on their cars, and essentially roadbound. NPS planners thought that by modernizing the park infrastructure to suit the day-use visitor, they could keep traffic flowing, reduce the feeling of crowding, and thereby increase the park's recreational carrying capacity. To this end, the driving tour would be encouraged; the car, the road, and the wayside exhibit would frame the common visitor experience to a greater extent than ever before. The park service's March 1956 press release on Mission 66 for Mount Rainier said as much. "Numerous scenic overlooks, picnic areas and campgrounds provided in the 10-year program will encourage the dispersal of visitors over a wide area and reduce the damaging overcrowding at Paradise and other popular centers within the park."[76] A memo on Mission 66 dated August 31, 1956, expressed even greater enthusiasm about the potential for roads to disperse the public. "This entire road system will be treated in such a way that the visitor will enjoy numerous scenic, recreational, and interpretive experiences as he drives through the park."[77]

Local business interests eagerly anticipated the completion of the Stevens Canyon Road. The Rainier National Park Advisory Board's Elmun R. Fetterolf thought that "the completion of this highway will do much to hold visitors within the park area."[78] Construction had begun in 1931, with most of the right-of-way completed when work stopped in World War II. After an eight-year hiatus, construction resumed in 1950. Between 1950 and 1952, contractors built bridges at the Muddy Fork and Nickel Creek, viaducts below Stevens Creek, a tunnel near the Muddy Fork, and masonry retaining walls and parapets. By the summer of 1952, the road was passable to trucks and was used to a limited extent for administrative purposes.[79] Mission 66 provided the last burst of funds to bring the project to completion, twenty-five years after it was begun.

The biggest item in the park's road construction program, however, was the new winter road to Paradise. From Marmot Point near Narada Falls the new road ascended the mountain by switchbacks to the relatively level ground known as Barn Flat, which stretched to the south of Paradise Lodge. The road served a dual purpose: in summer, it formed a loop with the existing road through Paradise Valley, easing weekend traffic congestion; in winter, it provided a safer route to Paradise, and the old road was no longer plowed.

The Paradise area had always been plagued by a shortage of parking, and it was clear that the new road would not alleviate the situation by itself; additional parking space must be developed, too. Mission 66 aimed to double or triple the amount of parking. The main question was whether to put the additional parking space underground, on the surface, or in a multilevel enclosed structure. To build a large parking garage in a national park was a novel concept. The plans for underground or multilevel parking were eventually rejected, primarily due to cost and aesthetics.[80]

NPS planners were optimistic that new campgrounds and picnic areas, like new roads, would disperse visitors more widely through the park. Mission 66 for Mount Rainier included plans to develop 1,200 new camping and picnic sites, or nearly four times what the park already had. The goal was to be able to accommodate 3,500 additional visitors per day by 1966. Two key components of the plan were to separate day use and overnight use areas, and to concentrate as much of the latter at lower elevations as possible. These developments would "enable the Park to absorb two or three times its present travel, satisfy more fully the needs of all visitors, and do so without further encroachment upon or impairment of the primary scenic areas."[81]

In 1956, the park had eight campgrounds and nine picnic areas, some of them quite small and primitive. There were three campgrounds at high elevations (one at Paradise and two at Sunrise) and five at low elevations (Longmire, Ohanapecosh, White River, Ipsut Creek, and Tahoma Creek). During the ten-year construction program, the park service added loops to the campgrounds at Ohanapecosh and Longmire, and sites to Ipsut Creek and White River campgrounds. In 1960 and 1961, it built a large campground at Cougar Rock, above Longmire, with the expectation of closing the campgrounds at Paradise and Sunrise thereafter. The environmental cost of operating campgrounds at high elevations was perhaps most evident at Sunrise, where the alpine tundra vegetation was especially vulnerable to trampling and wind erosion. Due to the pressure of visitor numbers, however, the campgrounds at

Paradise and Sunrise persisted beyond the Mission 66 era. Indeed, before converting the Paradise campground to a picnic area, the park service built a new campground a short distance below it on the new road to Paradise. Superintendent John Rutter soon realized that this was a mistake; built in a depression on the inside of a wide horseshoe bend in the road, the campground stayed snowbound until late July and had poor drainage for the rest of the summer. In 1973, the park service began to remove facilities from the campground, and in the 1980s it took steps to restore the area to a natural state. At Sunrise, meanwhile, Superintendent Rutter closed the smaller of the two campgrounds around 1965 but kept the larger one open. The latter was converted to walk-in campsites (mainly for the benefit of Wonderland Trail users) in 1973.[82]

The Mission 66 program to rehabilitate the national parks coincided with wilderness advocates' nine-year legislative campaign to establish a national wilderness system, which culminated in the Wilderness Act of 1964. The two movements were not unrelated. The Mission 66 emphasis on infrastructure underscored wilderness advocates' warnings that the national parks were in danger of being diced up by roads. It gave heat to their argument that a national wilderness system ought to encompass the national parks as well as the national forests. Even so, the wilderness movement directed most of its attention to the national forests. It was far more concerned about protecting the nation's remaining wilderness (considered at that time to amount to about 2 percent of the nation's total land area) from threats such as logging and mining. Existing wilderness areas in national forests could be invaded at any time under the U.S. Forest Service's mandate to manage for multiple use. Wilderness areas in national parks, by contrast, already had considerable protection under the laws framing the national parks. Picking their battles wisely, the campaigners for a wilderness act generally lauded the park service's efforts to protect wilderness in national parks.[83]

Congress held numerous hearings on the wilderness bill in cities and towns across the nation, and the hearings registered broad public support for a national wilderness preservation system. The Senate Committee on Interior and Insular Affairs held a two-day hearing in Seattle in March 1959. Senators Magnuson and Jackson took turns chairing the proceeding, at which ninety-one different witnesses testified, all having patiently waited for their allotted five minutes. Some witnesses represented organizations, many others spoke as individuals. There was Ellen Brooker, a self-described "typical Seattleite" with a passion for mountains, "whether looking to them from our unmatched city viewpoints, or straight up their precipices from the bank of a clear stream in a grove of soft-scented virgin timber." There was Johnellis Jones, a Boeing engineer, who said he had given up a day's wages to attend and testify in defense of wilderness. There was Richard Bayne, a student at the University of Washington, who protested "the need to build a road to the top of every mountain." There was Yvonne Prater of Ellensburg, a farmer's wife, whose farm lay in the path of Interstate 90, then under construction. Even the remote wildernesses in the Cascades, she and her husband had learned, could not be taken for granted. "The Federal laws that protect our wilderness are filled with enough loopholes," she said, "so that every once in a while a valuable chunk goes off down the drain in the form of a few dollars to line somebody's pockets and a short-term local boom." In addition to the many witnesses, the committee received an additional 423 statements from people who could not attend, of which all but 10 voiced support for the legislation.[84]

In all of the testimony presented at the Seattle hearing on the wilderness bill, not one witness questioned the park service's decision to build the Stevens Canyon Road or the new road to Paradise in Mount Rainier National Park. A few witnesses worried that Washington's national parks were not invulnerable to logging interests, but they focused their remarks on the national forests. The testimony was overwhelmingly focused on logging threats to wilderness (or, from another point of view, the need to manage those same areas for multiple use). Despite ongoing controversy over the Mission 66 plan for Mount Rainier, the many citizens who testified in this hearing gave the park service a virtual free pass.

In the broader context of conservation battles then raging over clear-cut logging, strip mining, and proposed hydroelectric dams, advocates of wilderness protection wanted to treat the park service as an ally and the national parks as examples of sound federal land management. Nevertheless, they did not go along with the view, held by Conrad Wirth and many others in the park service, that the national parks should be exempt from the Wilderness Act. In the end, this was what mattered for Mount Rainier. When the Wilderness Act was enacted in 1964, it started the clock running for the secretary of the interior to recommend areas in each national park for inclusion in the National Wilderness Preservation System. With the law behind them, citizens then felt empowered to engage the park service forcefully in a public debate about wilderness management inside the national park.[85]

CHAPTER 7

The Search for Limits (1965–2000)

IF REVAMPING VISITOR CIRCULATION WAS THE KEY TO park planning and management in the Mission 66 era, zoning became the management tool of choice in the 1960s and 1970s. Zoning would help managers restrict various types of development, public use, and administrative activity to appropriate areas in the park. Zoning would provide a more intensive and ecologically sensitive framework for land management. The change in focus from visitor circulation to land classification reflected the park service's deepening commitment to good environmental stewardship. It signaled a greater attentiveness to natural resources, a shift in the scales of preservation and use. Zoning offered a way to recognize different needs and challenges associated with each user group, and to begin a search for ways to limit visitor numbers in each zone or management context within the park.

The move toward zoning began with wilderness preservation. In 1964, Congress enacted the Wilderness Act, which required all federal agencies, including the park service, to recommend areas for inclusion in the wilderness preservation system within ten years. The NPS duly completed a wilderness proposal for Mount Rainier in 1972. It designated most of the backcountry (minus a corridor between Paradise and Camp Muir) as wilderness. Although the plan did not finally win legislative enactment until 1988, park officials administered the area as de facto wilderness for the next sixteen years. They recognized wilderness to be a finite resource and a crucial national park value, and they dedicated themselves to protecting wilderness from creeping development and overuse.

Wilderness preservation began with the question: what is Wilderness? (Land managers prefer to spell designated wilderness with a capital "W," to underscore that it is a legal construction.) Preservationists generally agreed that wilderness is a state of mind, an entity so subjective as to resist definition. Yet define it they must or wilderness would not have the protection of law. The Wilderness Act of 1964 defined wilderness as "an area where the earth and its community of life are untrammeled by man, where man himself is a visitor who does not remain." The key word in the definition, "untrammeled," was itself open to various interpretations; it connoted freedom from crowds, freedom from regulation, and freedom from physical traces of modern civilization.[1]

Given the subjective nature of the resource, wilderness managers recognized that it was impossible to preserve wilderness without protecting the "wilderness experience." In fact, park managers already had some familiarity with this problem. In view of the park service's dual mandate to preserve natural conditions while providing for the public's enjoyment, park managers sometimes found it necessary to identify and protect the "national park experience." This varied with time and place. During the winter seasons at Paradise in the 1930s, for example, park managers tried to prevent the development of a carnival-like atmosphere on the ski slopes precisely because they believed it would cheapen the park experience. After World War II, park managers provided campfire wood in the campgrounds and stocked Mount Rainier's lakes with fish— two examples of measures aimed at providing visitors with the desired "national park experience."

After the Wilderness Act of 1964, social scientists developed a more scientific method for defining the "wilderness experience" and the "national park experience." Their method was based on the concept of carrying capacity. Range and wildlife managers had developed the concept of carrying capacity many years earlier to define the amount of use (usually by grazing animals) that an area of land could support on a sustainable basis without damaging the resource. The social scientists proposed that wilderness and national park areas had a "recreational carrying capacity." According to sociologist J. A. Wagar, recreational carrying capacity was "the level of recreational use an area can withstand while providing a sustained quality of recreation."[2]

To define and measure "quality recreation," the concept of recreational carrying capacity evolved over the next decade into a dual system of psychological and ecological components. The psychological component of recreational carrying capacity comprised perceptions of crowding and user satisfaction, measured through visitor questionnaires; the ecological component included the effects of recreational activity on soils, vegetation, water quality, and wildlife behavior, measured through field study and analysis. The goal was to identify levels of sustainable use that would assist managers in achieving their twin objectives of preserving the resource and providing for the public's use and enjoyment of the resource.[3]

The concept of recreational carrying capacity first emerged on a policy level in the park service's backcountry management plans in the early 1970s. Backcountry management plans were implemented at Mount Rainier, Yosemite, Glacier, and several other national parks. Systemwide, the plan that attracted by far the most sociological study and media attention was one for restricting recreational use of the Colorado River in Grand Canyon National Park. Although Rainier did not get the same attention, its backcountry management plan was covered in the Seattle and Tacoma press, and eventually Rainier's backcountry users would be the subject of intensive sociological study, too. As much as park officials hated to restrict wilderness users (they generally sympathized with the notion that freedom from regulation was one of the essential qualities of wilderness), they came to the conclusion that unrestricted use was much worse. As one seasonal park ranger remarked, "I like to think that it isn't really wilderness when you have to find your assigned campsite along well-marked trails. It may not be wilderness but it's the best we have."[4]

The physical wear and tear on Rainier's backcountry had reached disturbing proportions by the 1960s. Trails were gullied, shortcuts were ubiquitous and badly eroded, and parallel trails were established across many meadow areas. Heavily used tent sites, easily recognizable from the sprawling bare patches that developed around them in the subalpine meadows, were sprinkled helter skelter around many of the park's most beautiful spots. Campfire rings abounded. John Rutter, superintendent of the park in the 1960s, recalled that the shoreline around Mowich Lake was "beaten to death," virtually denuded of vegetation. Gene Casey, who joined the ranger staff in 1974, thought Rainier was the most "beat up" national park he had ever seen.[5]

One instance of abuse in Berkeley Park, on the north side of the mountain, was particularly galling to Ranger John Dalle-Molle. In this verdant meadow, spangled with the billowy white blossoms of bear grass and fringed with stands of dark green fir, a party of Boy Scouts allowed a campfire to get out of control one evening in the summer of 1968. The incident created an enormous charcoal pit in the meadow. Dalle-Molle began yearly measurements of the revegetation of the blackened area. His study, which eventually spanned six years, demonstrated how slowly Rainier's subalpine meadows recovered from scarring. Dalle-Molle suggested the need to restrict backcountry use in order to give affected areas a respite. In particular he argued the need to control group sizes, convinced that large parties were causing a disproportional amount of damage, an intuition that research has since born out.[6]

The Seattle Mountaineers also recognized that Rainier's backcountry was in trouble. In a 1969 report, "Recommendations for Future Development of Mt. Rainier National Park," the club's conservation committee noted that many fragile areas in the park could not sustain the heavy use they received. Rainier's Spray Park, the committee cited for example, "suffers from typical back-packer abuse . . . and is in much the same situation as many of Mt. Rainier's meadow areas." The Seattle Mountaineers wanted the park service to close the Mowich Lake and Westside roads, making access to these areas more difficult and the hikes more rewarding.[7]

Anticipating that any move to limit numbers of people would be controversial, park officials helped organize a forum on overcrowding in the national parks at the University of Puget Sound. Held in observance of the Yellowstone centennial in 1972, the forum focused on the need to limit visitor access to the more popular national parks. "We're up to our ears in people," Rainier's Superintendent Daniel J. Tobin Jr. told the Tacoma-area audience, "and people cause trouble in managing a wilderness resource." Tobin announced that the park was formulating plans to restrict vehicular traffic, limit the number of backcountry campsites, and institute a reservation system for overnight backcountry use. Regional Director John A. Rutter emphasized that the impending changes at Rainier were part of a larger trend toward limiting park use. The N P S had restricted vehicular traffic in Mount McKinley and Yosemite the previous summer, Rutter said, and park officials had reported that the restrictions were "very well accepted" by the public. This forum, together with other N P S announcements on the coming backcountry management plan, received sympathetic coverage in the Seattle and Tacoma press.[8]

Superintendent Tobin unveiled the park's backcountry management plan the following year. Written by the ranger staff, the plan was directed at horse parties and overnight backpackers. Day hikers were unaffected. Horse parties were limited to six horses per group. They were restricted to just a few trails in the park and to designated campsites in those areas. Overnight backpackers were permitted to make campfires only in designated sites, and group sizes were similarly limited to six people per site. If backpackers camped off-trail, they had to comply with certain guidelines in selecting a site. They had to keep a minimum distance away from the trail and from any standing or running water. Finally, the plan divided the backcountry into three zones—trail, cross-country, and alpine—and divided each zone into numerous areas. Each area was assigned an overnight capacity, and when the capacity was reached, no more permits were issued for that area.

The public accepted most of the new restrictions without much complaint. Veteran backcountry users agreed in principle with the need for restrictions. One source of dissatisfaction, however, was the reservation system. Intended as a public convenience, the reservation system made 80 percent of sites available for advance booking by mail. The problem, park officials soon discovered, was that people who lived within sight of Rainier would make reservations for three or four different weekends with the expectation of postponing the trip until they could observe fair weather conditions at the mountain. As a result, people who drove to the park with the hope of obtaining a permit sometimes found themselves shut out, even as many backcountry campsites stood vacant. The reservation system was admirably suited for the Wonderland Trail hiker, who wished to plot the ninety-three-mile trip around the mountain weeks ahead of the event. But it utterly failed the whimsical weekend backpacker, who was apt to throw some gear in the trunk of the car on a Friday evening, check the late-night weather forecast, and drive to the park early the next morning. Park officials eliminated the reservation system at the end of 1973.[9] (A modified reservation system was reinstituted in about 2000; 60 percent of sites could be reserved in advance, but the user had to collect his or her reservation in person rather than obtain it by mail.)

With the unpopular reservation system behind them, park officials soon faced a more serious challenge to their backcountry management plan. Larry Penberthy, a professional mountaineer and founder of the Seattle-based outdoor equipment line, Mountain Safety Research, Inc. (MSR), opposed restrictions on the number of climbing parties per route in the alpine zone. Penberthy first objected to the restriction at a public hearing on the proposed new master plan for Rainier. Addressing Superintendent Tobin and Regional Director Rutter, he complained that the master plan had been prepared by "outsiders" who did not understand the local people's attachment to the park. "A park should be a park," Penberthy testified, "a place for the benefit and enjoyment of people. A place for restoration of tranquility. It should not be a wilderness. If it is, then lock the gates and put on guards. We need a park for the Sunday people, the weekend people." Penberthy was the only member of the public to speak at the hearing. Regional Director Rutter commented to a reporter afterward that it was unfortunate only one point of view had been presented.[10]

If Rutter knew anything about this mountaineer, he had probably heard of his feisty reputation. As local writer Harvey Manning commented, Penberthy would file lawsuits "at the snap of a carabiner."[11] In the 1960s, Penberthy had won a hefty settlement against a manufacturer of climbing equipment who allegedly infringed on his patented hardware, and around 1970 he had threatened similar action against the Seattle-based cooperative Recreational Equipment, Inc. (REI). As Pen-

THE SEARCH FOR LIMITS

berthy began his one-man crusade against the park's backcountry management plan, many N P S officials suspected he was laying the groundwork for a suit against the government.[12]

Penberthy began writing letters to Superintendent Tobin, requesting permits for large parties of climbers that he knew would be denied under the new regulations. Penberthy also complained when the park service did not supply him with a final copy of the backcountry management plan as it was printed in the *Federal Register* on June 24, 1975. That summer, after the park denied his request for a three-day climbing permit, Penberthy filed suit.[13]

In *Penberthy v. Tobin et al.*, the court upheld the right of the federal government to restrict park use. But the court also found merit in Penberthy's allegation that N P S regulations were "arbitrary and capricious." Consequently, the court ordered the park service to drop the restriction on the number of parties using each climbing route, to prepare an annual climbing report, and to submit any further restrictions to a process of public review.[14]

The Penberthy case underscored the need for research in determining the recreational carrying capacity of the backcountry. There had been no compilation of ecological or sociological data in the preparation of the original backcountry management plan. The rangers simply selected suitable campsites and established a limit for each area based on their experience and intuition. After a few years, they found that their carrying capacity estimates were low, and they revised them upward. When Penberthy sued the park service again in 1986, the park service had scientific data on climbers' and backpackers' environmental impacts, and the judge dismissed the case.[15]

The backcountry management plan had the desired effect on the condition of the wilderness. Many areas that were badly scarred began to recover in the 1970s and 1980s. Trail crews stabilized eroding sections of the trail, obliterated unplanned trails, covered up shortcuts with debris, and removed a number of overnight shelters that had fallen into disrepair.[16]

It remained doubtful whether the park's wilderness managers ever really identified a recreational carrying capacity. While park officials agreed that the condition of the backcountry improved markedly during the mid- to late 1970s and 1980s, their explanations for the improvement varied. Some felt that the restrictions placed on horse parties and large groups were decisive. Others believed that changes in camp procedures made the biggest difference. Either view underscored the fact that the recreational carrying capacity could not be expressed as a flat population limit but rather had to take into account the character and composition of the user population. Still others suggested that the condition of the backcountry improved primarily because overall backcountry use peaked in the early 1970s and then declined. One interpretation of the "peak" was based on demographics: baby boomers invaded the backcountry in force when they reached their young adult years, and retreated from the backcountry when they started having children. Another interpretation of the "peak" was based on climate change: a warm, dry period in the 1960s and early 1970s made Rainier's backcountry more accessible and vulnerable. Both of these interpretations suggest that the backcountry management plan was largely incidental to the recovery of heavily impacted areas. Whatever factors were at work in correcting the problem, park officials agreed that public use of the backcountry had been too heavy for the environment to sustain in the 1960s and early 1970s.

The backcountry management plan produced significant changes in the "wilderness experience" at Rainier. Backpackers now entered a more regulated environment, an area where backcountry rangers routinely checked whether they had a permit, and where the permit itself required that they camp in a certain designated campsite or cross-country area and that they follow certain camp procedures. The camp procedures had a slightly antiseptic quality, as backpackers now filtered or boiled their water, cooked on propane stoves rather than wood fires, hung their food at night, and conscientiously packed out every particle of trash. Gone were the days when backpackers could camp beside their favorite lake. Now they typically camped in forest settings such as that found at the new Devil's Dream camp, where eight numbered sites and a privy stairstepped down the densely wooded trail half a mile below the meadow known as Indian Henry's Hunting Ground. Yet if something in the wilderness experience had been lost in all of this, it was only necessary to contemplate the alternative of unrestricted use to appreciate how much had been preserved.[17]

Park officials contended with similar problems in the nonwilderness, or front country, portion of the park: environmental degradation, crowding, and public resistance to any form of visitor management that smacked of regimentation. As it had with the backcountry, the NPS used zoning as a device for prescribing limits on use and development. The 1972 master plan listed fifteen "developed areas" in the park, excluding the road system. Only three of the fifteen—Tahoma Woods (a new headquarters site located outside of the park), Cougar Rock (a campground), and Stevens Canyon Entrance (a fee station)—were of recent origin. The other twelve—Paradise, Longmire, Sunrise, Ohanapecosh, Nisqually Entrance, Carbon River Entrance, White River Entrance, Tipsoo Lake, Mowich Lake, Carbon River, Ipsut Creek, and Camp Muir—dated from the period 1900 to 1940. The master plan classified most of these areas as Class II lands, or "General Outdoor Recreation Areas." The master plan stated that "the area included in this classification is sufficiently large to accommodate projected use."[18] There would be no more developed areas in Mount Rainier National Park. By and large, the park facilities would be renovated or replaced but not expanded.

The master plan called for removal of some facilities. Automobile campgrounds at Sunrise and Mowich Lake would be changed to walk-in campgrounds, and the campground at Paradise would be eliminated altogether. The administrative offices at Longmire would be replaced with new offices at Tahoma Woods. Over the next few years, these plans were implemented. The changes to these facilities represented significant planning and policy choices that originated in the Mission 66 era but came to fruition only in the 1970s.

While the park service was fairly successful in holding the line against further growth of administrative sites and structures in the park, it had much more difficulty dealing with the growth of automobile traffic. Indeed, car use in the national park showed the same disturbing trend that it exhibited in cities and suburbs: as the years passed, there were fewer occupants per vehicle, more cars per capita. Determined not to build any more roads, park planners saw but one course for the future: mass transit. The problem with mass transit was that it conflicted with another aim of park planning, to preserve the visitors' sense of freedom in exploring the park. For most of the public, taking a scenic drive by automobile continued to be the quintessential national park experience.[19]

The master plan of 1972 proposed the development of an aerial tramway between the White River Valley and Sunrise, with the objective of eventually removing the automobile completely from the Sunrise area. Planners envisioned that the tramway would reduce the number of people going to Sunrise, alleviate the feeling of crowding in that development area, and lessen the human impact on the tundra vegetation around it. The visual blight of the vast parking lot would be removed. In the long run, the existing road cut on Sunrise Ridge would be restored to a natural condition.[20]

Although the Sunrise tramway proposal never reached the stage of detailed engineering studies, planners had a rough idea of what it would entail. A direct route of ascent from the White River Valley would involve an elevation rise of 2,500 feet; alternatively, a more gradual route of ascent from the east, up the length of Sunrise Ridge, would require an elevation rise of 2,700 feet with some nearly horizontal stretches along the route. Depending on the route, the tramway would carry 300 to 500 passengers per hour (3,000 to 5,000 per day), or about half of the existing peak daily use. Construction costs for a tramway and terminal building would be several million dollars. Visitors would presumably pay a fee to ride the tramway.

The public responded negatively to the proposal in hearings on the master plan. Fully 92 percent of comments on the proposal were opposed. Respondents mainly stated that a tramway would degrade the beauty of the area, that a shuttle bus would be less obtrusive, or that the existing road made it unnecessary. Interestingly, the public's rejection of the proposal came on the heels of a similar controversy over four proposed tramways in North Cascades National Park, where high-ranking Interior officials had insisted that the tramways would be unique to that national park. The NPS eliminated the proposal from the final master plan for Mount Rainier approved in 1976.[21]

The master plan of 1972 also proposed to eliminate automobile use in the northwest corner of the park along the Carbon River and Mowich Lake roads. Since these roads were both dead-ends, it appeared that banning cars would be relatively simple there. The master plan proposed to develop a parking area at the park boundary on the Carbon River Road and to limit access beyond that point to foot, bicycle, and public mini-

THE SEARCH FOR LIMITS

buses. It offered a similar formula for Mowich Lake, commenting: "Removal of the automobiles from the vicinity of this highly scenic area would greatly increase the quality of the visitor experience."[22]

Subsequently, the NPS quietly dropped the proposal to close the Carbon River Road to private vehicular traffic. One problem involved the spring and fall seasons, when public use diminished to the point that mini-bus service would absorb a disproportional share of park operating funds. Probably the main factor in the plan's abandonment, however, was the concern that closing the road to private vehicular traffic would only turn away visitors rather than get them out of their cars. These visitors would then be diverted to other areas of the park—Paradise and Sunrise—where problems of crowding were even more acute.[23]

Park service officials were somewhat more enthused about the Mowich Lake Road closure. For one thing, this proposal had the support of the Seattle Mountaineers. More important, the much-trodden shoreline of Mowich Lake was in greater need of a respite. The park service proposed to rehabilitate the historic Grindstone Trail so hikers would have a more pleasing experience getting from the park boundary to Mowich Lake.[24] For one reason or another, the road closure never happened.

Mass transit proposals elsewhere in the park were more complicated, because the south and east sides of the park were now linked by the Stevens Canyon Road. Indeed, it had been one of the purposes of the Stevens Canyon Road to encourage visitors to make a one-day drive around the mountain. Now the park's through-road system did not lend itself to mass transit. People were less willing to accept mandatory public transit on a through-road than a dead-end road. If visitors had to leave their cars at Longmire to take a shuttle bus to Paradise, for example, they would then want the option to continue onward through Stevens Canyon; otherwise, the public transit would be an inconvenience. This problem notwithstanding, the master plan of 1972 called for a transportation study "to determine the exact methods required to satisfy present and future needs."[25] The master plan explicitly aimed to reduce private vehicular use in the park.

Funding for the transportation study was delayed for many years. Finally, in 1987, Superintendent Neil Guse initiated a study of visitor attitudes toward a potential mass transit system. The study, undertaken by the Cooperative Park Studies Unit, University of Washington, used visitor surveys to test the public's receptivity to six mass transit scenarios involving various combinations of return-trip shuttles on the Nisqually-Paradise, Sunrise, and Carbon River roads. The study revealed that public opinion was almost evenly divided, with many people holding strong views for or against the proposal.[26]

In 1993, the NPS contracted with a Denver-based company, BRW Inc., to evaluate transportation needs at Rainier. BRW's study included an analysis of summer and winter visitor circulation patterns and an evaluation of the feasibility of implementing a mass transit or Visitor Transportation System (VTS) to reduce automobile congestion. On June 2, 1994, the park convened a Transportation Alternatives Workshop at which BRW presented its findings and preliminary VTS alternatives. Regional transit planning authorities attended, together with representatives from a wide range of organizations interested in the park. BRW submitted a final report in 1995.[27]

By the end of the century, park officials were once again backing away from mass transit proposals, however, citing high operating costs. Instead, they began limiting the number of people simply by limiting the number of parking spaces. When available parking filled up at Paradise, visitors were shunted past the parking lot and visitor center onto the old road through Paradise Valley, now known as the scenic loop drive, for a one-way trip out of the area. In this manner, park officials sought to discourage people from parking their cars willy-nilly along the roadway or driving in circles around the parking lot in the hope of seizing newly vacated parking spots. Collecting data in the late 1990s, researchers counted up to 1,400 cars at one time at Paradise—nearly twice the number of designated parking stalls.[28]

As park officials prepared a new general management plan for the park, they worked on making this ad hoc solution into policy. The plan's cornerstone, according to chief planner Eric Walkinshaw, was to use the recreational carrying capacity concept to limit numbers of people at Paradise and other popular developed areas. "Realizing there's no magic number out there, we're trying to set the bar right now," he told a reporter in 1999. Parked cars would be the index for tracking how many people were in an area, and parking stalls would be the limiting factor in ensuring that an area's carrying capacity was not exceeded. Just as at Paradise, when available parking at Mowich Lake reached capacity, the area would be closed to additional visitors. At Sunrise, where the number of parking stalls was 250, the recreational carrying capacity might be set a little higher, allowing visitors to leave their cars at a lower elevation and take a shuttle when the parking lot was full.[29]

If such a solution seemed rather compromising, it was worth recalling one line of development that the park service steadfastly opposed. The N P S refused to define the problem as a shortage of parking. In previous eras—notably in the first master planning effort at the end of the 1920s and again in Mission 66—park planners had pointed to a shortage of alternative destinations or through-roads in the park. They had recommended more development in order to take pressure off of existing developed areas. At the end of the century, park planners finally rejected that formula.

The search for limits extended to Mount Rainier's alpine zone. The mountain began to attract increasing numbers of climbers after World War II. The number of summit attempts grew from a few hundred per year in the late 1940s to approximately triple that number a decade later. It jumped into the range of 2,000 to 3,000 after 1965—boosted, it was thought, by the publicity that Rainier received as a training ground for the American Mount Everest expedition of 1963.[30] Repeat visitors to Rainier soon became familiar with the impressive mountaineering exhibit in the new Paradise visitor center, which included a life-size diorama of local hero Jim Whittaker planting his foot on the summit of Everest. The exhibit also offered tips on what was involved in making an ascent of Mount Rainier.

The park service welcomed this form of recreation at Rainier while encouraging the use of a professional guide service. Superintendent Tobin observed that a professional guide service gave many more people an opportunity to attempt a summit ascent. "To climb the mountain," Tobin wrote, "is a compelling reason to visit and use the Park."[31] As the popularity of climbing Rainier grew in the 1960s, the park service found it expedient to establish the guide service as a separate concession.

The park service found two willing entrepreneurs in Lou Whittaker and Jerry Lynch. Twin brothers Lou and Jim Whittaker had been guiding on Mount Rainier since 1951. As the years passed, Jim Whittaker focused on expeditions and his role in Recreational Equipment, Inc., while Lou Whittaker continued his association with Rainier and, with partner Jerry Lynch, opened an outdoor equipment store in Tacoma called Whittaker's Chalet. In 1968, Lou Whittaker and Jerry Lynch formed Rainier Mountaineering, Inc. (RMI). Their partnership was highly successful and the new company showed promise. In 1972, Whittaker got out of the outdoor equipment retail business and Lynch became an equal partner in RMI. "We made him president and me vice president," Whittaker wrote. "Jerry did the paperwork and I did the guiding. He's always been the detail man, I've always been the personality out front, hawking clients and guides."[32]

Whittaker and Lynch worked aggressively to secure their position in the park, pressing the NPS for a five-year contract, which they finally achieved in 1975. RMI received another five-year contract in 1980 and a seven-year contract after that. In 1985, some climbers formed an organization called "Open Rainier" to protest what they perceived to be RMI's unfair monopoly in the park, and park staff held at least two meetings with the organization to hear its concerns. But the park received only one application for the guide service in addition to RMI's and it was not competitive.[33]

RMI placed a strong emphasis on client safety. Fatalities were rare. But on June 21, 1981, ten RMI clients and one guide were killed by an icefall on the Ingraham Glacier. Survivors of the tragedy said that they saw a big serac collapse about 1,000 feet higher on the mountain, triggering a massive avalanche. Half of the party escaped; half were swept into a crevasse and buried under tons of ice. The event occurred shortly after sunrise. At 6:20 A.M., Superintendent William J. Briggle was banging on Whittaker's door in Ashford, telling him there had been an accident on the mountain. Whittaker rode with Briggle up to the Guide House at Paradise, where rescue operations were already under way and the families of the victims would shortly begin to gather. The survivors, bruised and shaken but not badly injured, straggled in at midday. It was the worst climbing disaster in North American history. Weeks later, following a detailed investigation by park officials and a team of glaciologists, it was found that RMI's guides had acted in a reasonable manner and the accident was classified as an act of God.[34]

RMI's guides generally served a three-year apprenticeship before they were given responsibility for whole climbing parties. An apprentice guide would work with two experienced guides, and if the new guide did not progress during the first season, he or she would not be hired back the following spring. RMI looked for "people skills" as well as climbing ability; guides had to be sensitive to their clients' level of confidence and fatigue. Apprentice guides could lead a rope of four or five clients, but RMI did not put them in charge of a whole climbing party. In 1994, RMI had nearly thirty guides who were qualified to lead parties to the summit.[35]

RMI guides sometimes assisted park rangers in search and rescue operations (SAR), but by and large this remained a park service responsibility. Most search and rescue operations on the upper mountain involved the evacuation of injured climbers; some required bringing out bodies after fatal climbing accidents or airplane crashes; others entailed searching for missing persons. Despite mounting costs and a surfeit of volunteer SAR groups in the Pacific Northwest who were willing to help, the park administration normally took the lead in organizing SAR operations. There were several reasons for this. First, quick response time was a critical concern in most search and rescue operations; typically the emergency call came late in the day, and the SAR team would be pushing daylight as it started toward the scene of the accident. The park staff, with its contingent of experienced "climbing rangers" assigned to the Paradise district, was in a much better position than any volunteer SAR group to respond quickly to an emergency. Second, park officials could readily coordinate with the army for helicopter support. A helicopter stationed at Gray Army Air Base at Fort Lewis assisted with medical evacuations on numerous occasions in the 1970s. Army helicopters were also used to insert SAR teams into inaccessible areas on the east, north, and west sides of the mountain, lowering rangers to the ground by a cable device known as a "jungle penetrator." Helicopters began assisting with high altitude (above 10,000 feet) SAR operations in the 1980s. Helicopters were also used for "short haul" rescue operations, in which a ranger and stretcher were carried in a sling below the helicopter to the scene of the accident. A third reason that the NPS did not rely on volunteer SAR groups was that these operations were frequently dangerous, as teams worked at night or in adverse weather conditions. Use of volunteers always carried the risk that the volunteers themselves would get into trouble. Volunteers could assist park rangers, but they were rarely put in charge of search and rescue operations. The NPS most often deployed volunteers in long ground evacuations or searches—the most labor-intensive kinds of SAR operations.[36]

In addition to visitor safety, the upper mountain presented other management challenges. Surprisingly, crowding became a concern. Climbers encountered extremes of solitude and crowding on Rainier. Those who were in search of solitude could probably find it during certain times of the year or days of the week or on lesser-used routes, and no doubt the cold, austere environment above 7,000 feet tended to accentuate whatever sense of desolation existed. But climbers who took the standard routes on weekends during the summer had a very different experience. They were apt to follow a beaten path over the snow, compete for cooking and bunk space at Camp Muir, and share the summit with a few dozen other climbers. As the number of climbers rose sharply from about 2,000 annually in the 1960s to 3,997 in 1972 and 4,471 in 1973, park officials worried that crowded conditions would diminish the wilderness experience.

Camp Muir presented an especially difficult problem. At 10,000 feet elevation, the camp was a popular destination for day hikers starting from Paradise. It was also a popular overnight shelter for independent climbers, a base of operations for guides, and an important staging area for search and rescue. Crowded conditions at the camp in the late 1960s and early 1970s raised a number of issues. How should the limited facilities be shared among these different users? How should sewage and water supply problems be resolved? Should the area be zoned for wilderness protection?

There were three old stone buildings at Camp Muir: a guide hut built in 1916, Muir Hut built in 1921, and a storage building of unknown date. In 1969 the park service built an A-frame rangers' shelter, and the following year it authorized RMI to build a prefabricated guide and client

THE SEARCH FOR LIMITS

shelter. The buildings provided a division of the camp between the public, the rangers, and the guide service. Although it now presented a rather haphazard appearance, visitors to Camp Muir generally felt that the camp's rough character was appropriate to the setting and a favorable part of the climbing experience.[37]

In the early 1970s, the park service wanted to exclude Camp Muir from wilderness designation, reasoning that the logistical requirements of the camp and its busy character made it impossible to manage as "Wilderness." On the other hand, the park service wanted to protect the wilderness experience on all the climbing routes. Thus, in the backcountry management plan of 1973, the NPS limited the number of climbing parties on each route to two per day on the northern side and three per day on the southern side of the mountain. The NPS eliminated these quotas in the aftermath of the court's decision in *Penberthy v. Tobin et al.* A 1980 user survey indicated that most climbers did not feel that the mountain was too crowded. Park officials discerned that backpackers and climbers held different expectations about their experience: backpackers by and large cared much more about obtaining a feeling of solitude. Nevertheless, the route from Paradise to Camp Muir was eventually included in the Mount Rainier National Park Wilderness Act approved by Congress in 1988. As the number of climbers on the mountain continued to grow—exceeding 11,000 in 1998—the park service cautioned that it still might have to impose an overall limit.[38]

Another concern was the human impact on the delicate flora in the alpine zone. Most vulnerable, it seemed, were the fell fields located between 7,000 and 10,000 feet elevation, where tiny, ground-hugging plants grew in the loose, volcanic soil and lay dormant under snow for ten months of the year. Each human footfall on these talus and pumice-covered slopes could set rock scraping against rock, disturbing whatever life-giving shelter each plant had secured against wind, sun, and cold. Park biologist Ola Edwards initiated a baseline study of Rainier's alpine biology in 1975, and expanded her work in the mid-1980s with the establishment of permanent sample plots along the most frequently traveled routes in the alpine zone. By 1991, the park administration was monitoring eleven areas in the alpine zone using infrared and low-elevation color photography, logging changes in vegetation in its Geographical

Information Systems (GIS) database. These studies showed pronounced effects in travel corridors and camping areas.[39]

Still another impact came to light in the early 1980s as climbers began complaining about the unpleasantness of encountering deposits of human waste on the upper mountain. Deposited on ice in an environment with few microorganisms, the feces refused to decompose. The deposits were most prolific on the Emmons Glacier, Ingraham Flats, the top of Disappointment Cleaver, and Columbia Crest. Not only were the deposits unsightly, but it seemed that human waste on the upper mountain might be linked to higher bacteria counts in stream run-off from these areas. The problem was not unique to Rainier; a 1980 report to Congress on "The State of the Parks" indicated that the accumulation of human waste posed a significant environmental threat in other national parks with alpine areas, too. Between 1982 and 1986, Rainier staff, guides, and climbers found themselves at the cutting edge of high-altitude human waste management.[40]

There were five points in the human waste management program. First, there was a program of helicopter support for removing barrels of waste that accumulated annually in the privy pits at Camp Muir. Second, the park service installed a solar-assisted toilet at Camp Muir. The unit was designed to dehydrate the material using passive solar energy, thereby making it lighter to airlift out. Third, the park administration experimented with privacy screens at Camp Schurman and Ingraham Flats. This system, requiring frequent ranger patrols to ensure site cleanliness, was later abandoned. Fourth, rangers dispensed "blue bags" to climbers at Camps Muir and Schurman so that they could carry out their defecated material themselves. This method proved most successful. Finally, the park service, together with RMI and Recreational Equipment, Inc., strove to educate the climbers about the problem.[41] Indeed, climber education paid other dividends as well. As with so many other forms of visitor use of the mountain, the most promising approach to dealing with the pressure of numbers seemed to be to change individuals' behavior. For example, climbers could be taught to walk and camp on snowfields rather than fell fields whenever the opportunity presented itself.

As the popularity of climbing Rainier grew, old hands saw a change in the kind of people that the mountain attracted. Jim Nelson, a climbing guidebook author, believed that the challenge of Rainier had assumed the character of a trophy-seeking experience. The seekers were people who went climbing once a year at most, and in his view, they were "not looking at the aesthetics of climbing" so much as bagging their trophy. Ranger David Gottlieb, who worked much of the summer at Camp Schurman, had a similar impression. "There's a cult in the Northwest," he told a reporter in 1999. "We here in the Northwest are creating our own personal mythos about what it's like to be a Pacific Northwest character, and part of it has to do with climbing Mount Rainier." After talking with many of these people, Gottlieb found them sympathetic. They were typically "midmanagement, middle-life, white collar climbers from the Puget Sound area." They worked in the city but loved the wilderness. They trained for the climb at the health club after a ten-hour day at the office, and they were so ensconced in their urban routines "that it took something like Rainier to excite them, to jolt them a little bit."[42]

To Mike Gauthier, chief climbing ranger on the park staff, it appeared there would be no turning back the horde of new mountaineers, if only because Rainier loomed so large on the horizon for so many thousands of people. "It's this billboard that everybody sees and deals with all the time," he mused. "It's the big dog sitting next to a big metropolitan area."[43]

The park service did engineer a visitor turnover of another kind, converting Rainier from a downhill skiers' winter resort to a haven for other kinds of outdoor winter recreation, notably cross-country skiing. If these two forms of recreation had once been quite similar, they diverged in the decade from 1965 to 1975. As the sport of downhill skiing became increasingly commercialized, more and more downhill ski enthusiasts shunned Paradise in favor of regional ski areas located in Mount Baker–Snoqualmie National Forest or destination ski resorts located in Idaho, Utah, and Colorado. To a certain extent, decisions by the park administration helped to reshape winter use of the park. Park officials felt a natural affinity for cross-country skiers and snowshoers, while they came to see downhill skiing as an inappropriate use. Park officials had a more ambivalent response to two other winter activities, snowmobiling and sliding (snowplay).

Even after the development of new ski areas at nearby Crystal Mountain and White Pass in the early 1960s, a few thousand downhill skiers continued to use the slopes above Paradise. Superintendent John Rutter, like his predecessor Preston Macy, wanted the Rainier National Park Company to operate rope tows and a snack bar to accommodate this winter use. Reluctantly, the RNPC maintained this food service on weekends and holidays. General Manager Paul Sceva grumbled to the company's stockholders that the winter season would never amount to anything "as long as the tows are the only means of up-hill ski transportation." Proposals for a permanent chairlift resurfaced for the last time in 1968.[44]

In the fall of 1966, the RNPC turned over winter operations at Paradise, together with summer guide service, to a subcontractor by the name of the Kendall Corporation. This was not a success. The Kendall Corporation made a marginal profit on the winter operations and lost money on its climbing equipment rentals and guided trips to the summit, glaciers, and Paradise ice caves. The Kendall Corporation filed for bankruptcy, the RNPC sued, and the rope tow equipment was turned over to the RNPC in a final settlement. At this point Lou Whittaker and Jerry Lynch took over the guide service, while a separate subcontractor, John R. Anderson of Mt. Rainier Ski & Guide Service, Inc., purchased the ski tow operation. The guide service began to flourish while the ski tow operation remained a marginal enterprise. The park service considered recombining the two in 1972, but decided against it.[45]

This was the correct decision, for the public's interest in summit climbs grew while its desire for downhill skiing at Paradise diminished. Despite a forty-year tradition of downhill skiing at Paradise, no strong sentiment emerged for keeping the tradition alive. Indeed, there was a growing sentiment that the rope tow operation was an inappropriate use of the area. Although the four rope tows were taken down after each winter season, there remained the necessity of putting up pole markers each fall. Park officials noted that the equipment used in transporting the poles up the hill damaged the meadows.[46] The park service separated the ski tow operation from the main concession contract in 1972 and negotiated one-year contracts over the next three years. It issued a final prospectus for a ski tow operator in 1975 and received only a single, inadequate response. This marked the end of Mount Rainier's tradition of downhill ski use.

Cross-country skiing, meanwhile, increased in popularity during the 1970s, and park service officials encouraged the sport. In 1972, park rangers marked a cross-country ski trail from the Paradise visitor center to Nisqually Vista, and organized volunteers into a unit of the National Ski Patrol to assist in the protection of visitors. Park officials estimated that cross-country skiers outnumbered snowshoers by ten to one in the Paradise area in 1980.[47]

Cross-country skiing remained solely an independent activity until January 1979, when RMI initiated a program of ski and snowshoe rental and cross-country ski instruction at Paradise. RMI ran the program for two years. On the east side of the park, meanwhile, Pete Sandvigen of Back and Beyond Trading Post, Inc., obtained a one-year permit in 1979 to operate a mobile cross-country ski and snowshoe rental facility in the Cayuse/Chinook Pass area, but this venture was not a commercial success either.[48]

Following a winter without any ski rental service (1981–82), park officials asked the main concession, Guest Services, Inc., to provide this service. In November 1982, GSI opened a Ski Touring Center at Longmire, which rented skis and snowshoes and offered skiing lessons. Park interpreters led snowshoe walks from the Paradise visitor center, and park staff marked three cross-country ski trails in the Paradise area. Beginning in the winter of 1993–94, the Washington Ski Touring Club provided weekend volunteers for ski patrols on the trails out of Paradise. This was the first such volunteer effort in nearly twenty years. With the use of volunteers and paid weekend seasonals, the ranger staff greatly increased the number of ranger patrols into the more distant areas around Paradise that were frequented by weekend skiers.[49]

A nonprofit corporation called Mt. Tahoma Trails Association initiated a system of cross-country ski trails and overnight huts on the west edge of the park in 1989. The association utilized existing logging roads, together with the Westside Road, to develop a trail system that grew to more than eighty-eight miles in extent by 1994. It included three large huts plus a cylindrical shelter called the Colonnade Yurt just west of Sunset Park on land belonging to Champion International Corporation. On November 20, 1990, Mount Rainier National Park entered a memorandum of understanding with the USDA Forest Service, Washington Department of Natural Resources, Champion International, and Mt. Tahoma Trails Association outlining how the huts and trails would be managed. Trail grooming, ski patrols, hut reservations, and handling of refundable damage deposits would be handled entirely by the Mt. Tahoma Trails Association. The park service's most important stipulation was that a hut located in the park would be dismantled and removed at the end of each winter season.[50]

Snowmobilers first appeared in the park in the mid-1960s. They used both the Paradise and Chinook Pass areas. At first the park administration took the passive approach that snowmobiling did no significant harm to the environment and had a legitimate place in the park along with other forms of winter recreation. This greatly disturbed former park naturalist Frank Brockman, who sent a protesting letter to the superintendent and copies to NPS Director George B. Hartzog Jr. and Supreme Court Justice William O. Douglas. "While your term 'oversnow vehicles' may give [snowmobiles] a nod of acceptance," Brockman wrote, "the fact remains that they are motor scooters on skis and that their exhausts are noxious and offensive to the sightseer and tourist who tries to find solitude and escape from city traffic and noises." Brockman noted that there was nothing in the park regulations to prevent snowmobilers from using cross-country ski trails around Paradise.[51]

Over the years, the attitude of park officials toward snowmobiles changed little. Other than to restrict snowmobiling to designated park roads, officials generally accepted this recreational use as long as numbers of snowmobilers remained low. Rainier never experienced the wave of snowmobile use that overtook Yellowstone, where 4,000 snowmobiles entered the park in one weekend during the winter of 1969–70.[52] Rainier officials were confident that the number of snowmobilers would remain small because Rainier's winter use was virtually all local, and Washington residents did not take to snowmobiling the way residents of New England or the Upper Midwest did. Washington's climate and topography were generally not favorable for snowmobiling, and park officials refused to look for a problem where they did not think one existed.

Numbers of actual snowmobilers in the park remained sketchy. The final environmental statement for the park's master plan, completed in 1976, registered 707 snowmobilers in the park in 1973, and described this use as "light." Superintendent Tobin's statement for management in 1977 estimated the number of snowmobiles as from 50 to 60 annually, and described this use as "almost nil." Subsequent statements for management offered no figures but maintained that snowmobile use was "very low" or "on the low side."[53]

Sliding, or "snowplay" as park officials termed this use, became a popular family activity at Paradise in the 1960s. The park administration encouraged this use by preparing a run or runs and by coordinating with the Emergency Search and Rescue Scouts of Tacoma for weekend volunteers to supervise the snowplay area. Although no records on snowplay were kept before 1981, the number of sliders grew perceptibly during the late 1970s, reaching an estimated 5,000 during the winter of 1979–80.[54]

Unfortunately, snowplay entailed a significant rate of injury for the participants. Park officials found that the injury rate dropped if rangers regularly groomed the runs and closely supervised the activity. Some park officials believed this supervision of the snowplay area put an undue burden on a dwindling ranger staff. Yet when Superintendent Briggle experimented with leaving the snowplay area unsupervised (in the winter of 1992–93), injuries rose by a whopping 900 percent. Caught between his desire to provide for the public safety and his wish to address more urgent park needs, Briggle looked for a way to eliminate snowplay at Paradise.[55]

The park service's handling of winter sports concessions after 1965 demonstrated that the park service could more effectively influence how visitors used the park in winter than in summer. Of course, the park service owed much of its success to the fact that the downhill ski industry found a home on the western national forests. Nonetheless, park officials made a concerted effort to encourage noncommercial winter sports—cross-country skiing, snowshoeing, and family snowplay—so that more people could enjoy Rainier apart from the summer crowds. By discouraging use of Rainier as a destination ski resort, the park service effectively managed the park in winter for the benefit of local people.

No user group at Rainier presented a greater challenge than day hikers. This group included everyone from the casual hiker who ventured half a mile or more from the road to the serious hiker who happily pounded out twenty miles in a day. So extensive were the roads and trails at Mount

Rainier that day hikers could get almost anywhere in the park excluding the upper mountain. The difficulty with day hikers was that they were almost completely unregulated. Short of requiring every park visitor who wanted to set foot off the pavement to obtain a permit (an option that park managers did not rule out for the future), the park service had no way of counting, tracking, or directing information to day hikers. In an era when so much of the effort to protect park resources depended on visitor education and management, day hikers were a frustratingly elusive constituency.

The biggest impact that day hikers had on the environment was almost as old as the park itself. As they rambled about the meadows above Paradise Inn, or strolled to the crest of Sourdough Ridge above Sunrise, or puttered about the shoreline of Mowich Lake, day hikers unwittingly created a spider web of unplanned foot trails through the ground cover. Once initiated, a trail soon became as pronounced as any deliberate trail built by the park service. The soil became compacted, turned to mud or a running stream in the rain, and froze hard when the temperature fell. These overabundant trails had been a concern of park managers since the early years. T. H. Martin, general manager of the Rainier National Park Company, wrote eloquently on the issue to Superintendent Toll in 1919:

> The natural beauty of Paradise Valley is being rapidly destroyed by promiscuous wandering of the great crowds that now visit that locality. There are no established trails or walk-ways, but ugly paths through the grass and flower fields are being worn and the landscape is becoming woefully marred by this ungoverned traffic. . . . The plain truth is that Paradise Valley trails, all of them, are voluntary and without plan. In the old days, when comparatively few people visited the place, very little damage resulted from promiscuous walking. Now that the Valley is visited by thousands daily the damage to grass and flowers is appalling, and the landscape is being rapidly despoiled.[56]

Not until the 1960s, however, did the park service take positive steps to obliterate these excess trails. It began with a pilot project at Sunrise in the late 1960s that included resodding, planting, and laying jute matting on areas of bare ground.[57] Finding some success, the park service extended the effort to backcountry areas in the 1970s. Then in the mid-

1980s, Superintendent Neil Guse Jr. chose to restore Paradise meadows, the most badly scarred subalpine area in the park. By the early 1990s, this effort involved the movement of hundreds of cubic meters of soil, gravel, and rock—much of it by helicopter—and the transplanting of some 29,150 plants, mostly raised in a greenhouse at Tahoma Woods. Despite its impressive results, however, the program was always in peril of being undone by the growing throng of day hikers. Rangers stationed at Paradise observed large numbers of people simply ignoring the "stay on trail" signs or stepping over subtle barriers. Ultimately, meadow restoration depended on training all members of this user group to stay on established trails.[58]

Superintendent Guse was the first to acknowledge that restoring the meadows was a dual problem involving the natural resource and visitor behavior. He conceived a two-pronged effort involving natural resource studies on the one hand and social science research on the other. Meadow restoration would succeed only if the park administration understood and even modified visitor behavior. In theory, the recreational carrying capacity of the meadows could be increased if "noncompliant" visitor behavior could be minimized.[59]

While park botanists and rangers went to work with soil and plants, Guse invited sociologist Darryll Johnson of the Cooperative Park Studies Unit, University of Washington, to initiate a sociological study of "noncompliant use" in the Paradise meadows. Based on the results of visitor questionnaires, Johnson found that noncompliant users were typically from the local four-county area, disproportionately nonwhite or foreign, less than twenty years old, not college educated, and usually traveling in large groups. Field observation, meanwhile, disclosed the relative effectiveness of different types of signs and nontextual cues for influencing visitor behavior. In general, signs were less effective than objects. A strategically placed boulder, for example, could form a subtle impediment to a tempting off-trail vantage point, or it could offer an attractive seat, thereby removing the temptation to sit on a cushion of plants. Most significant, the presence of uniformed personnel reduced the level of noncompliance.[60]

These sociological findings were incorporated into a Paradise Meadow Plan adopted in 1989. The park service made a concerted effort to manage visitor behavior. Rest areas along the trails were delineated by rock borders and surfaced with gravel to match the adjacent trail surface, and log benches and sitting rocks were flown to many of these locations by helicopter. Five new trailhead signs with maps and interpretive messages were installed, and a new museum exhibit was featured in the Paradise visitor center explaining the fragility of the meadow and the cost and complexity of the restoration effort. "Roving interpreters" patrolled the trails, providing friendly nature commentary to some visitors and a visual reminder of park rules to others.[61]

The meadow restoration effort at Paradise was portentous. Through the coordinated work of botanists, sociologists, rangers, and interpreters, the park service had succeeded in bringing about real improvement in the condition of the meadow even in the face of growing visitor use. It had raised the recreational carrying capacity of this most popular section of the national park. Maintenance costs after 1989 were not insignificant—a greenhouse operation at Tahoma Woods, occasional airlifts of soil, and more than 6,000 hours of labor per year—but the positive results were obvious to even the untrained eye. Building upon what it had learned about meadow restoration and visitor behavior at Paradise, the park service initiated studies of day hiker behavior and resource damage in popular backcountry areas such as Spray Park.

Visitors appeared to accept the increased social controls without serious complaint. Still, specialists in visitor management conceded that the use of questionnaires to obtain sociological data on public attitudes and perceptions contained an ominous blind spot. Were parks like Rainier losing patrons who could no longer abide the growing numbers of people or the creeping regimentation in the national park experience? If a portion of the park service's customer base was indeed becoming alienated, and these people were resorting to other places for their enjoyment of nature, the park service had no way of detecting it. These disaffected users simply vanished from the park service's radar screen. It was possible that park policies were in fact contributing to a shift in the user population. Rather than preserving the national park experience, park policies might have been reshaping it in ways that attracted a different set of people.

It is likely that the demographic profile of Mount Rainier visitors will change, and as it does there will be a shift in park values. Visitor surveys made in 1985 and 1990 indicated a trend toward shorter visits. In 1990, an astonishing 63 percent of respondents not only qualified as day users, but they were in the park for less than six hours. Asked what they did in the park, 80 percent of respondents said they drove to view scenery, 51 percent reported day hiking, and 30 percent enjoyed a picnic. Compared to survey results in 1985, a growing proportion of visitors did not use any park facilities and did not leave developed areas during their whirlwind tours of the park. The 1990 survey found that the park "was used predominantly by well-educated, professional men and women who came to the park with family members." In the latter survey, 59 percent of respondents were from the state of Washington and 44 percent came from the four counties surrounding the park.[62]

Viewed in historical perspective, a change in the user population at Mount Rainier would be nothing new. Beginning at the start of the twentieth century, different user groups competed with one another for access and amenities that best served their interests. The park service, acting on its own philosophy as well as reacting to external political pressures, privileged some user groups over others. In the park's early years, distinctions between user groups could be based on race, as when park rangers ejected Indians from Yakima Park, or they could be based on class, as when the park service foiled the Cooperative Campers. More often, however, competition arose between different user groups based on aesthetics. The park service had to mediate between the auto tourist and the hotel sojourner, between the horseback rider and the trail walker, between the downhill and the cross-country skier. Typically there was not much difference in the racial, ethnic, or economic background of these user groups, just sharp differences in values. As the nearby urban population expanded and as public spaces such as Mount Rainier National Park became increasingly precious commodities, even the finest differences in people's aesthetic appreciation of nature posed questions for park management. The Mount Rainier National Park experience today remains as contested as it is sublime.

CHAPTER 8

Conclusion

IT IS OFTEN REMARKED THAT THE NATIONAL PARK SER-
vice mission contains an insoluble tension between preservation and use.
Preserving nature and providing for the public's enjoyment of nature
represent a pair of directives that can never be absolutely compatible
with one another. This classic tension animated management decisions
in Mount Rainier National Park from its founding through the first century of its existence. Although park officials usually made the final decision on issues of preservation and use, park users—particularly the users
represented by Seattle- and Tacoma-based organizations—most often
framed the problem. If management decisions were usually couched in
terms of contemporary philosophical notions of what a national park
should be, those decisions ultimately rested on economic and political
considerations. User organizations such as The Mountaineers, lobby-
ists such as the Federation of Western Outdoor Clubs, stockholders in
the Rainier National Park Company as well as other private investors
in the park, and state politicians all exerted enormous influence. The
National Park Service responded to an agenda fashioned by local interests, and that agenda was heavily oriented toward public use.

As the history of Mount Rainier National Park demonstrates, the
tension in national park policy sprung largely from aesthetic and eco-

nomic issues surrounding public use. Park management dilemmas most often arose from tension between one type of recreational use and another, even tension between competing economic classes or interests. In the early twentieth century, park officials mediated between rival concessions, drove the shabbiest camps out of the park, suppressed game hunting, and invited in the car culture. During the Great Depression, the park service stretched notions of appropriate use to serve larger national objectives of unemployment relief and economic recovery. Amidst postwar prosperity, the national park became the contested terrain of downhill skiing organizations, mountaineers, automobile enthusiasts, and wilderness preservationists. Over the course of the twentieth century, key decisions affecting Mount Rainier National Park included such diverse considerations as the proper role of private capital in a national park, the sanctity of national park resources in the context of economic mobilization for total war, and the importance of national park visitation to the state or regional tourism economy.

Indeed, until fairly recently, the fiercest disagreements over proper development of Mount Rainer National Park took into account the park's natural resources only peripherally. Concession policy, road development, public works in the Depression era, the proper limits of winter use: these were the issues that attracted the most public discourse. It is only in recent decades that some of the most controversial issues of park management began to revolve around the protection of natural resources. Even as park officials took measures to restore meadows and to control human waste deposits on the upper mountain, for example, these efforts remained fundamentally tied to the aesthetics of certain kinds of public use.

To the individual park user it might seem that the national park hosts—the park service and to a lesser degree the concessions—were chiefly responsible for shaping a "national park experience." Yet viewed en masse, the park users were hardly passive participants in the process of making the national park a unique place to visit. The most perceptive park users had always understood this; they recognized that their own individual behavior, and the cumulative effect of other people like them, had everything to do with making the national park what it was.

The national park idea is at once ennobling and imbued with a disquieting sense of loss. Our urge to preserve pieces of wild nature springs directly from our national experience of westward expansion. Anxious about the loss of the frontier at the close of the nineteenth century, Americans fashioned a new view of wild nature, remaking North American wilderness into an indispensable and dwindling commodity. National parks were one answer to a vanishing frontier. They were monuments to our wilderness heritage. National parks became our relics, our ancient ruins. They were intrinsically nostalgic places.

Today, at the beginning of a new century, we face a recurrence of this cultural anxiety in the prospect of our national parks becoming so inundated with people that the national park experience is changed beyond recognition. Reflecting that concern for the national park system as a whole, the dominant public-use issue in Mount Rainier National Park in the foreseeable future will be how to contend with 2 million or more visitors annually while preserving the "national park experience."

The pattern of visitor use in Mount Rainier National Park has changed in remarkable ways over the past one hundred years. Visitor numbers have grown from an estimated 2,000 in 1899 to more than 2 million in the 1990s, a thousandfold increase. Automobile use has increased by an even greater percentage. Moreover, private vehicles have grown larger in size. Probably more people visit the park in gargantuan recreational vehicles today than ever came by bus or train in years past. Meanwhile, average visitor stays have grown shorter and shorter. Various visitor activities have fallen in and out of favor, from golf to mineral baths to downhill skiing. Obviously the "national park experience" is a malleable and evolutionary concept.

In one important respect, the pattern of visitor use at Mount Rainier has remained consistent. Visitor use began as a predominantly local phenomenon, and it appears to be continuing in that vein.

The challenge for park managers in the next century will lie in their ability to define preservation for the public. As park managers search for that elusive balance between preservation and use, they will need to articulate what the public wants its national parks to be, and they will need to direct that message to the individual users to an ever increasing degree.

Notes

I A TALE OF TWO CITIES

1. George Vancouver, *A Voyage of Discovery to the North Pacific Ocean and Round the World 1791–1795,* vol. 2, ed. W. Kaye Lamb (London: Hakluyt Society, 1984), 541–43, 551.

2. Leo Marx, *The Machine in the Garden* (New York: Oxford University Press, 1964), 89; Vancouver, *A Voyage of Discovery,* 513.

3. Earl Pomeroy, *In Search of the Golden West: The Tourist in Western America* (New York: Alfred A. Knopf, 1957), 18.

4. Gordon B. Dodds, *The American Northwest: A History of Oregon and Washington* (Arlington Heights, Ill.: Forum Press, 1986), 138.

5. Seattle Chamber of Commerce, *Seattle Illustrated* (Seattle: Baldwin, Calcutt, and Blakely, 1890), 12; *Washington, the Evergreen State, and Seattle, Its Metropolis* (Seattle: Crawford and Conover, 1890), 12; *Seattle, Washington, U.S.A.* (Seattle: Eshelman, Llewellyn, and Company, 1891), 12; J. W. Dodge, *Washington: The Sound, State, and Its Chief City, Seattle* (Seattle: Crawford and Conover, 1890); O. M. Moore, *Washington Illustrated, Including Views of Puget Sound Country and Seattle, Gateway to the Orient with Glimpses of Alaska* (Seattle: Metropolitan Press, 1901).

6. *Seattle and the Pacific Northwest* (Seattle: n.p., 1909), n.p.

7. Genevieve E. McCoy, "'Call It Mount Tacoma': A History of the Controversy over the Name of Mount Rainier," M.A.thesis, University of Wash-

ington, 1984; Arthur D. Martinson, "Mount Rainier or Mount Tacoma? The Controversy That Refused to Die," *Columbia: The Magazine of Northwest History* 3, no.2 (Summer 1989), 10–16; Murray Morgan, *Puget's Sound: A Narrative of Early Tacoma and the Southern Sound* (Seattle: University of Washington Press, 1979), 293–96.

8. William R. Catton Jr., "The Mountain with the Wrong Name," *Etc.: A Review of General Semantics* 11, no.4 (Summer 1954): 299. Some Tacomans, for their part, claimed that Seattle residents were beholden to the name "Rainier" because they wanted to support the Rainier Brewing Company.

9. Martinson, "Mount Rainier or Mount Tacoma?" 16.

10. Dee Molenaar, *The Challenge of Rainier* (Seattle: Seattle Mountaineers, 1971); Aubrey L. Haines, *Mountain Fever: Historic Conquests of Rainier* (Portland: Oregon Historical Society, 1962).

11. *Seattle Post-Intelligencer*, July 25, 1894.

12. Erwin N. Thompson, *Mount Rainier National Park, Washington, Historic Resource Study* (Washington, D.C.: National Park Service, 1981), 61.

13. Haines, *Mountain Fever*, 158–59.

14. *Tacoma Daily Ledger*, September 3, 1892.

15. Quoted in James Muhn, "Early Administration of the Forest Reserve Act: Interior Department and General Land Office Policies, 1891–1897," *Origins of the National Forests: A Centennial Symposium*, ed. Harold K. Steen (Durham, N.C.: Forest History Society, 1992), 260.

16. Cyrus A. Mosier, Special Agent, to Commissioner of General Land Office, November 14, 1891, National Archives II (NA II), Record Group 49— Records of the General Land Office (RG 49), Division "R," National Forest Files, Gifford Pinchot National Forest, Box 53A. Emphasis in original.

17. Preamble and Resolutions Relative to Reservation of Public Lands in the State of Washington, enclosed with Assistant Secretary, Seattle Chamber of Commerce, to Cyrus A. Mosier, Special Agent, December 7, 1892, and Commercial Club of Tacoma to President Benjamin Harrison, January 26, 1893, NA II, RG 49, Division "R," National Forest Files, Gifford Pinchot National Forest, Box 53A; Secretary of the Interior John Noble to President Benjamin Harrison, February 17, 1893, National Archives Microfilm Publication 620— Letters Sent by the Land & Railroad Division of the Office of the Secretary of the Interior, 1849–1904, Roll 122, 236–37.

18. The name Pacific Forest Reserve was chosen to avoid the controversy

over the name of Mount Rainier. "Forest reserve" was the official designation of national forests until 1905, when the administration of the forests was transferred from the General Land Office to the USDA Forest Service and these areas were redesignated "national forests."

19. A fine, recent study of this distinctive cultural environment is Matthew W. Klingle's "Urban by Nature: An Environmental History of Seattle, 1880–1970," Ph.D. dissertation, University of Washington, 2001.

2 THE CAMPAIGN TO ESTABLISH MOUNT RAINIER NATIONAL PARK

1. Bailey Willis was the son of poet Nathaniel Parker Willis. He was schooled in Germany and at Columbia University. See the essay by Aaron C. Waters in *Dictionary of Scientific Biography*, vol. 14, edited by Charles Coulston Gillespie (New York: Charles Scribners Sons), 402–3. It is likely that Willis first got the idea ten years earlier, in 1883, when he was invited to join a large party of American and foreign dignitaries in celebrating the completion of the Northern Pacific Railroad. After the ceremony, the Northern Pacific treated some of the party to a Yellowstone trip and others to a sightseeing tour of the Pacific Northwest. Willis chose the latter. Taking an excursion train out of Tacoma, he led a small group into the Carbon River high country; the group included the distinguished British writer and politician James Bryce and the German geologist Karl von Zittel. Bryce and Zittel wrote afterward of their hope "that the suggestion will at no distant date be made to Congress that Mount Rainier should, like the Yosemite Valley and the geyser region of the Upper Yellowstone, be reserved by the Federal Government and treated as a national park."

2. U.S. Congress, Senate, *Memorial from the Geological Society of America Favoring the Establishment of a National Park in the State of Washington*, 53rd Cong., 2nd sess., 1894, Misc. Doc. 247.

3. Joseph L. Sax, *Mountains Without Handrails: Reflections on the National Parks* (Ann Arbor: University of Michigan Press, 1980).

4. Alfred Runte, *National Parks: The American Experience* (Lincoln: University of Nebraska Press, 1979).

5. Theodore Winthrop, *Canoe and Saddle* (Portland, Ore.: n.p., first published in 1863), 80–82. See, for example, the respectful reference to Winthrop in John P. Hartman, "Creation of Mount Rainier National Park," address delivered at the

37th Annual Convention of the Washington Good Roads Association, September 27–28, 1935, no pagination, copy available at University of Washington Libraries, Special Collections and Preservation Division.

6. P. B. Van Trump, "Mount Tahoma," *Sierra Club Bulletin* 1, no. 4 (May 1894): 121.

7. Israel C. Russell, "Impressions of Mount Rainier," *Scribner's Magazine* 22, no. 2 (August 1897): 176; Carl Snyder, "Our New National Wonderland," *Review of Reviews* 9, no. 2 (February 1894): 171; *Congressional Record*, 53rd Cong., 2d sess., 1894, vol. 26, pt. 8, 7878.

8. *Memorial from the Geological Society of America*, 2–3.

9. Van Trump, "Mount Tahoma," p. 111; Snyder, "Our New National Wonderland," 166.

10. *Congressional Record*, 53rd Cong., 2d sess., 1894, vol. 26, pt. 8, 7878.

11. Edward S. Ingraham, *The Pacific Forest Reserve and Mt. Rainier: A Souvenir* (Seattle: Calvert Company, 1895), 4.

12. Snyder, "Our New National Wonderland," 171; Russell, "Impressions of Mount Rainier," 176.

13. *Tacoma Daily Ledger*, September 8, 1893, and September 14, 1893. Years later, John P. Hartman provided an eyewitness account of an incident of vandalism in Paradise Park in 1895: "A considerable party, probably fifty, were encamped on the ground about where the hotel stands, while a party of four young men had taken up their site to the east of Alta Vista, and on the west bank of Paradise River. On the third evening we observed that these men had a considerable camp fire under one of the tall pines, probably 125 feet high, making a perfect cone, with the lower limbs coming to within about ten feet of the ground. We watched the fire and became alarmed. We could see the men throwing on more and more dry wood. Finally the object of the vandal was accomplished, because the rather oily, dry needles ignited and in a short time the whole wonderful tree was ablaze, making a fiery pillar that ascended probably 150 feet above the tree. Of course, this was awe-inspiring and seemed greatly to please the vandals, but the rest of us, looking on, thought it was an unmitigated wrong that ought to be punished." John P. Hartman, "Creation of Mount Rainier National Park."

14. The two best statements of the problem are E. S. Ingraham, "It Rises Above All," *Seattle Post-Intelligencer*, August 12, 1894; and P. B. Van Trump, "Mount Tacoma Vandals," *Tacoma Daily Ledger*, September 14, 1893.

15. *Seattle Post-Intelligencer*, August 12, 1894; *Tacoma Daily Ledger*, September 14, 1893, and September 8, 1893.

16. Ibid., September 9, 1893, and September 3, 1893.

17. Snyder, "Our New National Wonderland," 171.

18. *Congressional Record*, 53rd Cong., 2d sess., 1894, vol. 26, pt. 8, 7878.

19. Ibid.

20. *Congressional Record*, 53rd Cong., 2d sess., 1893, vol. 26, pt. 1, 154; Snyder, "Our New National Wonderland," 164; *Congressional Record*, 53rd Cong., 2d sess., 1894, vol. 26, pt. 1, 498.

21. S. 1250, "A Bill to set apart certain lands, now known as Pacific forest reserve, as a public park, to be known as the Washington National Park"; John Ise, *Our National Park Policy: A Critical History* (Baltimore: Johns Hopkins University Press, 1961), 45.

22. *Congressional Record*, 53rd Cong., 2d sess., 1894, vol. 26, pt. 8, 7877–78.

23. Robert McIntyre, "A Short History of Mount Rainier National Park," mimeograph report prepared for the National Park Service, 1952, 87. The eastern boundary left the Cascade Crest entirely outside the park.

24. For example, "Elliot Denies Humphrey Charge," June 4, 1913, unidentified newspaper clipping in Minnesota Historical Society (MHS), Northern Pacific Railroad Company Papers, President Series, President's Subject Files, File 60 (1); Charles Donnelly, *The Facts about the Northern Pacific Land Grant*, Northern Pacific Railway Company, n.d., 12.

25. Lute Pease, "The Way of the Land Transgression," *Pacific Monthly* 18, no. 4 (October 1907): 488; S. A. D. Puter and Horace Stevens, *Looters of the Public Domain* (Portland, Ore.: n.p., 1908), 371. Contemporary charges of corruption were completely unsubstantiated. While there is a whiff of bribery in the company's records on this matter, the evidence is only fragmentary. Beginning in 1896, company officials took a keen interest in the legislation. The company's land commissioner, W. H. Phipps, advised the president, Edwin W. Winter, that it was "very desirable that the bill as reported to the House, be passed," and in another letter remarked, "I do not think the Northern Pacific ought to be prominent in advocating the passage of the bill, but the company has friends." While Phipps met with Doolittle in Tacoma, Winter placed the bill in the right "channel" in Washington, D.C., probably with a sympathetic member of the Committee on Public Lands. When Congress eventually passed the bill, one company official stated, "The company thought it achieved a great

success in securing the passage of the act in question, which gives it property of large value in place of something of no value." Though this evidence is fragmentary, it seems indisputable that the Northern Pacific was involved in the legislative process contrary to what it always maintained afterward. Edwin W. Winters (president) to W. H. Phipps (land commissioner), October 12, 1896, Phipps to Winters, November 7, 1896, and C. W. Bunn to W. J. Curtis, June 7, 1899, MHS, Northern Pacific Railroad Company Papers, President, President's subject files, File 60 (1).

26. Hartman, "Creation of Mount Rainier National Park," n.p.

27. U.S. Congress, House, *Washington National Park*, 54th Cong., 1st sess., 1896, H. Rept. 1699.

28. Barry Mackintosh, *The National Parks: Shaping the System* (Washington, D.C.: National Park Service, 1985), 11.

29. John Muir, "The National Parks and Forest Reservations," *Harper's Weekly* 41, no. 2111 (June 5, 1897): 563–67; John Muir, "The Wild Parks and Forest Reservations of the West," *Atlantic Monthly* 81, no. 488 (January 1898): 15–28; Hartman, "Creation of Mount Rainier National Park," n.p.

30. *Congressional Record*, 54th Cong., 1st sess., 1896, vol. 28, pt. 7, 6445; *Congressional Record*, 54th Cong., 2d sess., 1897, vol. 29, pt. 2, 1918, and pt. 3, 2717; *Congressional Record*, 55th Cong., 1st sess., 1897, vol. 30, pt. 1, 41; *Congressional Record*, 55th Cong., 2d sess., 1897–98, vol. 31, pt. 1, 21, 192, and pt. 3, 2792, and pt. 6, 5346, 5633, 5696.

31. Hartman, "Creation of Mount Rainier National Park," n.p.

32. *Congressional Record*, 55th Cong, 3rd sess., 1899, vol. 32, pt. 3, 2354, 2663, 2667, 2631, 2697, 2770, 2787.

3 THE NEW PLEASURING GROUND (1900–1915)

1. Chester Thorne to Secretary of the Interior, April 8, 1907, National Archives (NA), Record Group 79—Records of the National Park Service (RG 79), Entry 1—Records of the Secretary of the Interior, Box 38.

2. Mount Rainier National Park Act of March, 2, 1899, 30 Stat., 993.

3. Ada Woodruff Anderson, "To the Summit of Mt. Rainier," *Outing* 38, no. 4 (July 1901): 391.

4. Henry Carter and Walter A. Ashford to Secretary of the Interior, September 11, 1900, NA, RG 79, Entry 1—Records of the Secretary of the Interior,

Box 38. These men claimed that 520 tourists entered Paradise Park in 1900. The Acting Superintendent's Annual Report for 1904 confirmed 563 visits to the park for that year and suggested the actual number was much greater. Elcaine Longmire cut the trail to Indian Henry's Hunting Ground for prospecting purposes in 1902, according to E. T. Allen (forest inspector) to Secretary of the Interior, March 11, 1903, NA, RG 79, Entry 1—Records of the Secretary of the Interior, Box 38.

5. G. F. Allen to Secretary of the Interior, July 17, 1905, NA, RG 79, Entry 1—Records of the Secretary of the Interior, Box 38.

6. Henry S. Hayes to Senator A. G. Foster, December 16, 1899; Henry Carter and Walter A. Ashford to Secretary of the Interior Ethan A. Hitchcock, September 11, 1900; Representative Francis W. Cushman to Hitchcock, January 7, 1900; Joseph Stampfler to Hitchcock, February 7, 1901; D. B. Sheller to General Land Office Commissioner Binger Hermann, July 9, 1902; and Foster to Hitchcock, October 18, 1900, NA, RG 79, Entry 1—Records of the Secretary of the Interior, Box 38.

7. General Land Office Commissioner Binger Hermann to Secretary of the Interior Ethan A. Hitchcock, July 25, 1902; Ranger G. F. Allen to Forest Superintendent D. B. Sheller, July 8, 1902; and Forest Inspector E. T. Allen to Hitchcock, March 11, 1903, NA, RG 79, Entry 1—Records of the Secretary of the Interior, Box 38.

8. Snyder, "Our New National Wonderland," 171.

9. U.S. Congress, House, *Road into Mount Rainier National Park*, 58th Cong., 2nd sess., 1904, H. Doc. 631, 1.

10. A biographical abstract of Ricksecker can be found in Mount Rainier National Archives (MORA), Eugene Ricksecker Papers, File H18; James J. Flink, *America Adopts the Automobile, 1895–1910* (Cambridge, Mass.: MIT Press, 1970), 202–9; for a fuller treatment of Ricksecker's ideas and influence, see David B. Louter, "Windshield Wilderness: The Automobile and the Meaning of National Parks in Washington State," Ph.D. dissertation, University of Washington, 2000.

11. Eugene Ricksecker to John A. Millis, May 14, 1904, MORA, Eugene Ricksecker Papers, File H18.

12. Department of the Interior, *Annual Report of the Secretary of the Interior*, 1908, (Washington, D.C.: Government Printing Office, 1908), 470; hereafter cited as *Annual Report of the Secretary of the Interior* [year]. Nisqually Glacier has since receded from this point, but in 1908 the terminus of the glacier was

a major attraction. Ricksecker described it romantically: "From the river cross-ing the foot of the glacier looms up, a mass of delicate tinted snow capped ice, about 1,000 feet distant. A few minutes walk brings one within the pale of its icy breath and touch of its coldness. Have a care, though, for a watch-ful eye is necessary to dodge the boulders hurled down from its top by this old giant in wrathful indignation against intrusion." Eugene Ricksecker to John A. Millis, May 14, 1904, MORA, Eugene Ricksecker Papers, File H18.

13. *Annual Report of the Secretary of the Interior*, 1910, 695, and 1915, 975. Rick-secker's other accomplishments included the rim road in Crater Lake National Park and sections of road on the Oregon Coast.

14. McIntyre, "A Short History of Mount Rainier National Park," 187.

15. Asahel Curtis to G. F. Allen, September 25, 1908, University of Wash-ington Libraries, Special Collections and Preservation Division (UW), Asahel Curtis Papers, Box 1, Folder 4; Asahel Curtis to Co. Commissioners Pierce County, April 23, 1909, UW, Asahel Curtis Papers, Box 1, Folder 8.

16. G. F. Allen to A. Curtis, August 19, 1908, A. Curtis to G. F. Allen, Sep-tember 25, 1908, A. Curtis to Mr. Gleason, December 1, 1908, A. Curtis to Pierce County Commissioners, April 23, 1909, UW, Asahel Curtis Papers, Box 1, Fold-ers 3, 4, 6, 8; Asahel Curtis to R. A. Ballinger, July 13, 1909, UW, Asahel Curtis Papers, Box 1, Folder 11.

17. John H. Williams to Asahel Curtis, August 27, 1911, UW, Asahel Curtis Papers, Box 1, Folder 17; Asahel Curtis to Tacoma Eastern R.R. Co., Septem-ber 16, 1909, UW, Asahel Curtis Papers, Box 1, Folder 14; untitled, undated report on the 1909 outing of The Mountaineers, UW, Asahel Curtis Papers, Box 1, Folder 12.

18. Thompson, *Mount Rainier National Park*, 53–54.

19. Walter L. Fisher to Asahel Curtis, November 9, 1911, UW, Asahel Curtis Papers, Box 1, Folder 17.

20. Asahel Curtis to Walter L. Fisher, March 18, 1912, UW, Asahel Curtis Papers, Box 1, Folder 20.

21. Memorandum, March 7, 1912, NA, RG 79, Entry 6—Central Files, Box 135, File 12–7–2 on Roads, Trails, and Bridges.

22. Walter L. Fisher to T. H. Martin, May 8, 1912, NA, RG 79, Central Files, Box 135, File 12–7–2 on Roads, Trails, and Bridges.

23. Report of Samuel C. Lancaster, 1913, copy available at UW, Special Col-lections and Preservation Division.

24. Lancaster Report.

25. Mount Rainier National Park Act of March 2, 1899, 30 Stat., 993.

26. *Tacoma Daily Ledger*, September 8, 1893.

27. A. G. Foster (Senator) to Elihu Root (Secretary of War), July 19, 1901, NA, RG 79, Entry 1—Records of the Secretary of the Interior, Box 38; U.S. Congress, Senate, *Trespassing on Mount Rainier National Park, Washington*, 57th Cong., 1st sess., 1902, S. Rept. 729, 1–3; R. A. Ballinger (Secretary of the Interior) to N. R. Sibley (Seattle Commercial Club), January 11, 1910, NA, RG 79, Entry 6—Central Files, Box 139, File Troops for the Park.

28. Harold K. Steen, *The U.S. Forest Service: A History* (Seattle: University of Washington Press, 1976), 40. Henry Carter and Walter A. Ashford to Fitch & Harris, October 26, 1900, NA, RG 79, Entry 1—Records of the Secretary of the Interior, Box 38. The term *ranger* came from Bernhard E. Fernow, first chief of the Division of Forestry. As early as November 1898, the commissioner of the General Land Office informed the governor of Washington that Forest Supervisor F. C. Mathewson had a "force of Forest Rangers under his direction" who were prepared to cooperate with state officials in enforcing state forestry and fish and game laws. Binger Hermann to Governor of Washington, November 12, 1898, Olympia State Archives, Governor John Rogers Papers, Incoming Correspondence (1898), Box 2c-1-9.

29. C. Frank Brockman, *The Story of Mount Rainier National Park* (Longmire, Wash.: National Park Service, 1940), 56; E. T. Allen to Secretary of the Interior, March 11, 1903, NA, RG 79, Entry 1—Records of the Secretary of the Interior, Box 38; Grenville F. Allen to D. B. Sheller (Forest Superintendent of the State of Washington), July 8, 1902, NA, RG 79, Entry 1—Records of the Secretary of the Interior, Box 38.

30. Grenville F. Allen to D. B. Sheller (Forest Superintendent of the State of Washington), July 8, 1902, NA, RG 79, Entry 1—Records of the Secretary of the Interior, Box 38; W. A. Richards (commissioner) to Secretary of the Interior, April 29, 1903, NA, RG 79, Entry 1—Records of the Secretary of the Interior, Box 38.

31. Superintendent's Annual Report in *Annual Report of the Secretary of the Interior*, 1908, 469.

32. Ibid., 1904, 439, and 1908, 468. It was probably a good indication of Allen's priorities that the first two trails built primarily for their scenic value to tourists were completed after his tenure in 1910. These were the trails to Eagle Peak

and Rampart Ridge, both commencing at Longmire. See Superintendent's Annual Report in *Annual Report of the Secretary of the Interior*, 1910, 507.

33. William E. Colby to E. A. Hitchcock, March 15, 1905; G. F. Allen to William E. Colby, April 15, 1905; and G. F. Allen to Secretary of the Interior, August 16, 1905, and March 25, 1906, NA, RG 79, Entry 1—Records of the Secretary of the Interior, Box 38. See also Lisa Mighetto, "The Expedition of 1905: Two Hundred Climbers Tackle Mt. Rainier," *Columbia: The Magazine of Northwest History* 4, no. 3 (Fall 1990): 32–36.

34. Park superintendents maintained detailed statistics on visitation, including visitor numbers, methods of transportation, routes of access, length of stays, and visitor origins. On the proportion of use by car, see the superintendents' reports in *Annual Report of the Secretary of the Interior*, 1908, 471, and Department of the Interior, *Report of the Director of the National Park Service*, 1929, 108 (hereafter cited as *Report of the Director of the National Park Service* [year]).

35. *Annual Report of the Secretary of the Interior*, 1906, 679; 1908, 471; and 1909, 466. Also see Louter, "Windshield Wilderness," 26–38. Louter finds that concerns about the automobile tended toward aesthetic and philosophical considerations.

36. A. Woodruff McCully, "The Rainier Forest Reserve," *Overland Monthly* 55 (June 1910): 553; *Annual Report of the Secretary of the Interior*, 1915, 975; "Motoring Rules and Regulations in the National Parks," *Outing* 72 (August 1918): 334–35.

37. McIntyre, "A Short History of Mount Rainier National Park," 124; also see correspondence and permits in MORA, Concessions, Leases and Privileges, J. S. Reese.

38. Superintendent's Annual Report in *Annual Report of the Secretary of the Interior*, 1911, 624, 630.

39. McIntyre, "A Short History of Mount Rainier National Park," 122.

40. McCully, "The Rainier Forest Reserve," 554.

41. Virinda Longmire to Secretary of the Interior, August 22, 1902; G. F. Allen to Secretary of the Interior, July 2, 1905; Robert Longmire to Secretary of the Interior, July 6, 1905; Francis W. Cushman to Secretary of the Interior, July 31, 1905; G. F. Allen to Fred W. Stocking (acting GLO commissioner), April 23, 1906; E. A. Hitchcock (secretary of the Interior) to GLO commissioner, December 12, 1906; and J. R. Garfield (secretary of the Interior) to GLO com-

missioner, March 28, 1907, NA, RG 79, Entry 1—Records of the Secretary of the Interior, Box 38.

42. Harry M. Cunningham to G. F. Allen, January 9, 1908, MORA, L3025 Inholdings.

43. Superintendent's Annual Report in *Annual Report of the Secretary of the Interior*, 1908, 478.

44. Ibid., 1909, 466.

45. McIntyre, "A Short History of Mount Rainier National Park," 123.

46. Quoted in Edward S. Hall to George W. Hibbard, May 31, 1912, MORA, Concessions, Leases and Privileges, Tacoma Eastern Railroad Company.

47. Specifications were given in a proposed permit form, enclosed with Ethan Allen to Secretary of the Interior, December 8, 1913, MORA, Concessions, Folder George B. Hall. Also see Ethan Allen to Secretary of the Interior, October 10, 1914, MORA, Concessions, Folder George B. Hall.

48. George W. Hibbard to Edward S. Hall, May 28, 1912, MORA, Concessions, Leases and Privileges, Tacoma Eastern Railroad Company; Superintendent's Annual Report in *Annual Report of the Secretary of the Interior*, 1911, 630.

49. Section 5, a brief two lines appended to the end of the bill, was included at the insistence of local people, including James Longmire, in the late 1890s. Hartman, "The Creation of Mount Rainier National Park."

50. Superintendent's Annual Report in *Annual Report of the Secretary of the Interior*, 1907, 581; 1908, 472; and 1907, 582.

51. Eugene Ricksecker to Secretary of the Interior James R. Garfield, October 18, 1907, MORA, Eugene Ricksecker Papers, File H18, and Superintendent's Annual Report in *Annual Report of the Secretary of the Interior*, 1907, 582. The law provided that "hereafter the location of mining claims under the mineral land laws of the United States is prohibited within the area of the Mt. Rainier National Park in the State of Washington; Provided, however, that this provision shall not affect existing rights heretofore acquired in good faith under the mineral land laws of the United States to any mining location or locations in said Mt. Rainier National Park" (Act Making appropriations for sundry civil expenses of the Government for the fiscal year ending June thirtieth, nineteen hundred and nine, and for other purposes, May 27, 1908, 35 Stat. 365).

52. Superintendent's Annual Report in *Annual Report of the Secretary of the Interior*, 1906, 679.

53. G. F. Allen to Secretary of the Interior, November 10, 1908, and Assistant Secretary Frank Pierce to Allen, November 27, 1908, NA, RG 79, Entry 6—Central Files, Box 139, File 12–7–19, Part 2.

54. G. F. Allen to Secretary of the Interior, May 17, 1909; Clement S. Ucker to Mr. Carr, September 8, 1909; and G. F. Allen to Secretary of the Interior, December 27, 1909, NA, RG 79, Entry 6—Central Files, Box 139, File 12–7–19, Part 2.

55. L. A. Nelson and J. A. McCormick to Board of Directors, The Mountaineers, May 20, 1910, NA, RG 79, Entry 6—Central Files, Box 139, File 12–7–19, Part 2.

56. Eugene Ricksecker to C. W. Kutz, May 14, 1910, NA, RG 79, Entry 6—Central Files, Box 139, File 12–7–19, Part 2.

57. Edward W. Dixon to Secretary of the Interior, June 28, 1910; Secretary of the Interior to Clement S. Ucker, September 13, 1910, NA, RG 79, Entry 6—Central Files, Box 139, File 12–7–19, Part 2.

58. Quoted in Arthur D. Martinson, "Mount Rainier National Park: First Years," *Forest History* 10, no. 3 (October 1966): 27–28. The superintendent's annual reports also minimize this threat to the park. For example, G. F. Allen wrote in 1908: "The summit of the Cascades beyond the park is an open country and easily traveled, and is utilized for sheep pasturage. This stock is grazed under permit from the Department of Agriculture and the number and location of the bands are known to the rangers. There is no difficulty in keeping the sheep from crossing the park line." Superintendent's Annual Report in *Annual Report of the Secretary of the Interior*, 1908, 468.

59. Park superintendents made rough estimates of wildlife populations from year to year, and reported steady increases for most game species after about 1910. The increases were attributed to several factors: the suppression of poaching, the elimination of several cougars from the park, and two mild winters in 1913–14 and 1914–15. By the end of the era, deer were considered to be abundant and mountain goats were making a very encouraging comeback. The reappearance of a band of goats in Van Trump Park, a few miles above Christine Falls on the road to Paradise, in 1914, suggested that the goats had been driven out of the area by the noise of dynamite explosions some six years earlier rather than slaughtered by hunters as previously feared. Probably the mountain goats were acclimating to the growing human presence in the area. Superintendent's Annual Report in *Annual Report of the Secretary of the Interior*, 1915, 966.

60. Ibid., 1904, 440, and 1908, 468.

61. Karl Jacoby, *Crimes Against Nature: Squatters, Poachers, Thieves, and the Hidden History of American Conservation* (Berkeley: University of California Press, 2001).

62. Superintendent's Annual Report in *Annual Report of the Secretary of the Interior*, 1909, 465, and 1914, 780. Also see G. F. Allen to the Secretary of the Interior, March 9, 1909, NA, RG 79, Entry 6—Central Files, Box 138, File 12–7–4, Rules and Regulations.

63. Thomas E. O'Farrell to D. L. Reaburn, July 29, 1915; D. L. Reaburn to Secretary of the Interior, August 26, 1915; and Acting Assistant Secretary E. J. Ayers to Reaburn, August 9, 1915, NA, RG 79, Central Files, Box 140, File Wild Animals.

64. Michael F. Turek and Robert H. Keller Jr., "Sluskin: Yakima Guide to Mount Rainier," *Columbia: The Magazine of Northwest History* 5, no. 1 (Spring 1991): 2. On the National Park Service's policies toward Indians in other national parks in this era, see Robert H. Keller Jr. and Michael F. Turek, *American Indians and National Parks* (Tucson: University of Arizona Press, 1998), and Mark David Spence, *Dispossessing the Wilderness: Indian Removal and the Making of the National Parks* (New York: Oxford University Press, 1999).

65. Telegram, Reaburn to Secretary of the Interior, September 1, 1915, NA, RG 79, Central Files, Box 140, File Wild Animals.

66. Bo Sweeney to Assistant Secretary, September 2, 1915, NA, RG 79, Central Files, Box 140, File Wild Animals.

67. Preston C. West to Secretary of the Interior, September 23, 1915, NA, Record Group 48—Records of the Secretary of the Interior (RG 48), Entry 749, Central Classified Files, Box 1991, File 12–7, Part 1, Parks, Reservations and Antiquities.

68. L. E. Darwin to G. F. Allen, October 9, 1916; Ira D. Light (Game Warden) to Secretary of the Interior Franklin K. Lane, February 5, 1917; and J. J. Cotter to Ira D. Light, February 15, 1917, NA, RG 79, Central Files, Box 140, File Wild Animals 12–7–5.

69. J. J. Cotter to Files, no date, and Telegram, Robert Marshall to D. L. Reaburn, October 28, 1916, NA, RG 79, Central Files, Box 140, File Wild Animals 12–7–5.

70. *Tacoma Ledger*, October 6, 1917.

71. Horace M. Albright to Cato Sells (Commissioner of Indian Affairs), October 18, 1917; E. B. Meritt (Assistant Commissioner of Indian Affairs) to Albright, November 2, 1917; Meritt to Albright, November 23, 1917; Albright

to Meritt, November 24, 1917; and Albright to D. L. Reaburn, November 24, 1917, NA, RG 79, Central Files, Box 140, File Wild Animals 12–7–5.

4 STEVE MATHER AND THE RAINIER NATIONAL PARK COMPANY (1915–1930)

1. Robert Shankland, *Steve Mather of the National Parks* (New York: Alfred A. Knopf, 1951), 7.

2. Ise, *Our National Park Policy*, 193.

3. Yard quoted in Ise, *Our National Park Policy*, 193.

4. Shankland, *Steve Mather of the National Parks*, 78.

5. Anonymous, "A History of the Organization, Operation, Activities, and Aspirations of the Rainier National Park Company, Incorporated," undated, unpaginated manuscript given to Arthur D. Martinson by Paul H. Sceva and filed in the Nisqually Room of Pacific Lutheran University, Tacoma. Hereafter cited as "A History of the Rainier National Park Company" [year]. Note: this 153–page manuscript is presented in the form of narrative annual reports, but it appears to have been compiled and written by one author in the early 1960s. The original sources on which it is based have not been found.

6. These terms are taken from Sax, *Mountains Without Handrails*, 108.

7. *Report of the Director of the National Park Service*, 1925, 1–2.

8. Shankland, *Steve Mather of the National Parks*, 120–21.

9. "History of the Rainier National Park Company," 1919.

10. Ibid., 1916; R. B. Marshall to D. L. Reaburn, April 26, 1916, MORA, Concessions, File 920–02 Rainier National Park Company contracts. The RNPC's protection from competition was in the form of an understanding. It was actually written into the contract when the contract was renewed in 1928.

11. "History of the Rainier National Park Company," 1916.

12. T. H. Martin to D. L. Reaburn, November 27, 1917, MORA, File D34 Buildings; "History of the Rainier National Park Company," 1916.

13. Ibid., 1918.

14. Ibid., 1919, 1920; *Report of the Director of the National Park Service*, 1920, 130.

15. "History of the Rainier National Park Company," 1916, 1917; D. L. Reaburn to Horace M. Albright, September 19, 1918, MORA, Concessions, Cooperative Campers of the Pacific Northwest.

16. James Hughes to Chester Thorne, June 26, 1916, MORA, File D34 Buildings; "History of the Rainier National Park Company," 1916, 1918.

17. Superintendent to Director, July 5, 1918, MORA, File H2615 Superintendent's Monthly Reports; "History of the Rainier National Park Company," 1918; *Report of the Director of the National Park Service*, 1920, 130.

18. "History of the Rainier National Park Company," 1922.

19. *Report of the Director of the National Park Service*, 1921, 222.

20. Arno B. Cammerer to George W. McCoy (Hygienic Lab), September 15, 1920; A. M. Stimson (Public Health Service) to Cammerer, September 29, 1920; McCoy to Cammerer, March 21, 1921; Cammerer to Dr. William P. Parks (Superintendent, Hot Springs Reservation), March 26, 1921; Parks to Director, April 8, 1921; Cammerer to W. H. Peters, April 12, 1921; Peters to Director, November 4, 1921, NA, RG 79, Entry 6—Central Files, Box 140, File Water Analysis 12–7, Part 1.

21. Constitution and By Laws, no date, MORA, Concessions, File Cooperative Campers of the Pacific Northwest.

22. "Mount Rainier National Park Co-Operative Camps Run at Cost," July 10, 1917, MORA, Concessions, File Cooperative Campers of the Pacific Northwest.

23. Anna Louise Strong, Plans made by Camp Seattle for camps on Rainier, 1917, UW, Irving M. Clark Papers; "Mount Rainier National Park Co-Operative Camps Run at Cost," July 10, 1917, MORA, Concessions, File Cooperative Campers of the Pacific Northwest.

24. Ibid. In her autobiography, *I Change Worlds: The Remaking of an American* (Seattle: Seal Press, 1935), Strong describes her work for the Cooperative Campers as a salve for her deep disappointment in President Woodrow Wilson's decision to lead the United States into World War I: "I turned like a wounded beast to the hills for shelter. Like the pioneers of old I fled to the simpler wilderness from the problems of human society that I could not face. Week after week on the high slopes of Rainier I was busy with problems of pack-trains, commissary, cooking, hikes. Eight or ten hours a day I led parties on the glaciers. Few newspapers reached me; I did not read them. I shrank from every mention of the war. I drugged myself with twenty-four-hour climbs. It was the end of youth, the end of belief, the end of 'our America.' I could not face the ruins of my world."

25. Stephen Mather to D. L. Reaburn, December 21, 1917, MORA, Concessions, File Cooperative Campers of the Pacific Northwest.

26. Anna Louise Strong to D. L. Reaburn, December 17, 1917, MORA, Concessions, File Cooperative Campers of the Pacific Northwest.

27. Ibid., August 18, 1918.

28. D. L. Reaburn to Anna L. Strong, September 17, 1918, MORA, Concessions, File Cooperative Campers of the Pacific Northwest.

29. Superintendent to Horace M. Albright, September 19, 1918, MORA, Concessions, Cooperative Campers of the Pacific Northwest.

30. The Mountaineers, Inc., *The Administration of the National Parks* (Seattle: The Mountaineers, 1922), 7; John Barton Payne to Hugh M. Caldwell, December 16, 1920, NA, RG 79, Entry 7—Central Classified Files, Box 1991, File 12–7.

31. Arno B. Cammerer to Norman Huber, July 13, 1921, MORA, Concessions, Cooperative Campers of the Pacific Northwest.

32. Ibid.

33. W. H. Peters to Director, July 21, 1921, MORA, Concessions, Cooperative Campers of the Pacific Northwest.

34. Ibid., April 7, 1922.

35. Ibid.

36. Arno B. Cammerer to C. L. Nelson, July 14 and 18, 1922, MORA, Concessions, File Cooperative Campers of the Pacific Northwest.

37. Ibid., July 14, 1922.

38. Playground and Recreation Association of America, *Camping Out: A Manual on Organized Camping* (New York: n.p., 1924), 1–20. Perhaps some people of this category were able to equip themselves and make their own way to the Longmire campground. Superintendent Tomlinson noted in his annual report for 1923 (p. 138), "Those who desire to camp several weeks frequently choose the campground at Longmire, where the facilities are more adequate." The free public campgrounds in the national parks and forests would attract thousands of poor and unemployed people during the Depression years.

39. The Mountaineers, *The Administration of the National Parks*, 2.

40. Ibid.

41. Ibid.

42. The RNPC's transportation monopoly was abetted by the state of Washington. A state law required all new stage lines that proposed to operate over the state highways to obtain a permit from the Board of Public Utilities. The law's purpose was to prevent ruinous competition between different transportation venders. In the summer of 1921, the state highway director ruled that

the RNPC would be the only carrier between Seattle or Tacoma and points inside Rainier. Asahel Curtis to Walter H. Van Zwoll, March 1, 1922, UW, Asahel Curtis Papers, Box 2, File 1.

43. The Mountaineers, *The Administration of the National Parks*, 5–6.

44. Special Meeting, Board of Trustees, December 13 and 20, 1922, UW, The Mountaineers Papers, Acc. 1984–3, Mountaineers Minute Books, Roll 2; "A History of the Rainier National Park Company," 1922; Arno B. Cammerer to Edmund S. Meany, January 19, 1923, MORA, Concessions, Cooperative Campers of the Pacific Northwest.

45. Regular Monthly Meeting, March 8, 1923, UW, The Mountaineers Papers, Acc. 1984–3, Mountaineers Minute Books, Roll 2; *Seattle Post-Intelligencer*, February 20, 1923.

46. *Report of the Director of the National Park Service*, 1924, 46.

47. Ibid., 1918, 57. The report noted a fourth, unimproved campground at Van Trump Park. This presumably referred to a road construction camp near the Nisqually River, known as Van Trump Camp.

48. Ibid.

49. Ibid., 1920, 133.

50. H. B. Hammon, Report on Sanitation at Mount Rainier National Park, October 14, 1922, NA, RG 79, Entry 6—Central Files, Box 138, File Sanitation Part 1; *Report of the Director of the National Park Service*, 1921, 213.

51. Arno Cammerer to George E. Goodwin, May 22, 1923, NA, RG 79, Entry 22—Records of the Branch of Engineering, General Records of the Engineering Division, 1917–1926, Box 16, File Administration.

52. *Report of the Director of the National Park Service*, 1923, 61, 138.

53. Ibid., 1925, 100.

54. Ibid., 99.

55. Anonymous, "Sceva Expresses Park Co. Viewpoint," *Washington Sportsman* 3, no. 9 (November 1937): 7.

56. Annual Report of the General Manager, October 15, 1926, MORA, Concessions, File C2621.

57. D. L. Reaburn to Director, July 7, 1917, NA, RG 79, Entry 6—Central Files, Box 132, File Superintendent's Monthly Reports; "History of the Rainier National Park Company," 1921. Similarly, in June 1929, when the new Paradise Lodge opened one week before the road was opened, the RNPC conveyed visitors' luggage from Narada Falls to Paradise Valley via dogsled, while visitors

had to walk the remaining distance over the snow. T. H. Martin to Transportation Department, June 19, 1929, MORA, File D30 Associated Improvement Clubs of the South End.

58. *Report of the Director of the National Park Service*, 1924, 45–46, 116; Owen A. Tomlinson, "Development of our National Park," *The Mountaineer* 17, no. 1 (December 1924): 45; A. E. Demaray to Secretary of the Interior, October 28, 1927, NA, RG 48, Central Classified Files, Box 1991, File 12–7.

59. "History of the Rainier National Park Company," 1925, 1929.

60. T. H. Martin to Owen A. Tomlinson, July 23, 1924, and Tomlinson to Director, July 24, 1924, NA, RG 79, Entry 7—Central Classified Files, Box 394, File 900.05, Part 1.

61. T. H. Martin to Owen A. Tomlinson, January 21, 1928, MORA, Concessions, File Aerial Tram.

62. H. A. Rhodes to Director, March 7, 1928, MORA, Concessions, File 920.02 R.N.P. Co. Contract.

63. T. C. Vint to O. A. Tomlinson, April 13, 1928 and Stephen T. Mather to O. A. Tomlinson, April 21, 1928, MORA, File D34 Buildings; Tomlinson to Director, July 20, 1928, NA, RG 79, Entry 7—Central Classified Files, Box 394, File 900.05, Part I.

64. Stephen T. Mather to Superintendent, August 23, 1928, NA, RG 79, Central Classified Files, Box 394, File 900.05, Part II.

65. O. A. Tomlinson to Asahel Curtis, January 24, 1929, MORA, Concessions, File Aerial Tram.

66. Horace M. Albright to Files, March 8, 1929, MORA, Concessions, File Aerial Tramway.

67. A. E. Demaray to Superintendent, January 29, 1929, MORA, Concessions, File Aerial Tram.

68. *Report of the Director of the National Park Service*, 1929, 114.

69. Arno B. Cammerer to Assistant Director (Field), June 27, 1927, MORA, Concessions, File 920.02 RNPC Contracts; Horace M. Albright to O. A. Tomlinson, August 13, 1927, MORA, Concessions, File C34 RNPC—1927. The eighteen-page contract is contained in MORA, Concessions, File 920.02 RNPC Contract and Supplemental Agreements. The contract references the act of Congress on page 15, and RNPC President Rhodes alludes to the act in Rhodes to Director, March 7, 1928, same file.

70. Thom C. Vint to O. A. Tomlinson, April 13, 1928, MORA, File D34 Buildings.

71. Stephen T. Mather to O. A. Tomlinson, April 21, 1928, MORA, File D34 Buildings.

72. Conrad L. Wirth, *Parks, Politics, and the People* (Norman: University of Oklahoma Press, 1980), 60.

73. Linda Flint McClelland, *Presenting Nature: The Historic Landscape Design of the National Park Service, 1916 to 1942* (Washington, D.C.: National Park Service, 1993), 185–86.

74. Memorandum, July 19, 1928, MHS, Northern Pacific Railroad Company Papers, President's Subject Files, File 60(1). The meeting is described in R. W. Clark to Charles Donnelly, July 23, 1928, and reviewed in E. M. Willis to B. W. Scandrett, November 14, 1934, same file.

75. "History of the Rainier National Park Company," 1929; Memorandum of Portland Conference, February 10, 1929, MHS, Northern Pacific Railroad Company Papers, President's Subject Files, File 60 (1).

76. Horace M. Albright to Charles Donnelly, April 4, 1929, MHS, Northern Pacific Railroad Company, President's Subject Files, File 60 (1).

77. C. R. Gray to Charles Donnelly, June 11, 1929, and Ralph Budd to Donnelly, June 10, 1929, MHS, Northern Pacific Railroad Company, President's Subject Files, File 60 (1).

78. H. A. Noble, "Report on Operations and Proposed Developments of Rainier National Park," 1929, MHS, Great Northern Railway Company Papers, President's Subject Files, File 12824 Mt. Rainier National Park; Memorandum by B. W. Scandrett, January 3, 1930, MHS, Northern Pacific Railroad Company Papers, President's Subject Files, File 60 (1).

79. The letter is summarized in a review of correspondence relating to the railroads' financial involvement in the RNPC in E. M. Willis to Scandrett, November 14, 1934, MHS, Northern Pacific Railroad Company Papers, President's Subject Files, File 60 (1).

80. Charles Donnelly to Horace M. Albright, October 1, 1931, MHS, Northern Pacific Railroad Company Papers, President's Subject Files, File 60 (1). The history of the railroads' financial involvement in the RNPC is summarized in E. M. Willis to Scandrett, November 14, 1934, MHS, Northern Pacific Railroad Company Papers, President's Subject Files, File 60 (1).

1. Annual visitation statistics are compiled in Theodore Catton, *Wonderland: An Administrative History of Mount Rainier National Park* (Seattle: National Park Service, Cultural Resources Program, 1996), Appendix B.

2. Warren James Belasco, *Americans on the Road: From Autocamp to Motel, 1910–1945* (Cambridge, Mass.: MIT Press, 1979), 143.

3. *Report of the Director of the National Park Service*, 1932, 54.

4. Floyd Schmoe, *Our Greatest Mountain* (New York: G. P. Putnam's Sons, 1925), 115; "Rainier National Park: In the Heart of the Great Northwest," pamphlet, 1933, MHS, Northern Pacific Railroad Company Papers, President's Subject Files, File No. 60, Folder 1.

5. O. A. Tomlinson to Director, May 12, 1926, NA, RG 79, Entry 7—Central Classified Files, Box 1441, File 620–080 Shelter Cabins.

6. O. A. Tomlinson to Director, September 3, 1929, NA, RG 79, Entry 7—Central Classified Files, Box 1438, File 611.

7. Arno B. Cammerer to O. A. Tomlinson, July 20, 1932, and Demaray to Supt. (telegram), July 22, 1932, MORA, Administrative File, Folder N3031 Blasting Paradise Ice Caves 1932; Superintendent to Director, July 16, 1932, MORA, Administrative Files, Folder N3031 Blasting Paradise Ice Caves 1932.

8. Tomlinson, Annual Report, 1931, MORA, Administrative Files.

9. O. A. Tomlinson, "Sunrise, Mt. Rainier," *Argus*, December 12, 1931.

10. Ibid.

11. "Rainier National Park" pamphlet.

12. On the wilderness area designation, see O. A. Tomlinson to Director, June 11, 1928; A. E. Demaray to Tomlinson, July 10, 1928; and Tomlinson to Director, July 17, 1928, NA, RG 79, CCF, Box 382, File 601 Part 7 Mt. Rainier-Lands-General; and *Tacoma Daily Ledger*, August 31, 1928. A few years later the NPS made a cosmetic change in its park development plan, renaming all "highways" in the park "roads." On wilderness preservation and the national parks in this era, see Paul S. Sutter, *Driven Wild: How the Fight against Automobiles Launched the Modern Wilderness Movement* (Seattle: University of Washington Press, 2002).

13. The Wonderland Trail was also shortened in some places. Estimates of the original length varied from 100 to 115 miles; today it is given as 93 miles. See Schmoe, *Our Greatest Mountain*, 99; C. Frank Brockman, "The Wonders of Mount Rainier," *Natural History* 37, no. 3 (March 1936): 253; Paul Sadin, "Com-

ing Full Circle: The Development of Mount Rainier's Wonderland Trail, 1907–1939," *Columbia: The Magazine of Northwest History* 13, no. 4 (Winter 1999–2000): 24–33.

14. *Report of the Director of the National Park Service*, 1921, 222; Brockman, "The Wonders of Mount Rainier," 254. The trail shelters differed from back-country patrol cabins in that they were generally three-sided, with earthen floors, and were intended for public rather than administrative use. Thompson, *Mount Rainier National Park*, 169–73.

15. Alexander Baillie to Harold L. Ickes, April 14, 1933, U W, Preston Macy Papers, Accession 3211, Box 4, Folder 22.

16. Albright briefed Secretary of the Interior Ray Lyman Wilbur on the background to the company's financial straits in a memorandum on January 2, 1932. His interpretation was as follows: "The Rainier National Park Co. was organized in 1915 for the exclusive purpose of providing accommodations for tourists visiting Mount Rainier National Park. Its organization was the result of an appeal by the Government to the civic pride of the citizens of the State of Washington to make possible the satisfactory operation and development of Mount Rainier National Park by furnishing satisfactory accommodations for visitors within the park. The stock is not an attractive proposition, as but few dividends have been paid. Due to a marked change in the type of accommo-dations demanded by the public, it has been necessary in the past two years to install considerable additional facilities for the accommodation of the public. To finance these improvements the credit of the company has been stretched to the utmost. Besides, in the past substantially all the profits of the company have been used in the acquirement of new assets. Now, for the past two seasons, due to the economic depression, although the attendance at the park has been constantly increasing, the gross revenue and net profits have been steadily decreas-ing, making it impossible for the company to meet its obligations on account of these new installations from the new profits resulting from operations." U.S. Congress, House, *Electric Generating System, Mount Rainier National Park*, 72d Cong., 1st sess., 1932, H. Rept. 98, 2–3.

17. Alexander Baillie to Harold L. Ickes, April 14, 1932, U W, Preston Macy Papers, Accession 3211, Box 4, Folder 22; Rainier National Park Company, Esti-mate of Financial Condition January 14, 1932, to July 1, 1932, U W, Saint Paul & Tacoma Lumber Company Papers, Accession 315, Box 43; Charles Donnelly to H. A. Scandrett et al., June 30, 1931, and Horace Albright to Charles Donnelly,

September 14, 1931; E. M. Willis to Mr. Scandrett, November 14, 1934, MHS, Northern Pacific Railroad Company Papers, President's Subject File, File 60.

18. Tomlinson, Annual Report, 1931, 12.

19. Rainier National Park Company, Minutes of Meeting of the Board of Directors, January 15, 1932, UW, Saint Paul & Tacoma Lumber Company Papers, Accession 315, Box 43; *Congressional Record*, 72nd Cong., 1st sess., 1931, vol. 75, 442. In a memorandum written for the Secretary of the Interior, Albright explained that the company had used the majority of the electrical power supply when the plant was built in 1915. Now with the lighted public campground and numerous administrative and residential buildings at Longmire, the situation was reversed, with the government using most of the plant's power-generating capacity. Albright informed Secretary of the Interior Ray Lyman Wilbur that it was the government's policy to own such power plants in the national parks, and moreover, the purchase would provide the company with much needed capital. *Electric Generating System*, 3.

20. Alexander Baillie to Ray Lyman Wilbur, August 3, 1932, NA, RG 79, Entry 17—Records of Key Officials, Records of Horace M. Albright, Box 2, Folder Mount Rainier; Joseph M. Dixon to Alexander Baillie, August 12, 1932, NA, RG 79, Entry 17—Records of Key Officials, Records of Horace M. Albright, Box 2, Folder Mount Rainier.

21. "Dude Ranch at Rainier," *Town Crier*, July 15, 1933.

22. "A History of the Rainier National Park Company," 1933, 2; "Rainier National Park" pamphlet, 6–7.

23. O. A. Tomlinson, Annual Report, 1931, 12, MORA, Administrative Files; Horace M. Albright to Messrs. Cammerer and Demaray, July 24, 1930, NA, RG 79, Entry 7—Central Classified Files, Box 380, File 204–020, Part 1.

24. O. A. Tomlinson, Proposed Civil Works Program for Mount Rainier National Park, November 16, 1933, and Report on Civil Works Program Accomplishments in Mount Rainier National Park, May 10, 1934, NA, RG 79, CCF, Box 1440, File 619 Civil Works Administration; *Annual Report of the Secretary of the Interior*, 1939, 297; J. Haslett Bell, Annual Narrative Report to Chief of Planning, 1938, National Archives Pacific Sierra Region (NAPSR), RG 79, Western Region, Resident Landscape Architect, Reports to the Chief Architect 1927–40, Box 10, Folder Mount Rainier 1938; Mark H. Astrup to Director, June 24, 1939, NA, RG 79, CCF, Box 1439, File 618 Mount Rainier; O. A. Tom-

linson, Superintendent's Annual Report, 1940, MORA, Administrative Files; Edwin G. Hall, *In the Shadow of the Mountain: The Spirit of the CCC* (Pullman: Washington State University Press, 1990), 115–17.

25. O. A. Tomlinson to CCC Camp Superintendents, June 10, 1933, UW, Preston Macy Papers, Accession 3211, Box 1, Folder 7.

26. Harlan D. Unrau and G. Frank Williss, *Administrative History: Expansion of the National Park Service in the 1930s* (Washington, D.C.: National Park Service, 1983), 77.

27. John A. Salmond, *The Civilian Conservation Corps, 1933–1942: A New Deal Case Study* (Durham, N.C.: Duke University Press, 1967), 34–35.

28. General Statement of Operating Conditions and Appropriations, July 4, 1933, UW, Preston Macy Papers, Accession 3211, Box 1, Folder 7; O. A. Tomlinson, General Statement of Operating Conditions and Appropriations, July 4, 1933, UW, Preston Macy Papers, Accession 3211, Box 1, Folder 7.

29. O. A. Tomlinson, Annual Report, 1933, 1, MORA, Administrative Files; M. J. Bowen to Robert Fechner, June 16, 1934, NA, RG 35, Entry 115—Division of Investigations, Camp Inspection Reports, Box 230, File Washington NP-2; *Tacoma Daily Ledger*, November 29, 1933.

30. Hall, *In the Shadow of the Mountain*, xvi.

31. W. C. Pabst, Fifth Period Narrative Report for Camp Narada NP-2, 1935, NA, RG 79, Narrative Reports Concerning ECW (CCC) Projects in National Park Service Areas, 1933–1935, Box 36.

32. Phoebe Cutler, *The Public Landscape of the New Deal* (New Haven, Conn.: Yale University Press, 1985), 90.

33. Laura Soulliere Harrison, "By Motor through Wonderland: Historic Roads in the National Park System," National Park Service draft report, 1994, 4, copy provided to author by National Park Service, Cultural Resources Program, Seattle, Washington.

34. Robert Scharff, ed., *Ski Magazine's Encyclopedia of Skiing* (New York: Harper and Row, 1974), 16–18; Raymond Flower, *The History of Skiing and Other Winter Sports* (New York: Methuen, 1977), 120.

35. Scharff, *Ski Magazine's Encyclopedia of Skiing*, 47–48.

36. Flower, *The History of Skiing and Other Winter Sports*, 123.

37. Ibid., 7–8; Isabelle Story, "Winter Sports and Sportsmen," *Review of Reviews* 91, no. 2 (February 1935): 61–62.

38. Linda Helleson, "The History of Skiing in Mount Rainier National Park," undated typescript in Mount Rainier National Park Library, 8–9.

39. McIntyre, "A Short History of Mount Rainier National Park," 275–77; "A History of the Rainier National Park Company," 1936, 2. Mather's observation is in *Report of the Director of the National Park Service to the Secretary of the Interior*, 1922, 26–27.

40. McIntyre, "A Short History of Mount Rainier National Park," 277, 289. On the difficulties of providing first aid to skiers, see O. A. Tomlinson to Charles Flory, November 29, 1937; P. H. Sceva to Arno B. Cammerer, November 29, 1937; and Arno B. Cammerer to P. H. Sceva, December 23, 1937, MORA, Administrative Files, File W48 Law Enforcement.

41. E. A. Davidson to Tom C. Vint, April 24, 1937, NAPSR, RG 79, Western Regional Office, Classified Records—Mt. Rainier National Park, Box 111, File 868 Winter Use, Part I.

42. Helleson, "The History of Skiing in Mount Rainier National Park," 11.

43. O. A. Tomlinson to Arno B. Cammerer, April 4, 1934, UW, Preston Macy Papers, Accession 3211, Box 4, Folder 22.

44. Helleson, "The History of Skiing in Mount Rainier National Park," 11–12.

45. O. A. Tomlinson to John C. Preston, July 14, 1941, NA, RG 79, Entry 7—Central Classified Files, Box 1438, File 611.

46. "Resume of Proposed Bar-Type Ski Lift in Mount Rainier National Park," August 9, 1954, MORA, Administrative Files, File D18 Winter Use Study Mt. Rainier 1953–1954; Helleson, "The History of Skiing in Mount Rainier National Park," 17; McIntyre, "A Short History of Mount Rainier National Park," 290.

47. John C. Preston to Director, October 24, 1942, NAPSR, RG 79, Western Region, Classified Records—Mount Rainier National Park, Box 88, File 207 Reports, Part II.

48. History of Snow Removal Operations, Nisqually Entrance to Paradise Valley Road, November 4, 1953, NAPSR, RG 79, Western Region, Central Coded Subject Files, Box 15, File D-30.

49. *Report of the Director of the National Park Service*, 1943, 198.

50. "Experiments in Freezing," *Etc.* 3, no. 2 (February 1941): 10–11.

51. Thompson, *Mount Rainier National Park*, 174.

52. V. A. Firsoff, *Ski Track on the Battlefield* (New York: A. S. Barnes and Company, 1943), 104–8.

53. Ibid., 108. Also Hal Burton, *The Ski Troops* (New York: Simon and Schus-

ter, 1971), 95; Curtis W. Casewit, *The Saga of the Mountain Soldiers: The Story of the 10th Mountain Division* (New York: Julian Messner, 1981), 18.

54. Unidentified clipping in Gene Curtis, "History of Fort Lewis," scrapbook, Seattle Public Library; John C. Preston to Director, October 24, 1942, National Archives—Pacific Sierra Region, NAPSR, RG 79, Western Region, Classified Records—Mount Rainier National Park, Box 88, File 207 Reports Part II.

55. More army units were dispatched to Rainier for special training in the late fall of 1943. These included a detachment of ski troops from the 10th Mountain, a small force from the 938th Aviation Engineers who undertook snow camouflage tests, and photographers from the Army Signal Corps who made an army training film. These units pulled out by December 1943, ending Mount Rainier National Park's role in World War II as a training and testing ground. Thompson, *Mount Rainier National Park*, 175; John C. Preston, Plan of Operation for use of Mount Rainier National Park Ski Lodge by the U.S. Army, October 11, 1943, MORA, Administrative Files, File H14 Mountain Infantry Regiment.

6 THE CONTENTIOUS YEARS (1945–1965)

1. *Tacoma News Tribune*, August 12, 1999; John C. Preston to the Director, June 23, 1945, NAPSR, RG 79, Western Region, Classified Records—Mount Rainier National Park, Box 88, File 204.21, Visitors, Part 1.

2. *Seattle Post-Intelligencer*, June 18, 1946.

3. For an overview of NPS concession policy, see Ise, *Our National Park Policy*, 606–18. See also Mark Daniel Barringer, *Selling Yellowstone: Capitalism and the Construction of Nature* (Lawrence: University Press of Kansas, 2002), for an examination of government-concessionaire relations in Yellowstone, and Alfred Runte, *Yosemite: The Embattled Wilderness* (Lincoln: University of Nebraska Press, 1990), for details on the concession in that park.

4. *Annual Report of the Director, National Park Service*, 1947, 320; U.S. House Committee on Public Lands, *Hearings before the Subcommittee on Irrigation and Reclamation and the Subcommittee on Public Lands*, 80th Cong., 1st sess., September 8, 1947—Salt Lake City, Utah, and September 15, 1947—Mount Rainier National Park, Wash., 1948, 249.

5. Paul H. Sceva to Newton B. Drury and enclosure, June 5, 1946, MORA, Administrative Files, File 920.02 RNPC Contract 1935–1949.

6. *Annual Report of the Director, National Park Service,* 1946, 313.

7. Paul H. Sceva to Newton B. Drury, March 22, 1947; Drury to Sceva, March 25, 1947; and Drury to Regional Director, March 25, 1947, MORA, Administrative Files, File 920.08–3 Purchase of RNPC Facilities by Government.

8. Quoted in U.S. House Committee on Public Lands, *Concessions in National Parks, Committee Hearing No. 28,* 81st Cong., 1st sess., November 12, 1949, 18.

9. Ibid., 17.

10. The concession advisory group's report is quoted in *Concessions in National Parks,* 17.

11. *Annual Report of the Director, National Park Service,* 1950, 320.

12. History of the Rainier National Park Company, 1948, 3; *Concessions in National Parks,* 17–20.

13. Paul H. Sceva to Julius A. Krug, September 30 and October 4, 1948, MORA, Administrative Files, File 920.02 RNPC Contract.

14. Harthon L. Bill to Director, November 26, 1948, MORA, Administrative Files, File 920.02 RNPC Contract.

15. *Tacoma News Tribune,* July 28, 1949; Paul H. Sceva to Secretary of the Interior, August 30, 1949; Secretary of the Interior to Sceva, September 13, 1949; Sceva to John C. Preston, September 21, 1949; Newton B. Drury to Girard C. Davidson, October 5, 1949, MORA, Administrative Files, File 920.02 RNPC Contract 1934–1949.

16. Paul H. Sceva to Henry M. Jackson, January 3, 1950; Newton B. Drury to Superintendent, August 18, 1950, MORA, Administrative Files, File Purchase of RNPC Facilities by Government.

17. 64 Stat. 896; U.S. Congress, Senate, *Authorizing the Secretary of the Interior to Acquire on Behalf of the United States Government All Property and Facilities of the Rainier National Park Co.,* 81st Cong., 2nd sess., 1950, S. Rept. 2448, August 28, 1950, 1; Press Release, August 15, 1968; and Leslie W. Scott to Paul H. Sceva, April 10, 1968, Washington State Historical Society, Paul H. Sceva Collection, Box 1, Folder 5; Amendment to Agreement and Plan of Reorganization Between Amfac, Inc. (a Hawaii Corporation), Fred Harvey, Inc. (a Delaware Corporation), and Rainier National Park Company (a West Virginia Corporation), January 1969, Paul H. Sceva Collection, Box 1, Folder 12.

18. *Authorizing the Secretary of the Interior to Acquire on Behalf of the United States Government,* H. Rept. 2721, July 24, 1950, 4.

19. *Annual Report of the Secretary of the Interior,* 1950, p. 320; U.S. Senate Com-

mittee on Interior and Insular Affairs, *Mount Rainier National Park*, 84th Cong., 2nd sess., October 15, 1956, 6.

20. Arno B. Cammerer, Memorandum for the Washington Office and all Field Offices, January 27, 1940, NAPSR, RG 79, Western Region Office, Central Files 1937–53, Box 100, File 201.15 Winter Use Policy; Newton B. Drury, Memorandum for the Director's Office and the Regional Directors, August 13, 1945, NAPSR, RG 79, Western Region Office, Central Files 1937–53, Box 100, File 201.15 Winter Use Policy; Newton B. Drury, Memorandum for the Director's Office and all Field Offices, March 21, 1946, MORA, Administrative Files, File 868 Winter Use.

21. O. A. Tomlinson to Superintendent, January 6, 1943, NAPSR, RG 79, Western Region Office, Central Files 1937–53, Box 100, File 201.15 Winter Use Policy.

22. Preston to Regional Director, May 21, 1946, MORA, Administrative Files, File 868 Winter Use.

23. Some individuals in The Mountaineers confided to Superintendent Preston that they believed the club had been railroaded into taking that position by a few ardent ski enthusiasts among its membership. Arthur P. Winder to John C. Preston, April 1, 1944, and Preston to Regional Forester, November 21, 1945, NAPSR, RG 79, Western Region, Classified Records, Mt. Rainier National Park, Box 98, File 600 Jobs Part VI; O. A. Tomlinson to Files, October 24, 1945, NAPSR, RG 79, Western Region Office, Central Files 1937–53, Box 100, File 201.15 Winter Use Policy; Preston to Regional Director, December 10, 1945, NAPSR, RG 79, Western Region Office, Classified Records Mt. Rainier National Park, Box 111, File 868 Winter Use, Part 2.

24. Newton B. Drury, Memorandum for the Director's Office and All Field Offices, March 21, 1946, MORA, File 868 Winter Use.

25. *Seattle Post-Intelligencer*, October 25 and 26, 1945; *Annual Report of the Director, National Park Service*, 1946, 319.

26. John C. Preston to Director, July 21, 1947, NAPSR, RG 79, Western Region, Classified Records—Mt. Rainier National Park, Box 88, File 207 Reports, Part 4.

27. Harthon L. Bill to Director, November 26, 1948, NA, RG 79, Central Classified Files, Box 1423, File 201–11 Advisory Board.

28. A. E. Demaray to Director, May 10, 1946, NAPSR, RG 79, Western Region, Classified Records—Mt. Rainier National Park, Box 87, File 0.1 Conferences, Part 1; John C. Preston to Regional Director, June 24, 1946, NAPSR, RG 79,

Western Region, Classified Records—Mt. Rainier National Park, Box 98, File 600 Development, Part 7.

29. Tom C. Vint to Director, May 21, 1946, N A P S R, R G 79, Western Region, Classified Records—Mount Rainier National Park, Box 98, File 600 Development, Part 7.

30. Tom C. Vint to Director, May 11, 1948, N A, R G 79, Central Classified Files, Box 1411, File 630 Roads (General).

31. Winter Use Committee to Regional Director, April 8, 1952, N A P S R, R G 79, Western Region Office, Classified Records—Mt. Rainier National Park, Box 112, File 868 Winter Use, Part 6.

32. Preston P. Macy to Director, May 29, 1953, M O R A, Administrative Files, File H2621 Annual Reports; History of Snow Removal Operations Nisqually Entrance to Paradise Valley Road, prepared November 4, 1953, N A P S R, R G 79, Western Region Central Coded Subject Files, Box 15, D-30.

33. Preston P. Macy to Regional Director, November 6, 1953, N A P S R, R G 79, Western Region Central Coded Subject Files, Box 15, File D-30.

34. Brief of Contacts with Governor Langlie on Developments for Mount Rainier, no date, M O R A, Administrative Files, File D18 Winter Use Study Mt. Rainier 1953–1954.

35. Conrad L. Wirth to Regional Director, November 6, 1953, N A P S R, R G 79, Western Region, Central Files 1953–62 (L,S, & P), 9 N S S 79–92–001, Box 3, File L3427, vol. 1, M O R A.

36. Mount Rainier National Park Development Study Committee to Arthur B. Langlie, July 15, 1955, Olympia State Archives, Albert Rosellini Papers, Box 63, File Mount Rainier Development.

37. Regional Director to Director, December 9, 1953, N A P S R, R G 79, Western Region, Central Files 1953–62 (L, S, & P) 9 N S S 79–92–001, Box 3, File L3427, vol. 1, M O R A.

38. Brief of Contacts with Automobile Club of Washington Officials, no date, N A P S R, R G 79, Western Region, Central Files 1953–62 (L,S, & P) 9 N S S 79–92–001, Box 3, File L3427 Report—Proposed Developments Mount Rainier from the Director to the Secretary.

39. National Parks Association, News Release No. 75, August 27, 1954, M O R A, Administrative Files, File L3427 Winter Sports—Paradise.

40. Conrad L. Wirth, Report on Proposed Developments for Mount Rainier National Park, September 29, 1954, M O R A, Administrative Files;

Olympic Park Associates, Inc., Mount Rainier Emergency, no date, MORA, Administrative Files, File L3427 Winter Sports—Paradise.

41. Conrad L. Wirth to Secretary of the Interior, September 29, 1954, MORA, Administrative Files, File Report on Proposed Developments for Mount Rainier.

42. Douglas McKay to Arthur Langlie, December 17, 1954, MORA, Administrative Files, File L3427 Winter Sports—Paradise.

43. Polly Dyer to Preston Macy, April 19, 1955, MORA, Administrative Files, File L3427 Winter Sports—Paradise.

44. Sigurd Olson to Devereux Butcher, December 29, 1954, Charles G. Woodbury to Butcher, December 29, 1954, and Conrad L. Wirth to Olson, February 15, 1955, Fred M. Packard to Olson, February 16, 1955, MHS, Sigurd F. Olson Papers, Box 24. Butcher's split with the NPA soon had wider implications. See Barringer, *Selling Yellowstone*, 145–46.

45. Virlis L. Fischer to Howard Zahniser, October 27, 1958, NAPSR, RG 79, Western Region, Central Files 1953–1962 (A & C) 9NSS 79 92 002, Box 6, File A9815 #18 Areas Mt. Rainier.

46. Philip A. Zalesky to Director, Bureau of the Budget, December 14, 1953, UW, Warren Magnuson Papers, Accession 3181–3, Box 100, Folder 25.

47. Conrad L. Wirth, *Parks, Politics, and the People* (Norman: University of Oklahoma Press, 1980), 242.

48. National Park Service, Mission 66 for Mount Rainier National Park, January 1957, 1.

49. However, see Barringer, *Selling Yellowstone*, on the park service's difficulties with Mission 66 in Yellowstone.

50. U.S. Senate Committee on Interior and Insular Affairs, *Mount Rainier National Park*, 84th Cong., 2nd sess., October 15, 1956, 66.

51. National Park Service, Mission 66 for Mount Rainier National Park, January 1957, 10–12.

52. National Park Service, Improving Visitor Use of Mount Rainier National Park, March 26, 1956, MORA, Administrative Files, File D18 Planning Program Mission 66. Opinions varied about whether the park boundary should be extended to bring the Skate Creek site inside the park. The advantage of a boundary extension would be to bring the development under the control of the park service; the disadvantage would be that the park would then include some cutover forest land.

53. *Mount Rainier National Park*, 2, 38.

54. National Park Service, Preliminary Planning Data for a Proposed Hotel Development at Paradise to Mount Rainier National Park, and Henry M. Jackson to Conrad L. Wirth, May 16, 1957, U W, Henry M. Jackson Papers, Accession 3560–3, Box 32, File 13.

55. Henry M. Jackson to Laurance S. Rockefeller, July 2, 1957, U W, Henry M. Jackson Papers, Accession 3560–3, Box 32, File 13.

56. Laurance S. Rockefeller to Henry M. Jackson, January 22, 1959, U W, Preston P. Macy Papers, Accession 3211, Box 4, File 23.

57. Roger Ernst to Elmer L. Alverts, April 21, 1960, M O R A, Administrative Files, File C58 Rockefeller Survey.

58. U.S. Congress, Senate, *To Authorize the Construction of a Hotel and Related Facilities in Mount Rainier National Park*, 86th Cong., 2nd sess., 1960, S. J. Res. 193, May 17, 1960; *Congressional Record*, 86th Cong., 2nd sess., 1960, vol. 106, 10397 and 14831; Thor C. Tollefson to Stewart L. Udall, January 21, 1961, M O R A, Administrative Files, File C58 Rockefeller Survey.

59. Conrad L. Wirth to Legislative Counsel, February 14, 1961, M O R A, Administrative Files, File C58 Rockefeller Survey.

60. Hillory A. Tolson to Wayne S. Pritchard, September 1, 1961, M O R A, File C58 Rockefeller Survey; *Seattle Times*, October 18, 1961; *Tacoma News Tribune*, October 19, 21, and 22, 1961.

61. Stewart L. Udall to Albert D. Rosellini, November 8, 1961, Olympia State Archives, Governor Albert D. Rosellini Papers, Box 286, File Mt. Rainier Study; John A. Rutter to Lawrence Merriam, January 23, 1962, M O R A, Administrative Files, File Governor's Study Committee; *Tacoma News Tribune*, January 5, 10, 15, and 17, 1962; *Seattle Times*, January 2 and 11, 1962; Albert D. Rosellini to Stewart L. Udall, January 31, 1962, Olympia State Archives, Governor Albert D. Rosellini Papers, Box 286, File Mt. Rainier Study.

62. Department of the Interior and Washington State Department of Commerce and Economic Development, *Report on Study of the Public Need with Respect to Visitor Facilities in Mount Rainier National Park*, by Harris, Kerr, Forster & Company, November 1963, 1–5.

63. John A. Rutter to Regional Director, August 12, 1963, M O R A, Administrative Files, File Governor's Study Committee; George F. Prescott to Members of Governor's Mount Rainier Study Committee, September 16, 1963, M O R A, Administrative Files, File Governor's Study Committee; *Report on Study of the Public Need with Respect to Visitor Facilities*, 1–5.

64. "Commercial Development in Mt. Rainier National Park," *The Mountaineer* 55, no. 3 (March 1962): 5; Leo Gallagher, "The Old Hotel in Paradise," *National Parks Magazine* 38, no. 198 (January 1964): 4–7.

65. John A. Rutter to Lawrence Merriam, June 14, 1963, and Paul H. Sceva to Board of Directors, June 13, 1963, MORA, Administrative Files, File RNPC 1962–63; *Seattle Times*, July 24, 1963; Wimberly, Whiseand, Allison and Ton and McGuire and Muri, "Report on Construction Program for a Day Use Facility at Paradise Park in Mount Rainier National Park, State of Washington," prepared for the National Park Service, no date, UW, Henry M. Jackson Papers, Accession 3560–3, Box 94, File 11; Barry Head, "Is It a Boon or a Boondoggle?" *Seattle Magazine* 4, no. 34 (January 1967): 51.

66. Paradise Visitor Center, Mount Rainier National Park, Washington (flyer for opening ceremony, September 3, 1966), UW, Henry M. Jackson Papers, Accession 3560–4, Box 231, File 42.

67. Head, "Is It a Boon or a Boondoggle?" 15–16, 50–51.

68. *Tacoma News Tribune*, June 11, 1965.

69. National Park Service, *Environmental Statement/Master Plan, Mount Rainier National Park, Washington*, PNRO, File Report MORA 73–64, 26.

70. Stephanie S. Toothman, "Cultural Resource Management in Natural Areas of the National Park System," *Public Historian* 9, no. 2 (Spring 1987): 65.

71. Acting Regional Director to Superintendent, June 4, 1976, PNRO, Administrative Files, File Classified Structure Field Inventory Report, Mount Rainier National Park, January 1976; Laurin Huffman, interview by the author, March 31, 1995. The buildings were recommended for listing on the park service's List of Classified Structures (LCS), which predated the National Register of Historic Places and was used by the NPS for tracking all of the agency's historic structures.

72. James Mote to Harry Pfanz, August 2, 1977, MORA, Administrative Files (Longmire), File H30 Historic Resource Survey 1975–1977.

73. Russell E. Dickenson to Associate Director, September 30, 1977; Dickenson to Manager, Denver Service Center, September 30, 1977, Development/Study Package Proposal No. 207, 1977; Acting Chief, Cultural Resources Management Division to Associate Manager, Denver Service Center, August 25, 1977; Chief Historian to Manager, Historic Preservation Team, Denver Service Center, June 13, 1977, MORA, Administrative Files (Longmire), File H30 Historic Resource Survey 1975–1977.

74. Thompson, *Historic Resource Study*.

75. Ethan Carr, *Wilderness by Design: Landscape Architecture and the National Park Service* (Lincoln: University of Nebraska Press, 1998).

76. National Park Service, press release, March 15, 1956, MORA, Administrative Files, File D18 Planning Program Mission 66.

77. Preston P. Macy to Park Staff, August 31, 1956, MORA, Administrative Files, File D18 Planning Program Mission 66.

78. E. R. Fetterolf to Newton B. Drury, May 27, 1949, NA, RG 79, Entry 7—Central Classified Files, Box 1441, File 630 Roads (General).

79. Anonymous memo, Stevens Canyon Road Project, 1953, UW, Preston P. Macy Papers, Accession 3211, Box 3, File 15.

80. Thomas E. Carpenter to Regional Director, February 15, 1955, NAPSR, RG 79, Western Region Central Coded Subject Files, Box 29, File A4067, vol. 1, MORA.

81. National Park Service, Mission 66 for Mount Rainier National Park, MORA, Administrative Files, File D18, Mission 66.

82. John A. Rutter, interview by the author, February 3, 1995; Superintendent's Annual Report, 1973, MORA, Administrative Files, File H2623; Gene Casey, interview by the author, February 9, 1995.

83. Mark Harvey, *Wilderness Forever: Howard Zahniser and the Path to the Wilderness Act* (Seattle: University of Washington Press, 2005).

84. U.S. Senate Committee on Interior and Insular Affairs, *National Wilderness Preservation Act*—1959, 86th Cong., 1st sess., March 30–31, 1959, 80, 131, 162, 236, 312.

85. Roderick Nash, *Wilderness and the American Mind*, 3rd rev. ed. (New Haven, Conn.: Yale University Press, 1982), 226.

7   THE SEARCH FOR LIMITS (1965–2000)

1. William C. Everhart, *The National Park Service* (Boulder, Colo.: Westview, 1983), 98–101. See also Harvey, *Wilderness Forever*.

2. Jeffrey Mason, David Cole, and David Reynolds, "Limits of Acceptable Change: A Framework for Assessing Carrying Capacity," *Park Science: A Resource Management Bulletin* 6, no. 1 (Fall 1985), 9; Wagar quoted in Patricia E. Aspland and Katherine A. Pawelko, "Carrying Capacity: Evolution of Management Concepts for the National Parks," *Trends* 20, no. 3 (1983), 22.

3. Aspland and Pawelko, "Carrying Capacity," 23. See also James Morton Turner, "From Woodcraft to 'Leave No Trace': Wilderness, Consumerism, and

Environmentalism in Twentieth-Century America," *Environmental History* 7, no. 3 (July 2002), 477–78.

4. Quoted in Everhart, *The National Park Service*, 102.

5. John Wilcox, interview by the author, February 11, 1995, and February 3, 1995; Gene Casey, interview by the author, February 9, 1995.

6. Ibid.; John Wilcox, interview by the author, February 11, 1995.

7. The Seattle Mountaineers, "Recommendations for Future Development of Mt. Rainier National Park," October 29, 1969, u w, Brock Evans Papers, Accession 1776, Rainier National Park, Box 20.

8. *Tacoma News Tribune*, December 3, 1972; *Seattle Post-Intelligencer*, May 16, November 14, 1973.

9. Larry Zelanak, interview by the author, October 12, 1993; John Wilcox, interview by the author, February 11, 1995. Similar relaxation of backcountry management occurred in other national parks. See Turner, "From Woodcraft to 'Leave No Trace,'" 477–78.

10. *Seattle Times*, January 17, 1974.

11. Harvey Manning, *R E I: 50 Years of Climbing Together* (Seattle: Recreational Equipment, Inc., 1988), 121.

12. Larry Zelanak, interview by the author, October 12, 1993.

13. *Seattle Times*, July 24, 1975.

14. John Wilcox, interview, February 11, 1995.

15. John Wilcox, interview, February 11, 1995; Superintendent's Annual Report, 1986, m o r a, Administrative Files, File H2623.

16. Gene Casey, interview by the author, February 9, 1995.

17. For an excellent treatment of consumer culture and the changing wilderness experience, see Turner, "From Woodcraft to 'Leave No Trace,'" 462–84.

18. National Park Service, *Master Plan, Mount Rainier National Park, Washington* (Washington, D.C.: National Park Service, 1972), 22–24, 28–30.

19. In a 1990 visitor survey, 80 percent of visitors selected "driving to view scenery" among the activities engaged in while in the park, and 38 percent named "driving to view scenery" as the most important activity to their enjoyment of the park. "Driving to view scenery" placed first in this category, ahead of "day hiking—self led," at 21 percent. Only 1 to 2 percent of respondents gave other front country uses such as camping, picnicking, staying at a lodge or inn, or visiting museums as the most important activity to their enjoyment of the park. Darryll R. Johnson, Karen P. Foster, and Katherine L. Kerr, *Mount Rainier*

National Park 1990 Visitor Survey (Seattle: National Park Service, Cooperative Park Studies Unit, University of Washington, 1990), 22–23.

20. National Park Service, *Master Plan, Mount Rainier National Park*, 16.

21. John C. Hendee et al., "Public Response to the Mt. Rainier National Park Draft Wilderness Proposal and Master Plan—Analysis and Summary," 71, MORA, Administrative Files. On proposed tramways in North Cascades, see David Louter, *Contested Terrain: North Cascades National Park Service Complex, an Administrative History* (Seattle: National Park Service, 1998), 74.

22. National Park Service, *Master Plan, Mount Rainier National Park*, 17–18.

23. Hendee et al., "Public Response," 73.

24. Seattle Mountaineers, "Recommendations for Future Development of Mt. Rainier National Park," October 29, 1969, UW, Brock Evans Papers, Accession 1776, Rainier National Park, Box 20; Environmental Review, Proposed Mowich Lake Access Route, Mount Rainier National Park, Washington, October 31, 1975, Columbia-Cascade Support Office (CCSO), File Report MORA D81.

25. National Park Service, *Master Plan, Mount Rainier National Park*, 15.

26. Darryll R. Johnson, *A Study of Visitor Attitudes toward Initiation of a Visitor Transportation System at Mount Rainier National Park* (Seattle: National Park Service, Cooperative Park Studies Unit, University of Washington, 1990), passim.

27. "Transportation Feasibility Study," undated briefing statement provided to the author by Eric Walkinshaw.

28. *Tacoma News Tribune*, August 29, 1999.

29. Ibid.

30. Molenaar, *The Challenge of Rainier*, 228.

31. Daniel J. Tobin Jr., "Assessment of the Environmental Impact of Proposed Concession Contract, Mount Rainier National Park," MORA, File C38 Concession—Prospectus—Guide Service, 1972–73–74.

32. Lou Whittaker and Andrea Gabbard, *Lou Whittaker: Memoirs of a Mountain Guide* (Seattle: Seattle Mountaineers, 1994), 95.

33. Superintendent's Annual Reports, 1975, 1980, 1985, 1993, MORA, Administrative Files, File H2623; Rick Kirshner, interview by the author, February 11, 1995.

34. Whittaker and Gabbard, *Lou Whittaker*, 61, 175.

35. Ibid., 173.

36. Rick Kirshner, interview by the author, February 11, 1995; Superintendent's Annual Reports, 1973, 1976, 1977, 1978, 1980, MORA, Administrative Files, File H2623; John Krambrink, interview by the author, February 10, 1995.

37. John Morse & Associates/Architects, "Camp Muir, Mount Rainier National Park," November 15, 1973, CCSO, file report, MORA 52, 2, 12–16.

38. Mount Rainier National Park, Backcountry Management Plan, February 1981, CCSO, file report, MORA D97 Backcountry Management Plan. In part to contain this growth, the park service proposed a $100 fee for each summit attempt. When the public protested, it established a climbing fee of $15 per person per climb. In 2003, it raised the fee to $30.

39. Superintendent's Annual Report, 1985, MORA, Administrative Files, File H2621; Regina Rochefort, e-mail communication with the author, June 1995.

40. Human Waste Management Program–1986, MORA, Central Files, File D18 High Altitude Human Waste Management.

41. Ibid.; John Wilcox, interview by the author, February 11, 1995; *Tacoma News Tribune*, July 25, 1999.

42. *Tacoma News Tribune*, July 25, 1999.

43. Ibid.

44. Paul Sceva, President-General Manager's Annual Report, 1963, Washington State Historical Society, Paul Sceva Papers, Box 1, File 16; John R. Anderson to John Townsley, June 28, 1968, MORA, Administrative Files, File D18 Ski Area Proposal Mount Rainier National Park.

45. Paul Sceva, President-General Manager's Annual Report for the Fiscal Year 1967, Washington State Historical Society, Paul H. Sceva Papers, Box 1, File 16; Rick Kirshner, interview by the author, February 11, 1995.

46. Rick Kirshner, interview by the author, February 11, 1995.

47. Superintendent's Annual Reports, 1972, 1980, MORA, Administrative Files, File H2623.

48. Superintendent's Annual Reports, 1979, 1980, 1981, MORA, Administrative Files, File H2623.

49. Superintendent's Annual Report, 1983, 1993, MORA, Administrative Files, File H2623.

50. John Wilcox, interview by the author, February 11, 1995.

51. C. Frank Brockman to David A. Ritchie, December 5, 1966, UW, Frank Brockman Papers, Accession 1802–72–5, Box 1, File 2.

52. Malcolm F. Baldwin, "The Snowmobile and Environmental Quality," *Trends* 6, no. 2 (April 1970): 15–17.

53. National Park Service, *Final Environmental Impact Statement, Master Plan, Mount Rainier National Park, Washington* (Washington, D.C.: National Park

Service, 1976), 45; Daniel J. Tobin Jr., Statement for Management, Mount Rainier National Park, January 1977, MORA, Administrative Files, File D18; Neil Guse Jr., Statement for Management, Mount Rainier National Park (revised), 1985, 1988, MORA, Central Files, File D18 Statement for Management.

54. Paradise Park Ranger to Assistant Chief Ranger, May 16, 1966, MORA, Administrative Files, File L3415 Recreational Activities; Superintendent's Annual Report, 1972, MORA, Administrative Files, File H2623; William J. Briggle, interview by the author, February 10, 1995; Superintendent's Annual Report, 1991, MORA, Administrative Files, File H2623.

55. Superintendent's Annual Report, 1993, MORA, Administrative Files, File H2623; William J. Briggle, interview by the author, February 10, 1995.

56. T. H. Martin to Roger W. Toll, September 9, 1919, NA, RG 79, Central Files, Box 137, File 12–7.

57. John Rutter, interview by the author, February 3, 1995; Gary Ahlstrand, telephone communication with the author, February 9, 1995.

58. Regina M. Rochefort and Stephen T. Gibbons, "Mending the Meadow: High-Altitude Meadow Restoration in Mount Rainier National Park," *Restoration and Management Notes* 10, no. 2 (Winter 1992), 126.

59. Neal Guse Jr., interview by the author, February 6, 1995.

60. Rochefort and Gibbons, "Mending the Meadow," 121–22.

61. Ibid., 124.

62. "A Profile of Mount Rainier National Park Visitors," undated pamphlet, National Park Service, Cooperative Park Studies Unit, College of Forest Resources, University of Washington.

Bibliography

ARCHIVES

Minnesota Historical Society, St. Paul, Minnesota
    Northern Pacific Railroad Company Papers
    Sigurd F. Olsen Papers
Mount Rainier National Park, Ashford, Washington
    Administrative Files
    Archives: Administrative Records, Eugene Ricksecker Papers
Mount Rainier National Park, Longmire, Washington
    Concessionaire Files
National Archives, Washington, D.C.
    Record Group 48—Records of the Secretary of the Interior
    Record Group 79—Records of the National Park Service
National Archives Pacific Sierra Region, San Bruno, California
    Record Group 79—Records of the National Park Service
Olympia State Archives, Olympia, Washington
    Governor John Rogers Papers
    Governor Albert D. Rosellini Papers
Pacific Lutheran University, Nisqually Room, Tacoma, Washington
    Rainier National Park Company Papers
University of Washington Libraries, Special Collections and Preservation
    Division, Seattle, Washington

Asahel Curtis Papers
Irving Clark Papers
Brock Evans Papers
Henry M. Jackson Papers
Preston Macy Papers
Warren Magnuson Papers
The Mountaineers Papers
Saint Paul & Tacoma Lumber Company Papers

MANUSCRIPTS AND PAMPHLETS

Curtis, Gene. "History of Fort Lewis." Scrapbook. Copy available at Seattle Public Library.

Dodge, J. W. *Washington: The Sound, State, and Its Chief City, Seattle*. Seattle: Crawford and Conover, 1890.

Donnelly, Charles. *The Facts about the Northern Pacific Land Grant*. Northern Pacific Railway Company, n.d.

Harrison, Laura Soulliere. "By Motor through Wonderland: Historic Roads in the National Park System." National Park Service draft report, 1994. Copy provided to author by National Park Service, Cultural Resources Program, Seattle, Washington.

Hartman, John P. "Creation of Mount Rainier National Park." Address delivered at the 37th Annual Convention of the Washington Good Roads Association, September 27–28, 1935, no pagination. Copy available at University of Washington Libraries, Special Collections and Preservation Division, Seattle, Washington.

Helleson, Linda. "The History of Skiing in Mount Rainier National Park." Unpublished typescript. Copy available at Mount Rainier National Park Library, Longmire, Washington.

Lancaster, Samuel C. Report, 1913. Copy available at University of Washington Libraries, Special Collections and Preservation Division, Seattle, Washington.

Moore, O. M. *Washington Illustrated, Including Views of Puget Sound Country and Seattle, Gateway to the Orient with Glimpses of Alaska*. Seattle: Metropolitan Press, 1901.

The Mountaineers, Inc. *The Administration of the National Parks*. Seattle: The Mountaineers, 1922.

"A Profile of Mount Rainier National Park Visitors." Undated pamphlet. National Park Service, Cooperative Park Studies Unit, College of Forest Resources, University of Washington.

Seattle Chamber of Commerce. *Seattle Illustrated*. Seattle: Baldwin, Calcutt, and Blakely, 1890.

Seattle and the Pacific Northwest. Seattle: n.p., 1909.

Seattle, Washington, U.S.A. Seattle: Eshelman, Llewellyn, and Company, 1891.

Washington, the Evergreen State, and Seattle, Its Metropolis. Seattle: Crawford and Conover, 1890.

NEWSPAPERS AND PERIODICALS

Seattle Post-Intelligencer
Seattle Times
Tacoma Daily-Ledger
Tacoma Ledger
Tacoma News Tribune

GOVERNMENT DOCUMENTS AND PUBLIC REPORTS

Brockman, C. Frank. *The Story of Mount Rainier National Park*. Longmire, Wash.: National Park Service, 1940.

Catton, Theodore. *Wonderland: An Administrative History of Mount Rainier National Park*. Seattle: National Park Service, Cultural Resources Program, 1996.

Congressional Record. 1893–99. Washington, D.C.

Department of the Interior. *Annual Report of the Director, National Park Service*. Washington, D.C.: Government Printing Office, 1946, 1947, 1950.

Department of the Interior. *Annual Report of the Secretary of the Interior*. Washington, D.C.: Government Printing Office, 1904, 1906, 1907, 1908, 1909, 1910, 1911, 1914, 1915, 1918, 1923, 1924, 1939, 1950.

Department of the Interior. *Report of the Director of the National Park Service*. Washington, D.C.: Government Printing Office, 1920, 1921, 1925, 1929, 1932, 1943.

Department of the Interior and Washington State Department of Commerce and Economic Development. *Report on Study of the Public Need with Respect* to *Visitor Facilities in Mount Rainier National Park.* Prepared by Harris, Herr, Forster & Company, November 1963.

Mackintosh, Barry. *The National Parks: Shaping the System.* Washington, D.C.: National Park Service, 1985.

McIntyre, Robert. "A Short History of Mount Rainier National Park." Mimeograph report prepared for the National Park Service, 1952.

National Park Service. *Master Plan, Mount Rainier National Park, Washington.* Washington, D.C.: National Park Service, 1972.

National Park Service. *Final Environmental Input Statement, Master Plan , Mount Rainier National Park, Washington.* Washington, D.C.: National Park Service, 1976.

Playground and Recreation Association of America. *Camping Out: A Manual on Organized Camping.* New York: n.p., 1924.

Thompson, Erwin N. *Mount Rainier National Park, Washington, Historic Resource Study.* Washington, D.C.: National Park Service, 1981.

U.S. Congress. House. *Authorizing the Secretary of Interior to Acquire on Behalf of the United States Government All Property and Facilities of Rainier National Park Co.* 81st Cong., 2nd sess., 1950, H. Rept. 2721.

U.S. Congress. House. *Electric Generating System, Mount Rainier National Park.* 72nd Cong., 1st sess., 1932, H. Rept. 98.

U.S. Congress. House. *Road into Mount Rainier National Park.* 58th Cong., 2nd sess., 1904, H. Doc. 631.

U.S. Congress. House. *Washington National Park.* 54th Cong., 1st sess., 1896, H. Rept. 1699.

U.S. Congress. Senate. *Authorizing the Secretary of the Interior to Acquire on Behalf of the United States Government All Property and Facilities of the Rainier National Park Co.* 81st Cong., 2nd sess., 1950, S. Rept. 2448.

U.S. Congress. Senate. *Memorial from the Geological Society of America Favoring the Establishment of a National Park in the State of Washington.* 53rd Cong., 2nd sess., 1894, Misc. Doc. 247.

U.S. Congress. Senate. *To Authorize the Construction of a Hotel and Related Facilities in Mount Rainier National Park.* 86th Cong., 2nd sess., 1960, S.J. Res. 193, May 17, 1960.

U.S. Congress. Senate. *Trespassing on Mount Rainier National Park, Washington.* 57th Cong., 1st sess., 1902, S. Rept. 729.

U.S. House Committee on Public Lands. *Hearings before the Subcommittee on*

Irrigation and Reclamation and the Subcommittee on Public Lands. 80th Cong., 1st sess., September 8, 1947—Salt Lake City, Utah, and September 15, 1947—Mount Rainier National Park, Wash., 1948.

U.S. House Committee on Public Lands. *Concessions in National Parks, Committee Hearing No. 28.* 81st Cong., 1st sess., November 12, 1949.

U.S. House Committee on Public Lands. *Concessions in National Parks, Committee Hearing No. 41.* 80th Cong., 2nd sess., 1948.

U.S. Senate Committee on Interior and Insular Affairs. *Mount Rainier National Park.* 84th Cong., 2nd sess., October 15, 1956.

U.S. Senate Committee on Interior and Insular Affairs. *National Wilderness Preservation Act—1959.* 86th Cong., 1st sess., March 30 and 31 and April 2, 1959.

BOOKS, ARTICLES, AND DISSERTATIONS

Albright, Horace M., and Robert Cahn. *The Birth of the National Park Service.* Salt Lake City: Howe Brothers, 1985.

Anderson, Ada Woodruff. "To the Summit of Mt. Rainier." *Outing* 38, no.4 (July 1901): 390–92.

Aspland, Patricia E., and Katherine A. Pawelko. "Carrying Capacity: Evolution of Management Concepts for the National Parks." *Trends* 20, no. 3 (1983): 22–24.

Baldwin, Malcolm F. "The Snowmobile and Environmental Quality." *Trends* 6, no. 2 (April 1970): 15–17.

Barringer, Mark Daniel. *Selling Yellowstone: Capitalism and the Construction of Nature.* Lawrence: University of Kansas Press, 2002.

Belasco, Warren James. *Americans on the Road: From Autocamp to Motel, 1910–1945.* Cambridge, Mass.: MIT Press, 1979.

Brockman, C. Frank. "The Wonders of Mount Rainier." *Natural History* 37, no. 3 (March 1936): 253–65.

Burton, Hal. *The Ski Troops.* New York: Simon and Schuster, 1971.

Carr, Ethan. *Wilderness by Design: Landscape Architecture and the National Park Service.* Lincoln: University of Nebraska Press, 1998.

Casewit, Curtis W. *The Saga of the Mountain Soldiers: The Story of the 10th Mountain Division.* New York: Julian Messner, 1981.

Catton, William R., Jr. "The Mountain with the Wrong Name." *Etc.: A Review of General Semantics* 11, no.4 (Summer 1954): 299–304.

"Commercial Development in Mt. Rainier National Park." *The Mountaineer* 55, no. 3 (March 1962): 5.

Cutler, Phoebe. *The Public Landscape of the New Deal.* New Haven, Conn.: Yale University Press, 1985.

Dodds, Gordon B. *The American Northwest: A History of Oregon and Washington.* Arlington Heights, Ill.: Forum Press, 1986.

"Dude Ranch at Rainier." *Town Crier,* July 15, 1933.

Everhart, William C. *The National Park Service.* Boulder, Colo.: Westview, 1983.

"Experiments in Freezing." *Etc.: A Review of General Semantics* 3, no. 2 (February 1941): 10–11.

Firsoff, V. A. *Ski Track on the Battlefield.* New York: A. S. Barnes and Company, 1943.

Flink, James J. *America Adopts the Automobile, 1895–1910.* Cambridge, Mass.: MIT Press, 1970.

Flower, Raymond. *The History of Skiing and Other Winter Sports.* New York: Methuen,, 1977.

Gallagher, Leo. "The Old Hotel in Paradise." *National Parks Magazine* 38, no. 196 (January 1964): 4–7.

Haines, Aubrey. *Mountain Fever: Historic Conquest of Mount Rainier.* Portland: Oregon Historical Society, 1962.

Hall, Edwin G. *In the Shadow of the Mountain: The Spirit of the CCC.* Pullman: Washington State University Press, 1990.

Harvey, Mark. *Wilderness Forever: Howard Zahniser and the Path to the Wilderness Act.* Seattle: University of Washington Press, 2005.

Head, Barry. "Is It a Boon or a Boondoggle?" *Seattle Magazine* 4, no. 34 (January 1967): 15–16, 50–51.

Ingraham, Edward S. *The Pacific Forest Reserve and Mt. Rainier: A Souvenir.* Seattle: Calvert Company, 1895.

Ise, John. *Our National Park Policy: A Critical History.* Baltimore: Johns Hopkins University Press, 1961.

Jacoby, Karl. *Crimes Against Nature: Squatters, Poachers, Thieves, and the Hidden History of American Conservation.* Berkeley: University of California Press, 2001.

Johnson, Darryll R. *A Study of Visitor Attitudes toward Initiation of a Visitor Transportation System at Mount Rainier National Park.* Seattle: National Park Service, Cooperative Park Studies Unit, University of Washington, 1990.

Johnson, Darryll R., Karen P. Foster, and Katherine L. Kerr. *Mount Rainier*

National Park 1990 Visitor Survey. Seattle: National Park Service, Cooperative Park Studies Unit, University of Washington, 1990.

Keller, Robert H., Jr., and Michael F. Turek. *American Indians and National Parks.* Tucson: University of Arizona Press, 1998.

Klingle, Matthew W. "Urban by Nature: An Environmental History of Seattle, 1880–1970." Ph.D. dissertation, University of Washington, 2001.

Louter, David B. *Contested Terrain: North Cascades National Park Service Complex, an Administrative History.* Seattle: National Park Service, 1998.

———. "Windshield Wilderness: The Automobile and the Meaning of National Parks in Washington State." Ph.D. dissertation, University of Washington, 2000.

Manning, Harvey. REI: *50 Years of Climbing Together.* Seattle: Recreational Equipment, Inc., 1988.

Martinson, Arthur D. "Mount Rainier National Park: First Years." *Forest History* 10, no. 3 (October 1966): 26–33.

———. *Wilderness above the Sound: The Story of Mount Rainier National Park.* Flagstaff, Ariz.: Northland Press, 1986.

———. "Mount Rainier or Mount Tacoma? The Controversy That Refused to Die." *Columbia: The Magazine of Northwest History* 3, no.2 (Summer 1989): 10–16.

Marx, Leo. *The Machine in the Garden.* New York: Oxford University Press, 1964.

Mason, Jeffrey, David Cole, and David Reynolds. "Limits of Acceptable Change: A Framework for Assessing Carrying Capacity." *Park Science: A Resource Management Bulletin* 6, no. 1 (Fall 1985): 8–10.

McClelland, Linda Flint. *Presenting Nature: The Historic Landscape Design of the National Park Service, 1916 to 1942.* Washington, D.C.: National Park Service, 1993.

McCoy, Genevieve E. "'Call It Mount Tacoma': A History of the Controversy over the Name of Mount Rainier." M.A. thesis, University of Washington, 1984.

McCully, A. Woodruff. "The Rainier Forest Reserve." *Overland Monthly* 55 (June 1910): 552–60.

Mighetto, Lisa. "The Expedition of 1905: Two Hundred Climbers Tackle Mt. Rainier." *Columbia: The Magazine of Northwest History* 4, no. 3 (Fall 1990): 32–36.

Molenaar, Dee. *The Challenge of Rainier.* Seattle: Seattle Mountaineers, 1971.

Morgan, Murray. *Puget's Sound: A Narrative of Early Tacoma and the Southern Sound*. Seattle: University of Washington Press, 1979.

"Motoring Rules and Regulations in the National Parks." *Outing* 72 (August 1918): 334–35.

Muhn, James. "Early Administration of the Forest Reserve Act: Interior Department and General Land Office Policies, 1891–1897." In *Origins of the National Forests: A Centennial Symposium*, edited by Harold K. Steen. Durham, N.C.: Forest History Society, 1992.

Muir, John. "The National Parks and Forest Reservations." *Harper's Weekly* 41, no. 2111 (June 5, 1897): 563–67.

———. "The Wild Parks and Forest Reservations of the West." *Atlantic Monthly* 81, no. 488 (January 1898): 15–28.

Nash, Roderick. *Wilderness and the American Mind*. 3rd rev. ed. New Haven, Conn.: Yale University Press, 1982.

Pease, Lute. "The Way of the Land Transgression." *Pacific Monthly* 18, no. 4 (October 1907).

Pomeroy, Earl. *In Search of the Golden West: The Tourist in Western America*. New York: Alfred A. Knopf, 1957.

Puter, S. A. D., and Horace Stevens. *Looters of the Public Domain*. Portland, Ore.: n.p., 1908.

Rochefort, Regina M., and Stephen T. Gibbons. "Mending the Meadow: High-Altitude Meadow Restoration in Mount Rainier National Park." *Restoration and Management Notes* 10, no. 2 (Winter 1992): 121–26.

Rothman, Hal K. *Devil's Bargains: Tourism in the Twentieth-Century American West*. Lawrence: University Press of Kansas, 1998.

Runte, Alfred. *National Parks: The American Experience*. Lincoln: University of Nebraska Press, 1979.

Russell, Israel C. "Impressions of Mount Rainier." *Scribner's Magazine* 22, no. 2 (August 1897): 169–76.

Sadin, Paul. "Coming Full Circle: The Development of Mount Rainier's Wonderland Trail, 1907–1939." *Columbia: The Magazine of Northwest History* 13, no. 4 (Winter 1999–2000): 24–33.

Salmond, John A. *The Civilian Conservation Corps, 1933–1942: A New Deal Case Study*. Durham, N.C.: Duke University Press, 1967.

Sax, Joseph L. *Mountains Without Handrails: Reflections on the National Parks*. Ann Arbor: University of Michigan Press, 1980.

"Sceva Expresses Park Co. Viewpoint." *Washington Sportsman* 3, no. 9 (November 1937): 7.

Scharff, Robert, ed. *Ski Magazine's Encyclopedia of Skiing.* New York: Harper and Row, 1974.

Schmoe, Floyd. *Our Greatest Mountain.* New York: G. P. Putnam's Sons, 1925.

Sellars, Richard W. "Manipulating Nature's Paradise: National Park Management under Stephen T. Mather, 1916–1929." *Montana: The Magazine of Western History* 43, no. 1 (Spring 1993): 2–13.

———. *Preserving Nature in the National Parks: A History.* New Haven, Conn.: Yale University Press, 1997.

Shaffer, Marguerite S. *See America First: Tourism and National Identity, 1880–1940.* Washington, D.C.: Smithsonian Institution Press, 2001.

Shankland, Robert. *Steve Mather of the National Parks.* New York: Alfred A. Knopf, 1951.

Snyder, Carl. "Our New National Wonderland." *Review of Reviews* 9, no. 2 (February 1894): 163–72.

Spence, Mark David. *Dispossessing the Wilderness: Indian Removal and the Making of the National Parks.* New York: Oxford University Press, 1999.

Steen, Harold K. *The U.S. Forest Service: A History.* Seattle: University of Washington Press, 1976.

Story, Isabelle. "Winter Sports and Sportsmen." *Review of Reviews* 91, no. 2 (February 1935): 61–62.

Sutter, Paul S. *Driven Wild: How the Fight against Automobiles Launched the Modern Wilderness Movement.* Seattle: University of Washington Press, 2002.

Tomlinson, O. A. "Sunrise, Mt. Rainier." *Argus*, December 12, 1931.

Toothman, Stephanie S. "Cultural Resource Management in Natural Areas of the National Park System," *Public Historian* 9, no. 2 (Spring 1987).

Turek, Michael F., and Robert H. Keller Jr., "Sluskin: Yakima Guide to Mount Rainier." *Columbia: The Magazine of Northwest History* 5, no. 1 (Spring 1991): 2–7.

Turner, James Morton. "From Woodcraft to 'Leave No Trace': Wilderness, Consumerism, and Environmentalism in Twentieth-Century America." *Environmental History* 7, no. 3 (July 2002): 462–84.

Unrau, Harlan D., and G. Frank Williss. *Administrative History: Expansion of the National Park Service in the 1930s.* Washington, D.C.: National Park Service, 1983.

Vancouver, George. *A Voyage of Discovery to the North Pacific Ocean and Round the World, 1791–1795.* Vol. 2. Edited by W. Kaye Lamb. London: Hakluyt Society, 1984.

Van Trump, P. B. "Mount Tahoma." *Sierra Club Bulletin* 1, no. 4 (May 1894).

———. "Mount Tahoma Vandals." *Tacoma Daily Ledger,* September 14, 1893.

Waters, Aaron C. "Bailey Willis." *Dictionary of Scientific Biography* 14. Edited by Charles Coulston Gillespie, 402–3. New York: Charles Scribner's Sons, 1976.

Whittaker, Lou, and Andrea Gabbard, *Lou Whittaker: Memoirs of a Mountain Guide.* Seattle: Seattle Mountaineers, 1994.

Winthrop, Theodore. *Canoe and Saddle.* Portland, Ore.: Binford and Morts, 1955; orig. n.p., 1863.

Wirth, Conrad L. *Parks, Politics, and the People.* Norman: University of Oklahoma Press, 1980.

Index

Bayley, George B., 10, 17
Bayne, Richard, 145
Beader, Henry, 45
Belasco, Warren James, 91
Berkeley Park, 94, 150
Big Creek Shingle Company, 53–54
Bill, Harthon L., 119
boosters, 7–9, 41, 63, 115
Boy Scouts (of America), 70, 150
Briggle, William J., 160, 169
Brockman, Frank, 168
Brooker, Ellen, 145
Brougham, Royal, 123
Brower, David, 134–35
BRW Inc., 158
Bryce Canyon National Park, 88, 118
Budd, Ralph, 88
Butcher, Devereux, 130

Caldwell, Hugh M., 73
Cammerer, Arno B.: and access to
    Paradise ice caves, 93; and chal-
    lenge to concession policy, 73–75,
    77; and development at Paradise,
    107; and winter use policy, 121–
    22, 129
campfire programs, 80
camping: and appropriate use, 59;
    by Cooperative Campers, 3, 69–
    70, 72, 76; and harm to vegeta-
    tion, 45; in hotel camps, 78; at
    Paradise, 82, 137; and prospecting,
    52; sites developed under Mis-
    sion, 66, 143
Camp Muir: hiking destination, 92;
    and human waste management,

164; proposed, 39–40; and wilder-
    ness experience, 162–63; and zon-
    ing, 147, 155
Camp of the Clouds, 47
Cannon, Joseph, 30
Canoe and Saddle, 9, 19
Carbon River: access to, 40, 45;
    CWA camp at, 99; hunters at,
    55; and master plan of 1972, 155–
    56; ranger at, 44; trips to, 38, 62
Carbon River Road, 156–58
Carper, Robert L., 140
Carr, Don M., 59
carrying capacity: and automobile
    use, 158–59; effort to increase, 142;
    mentioned in hearing, 134, 142; in
    Paradise Meadows; 171–72; and
    wilderness, 148, 151, 153–54
Casey, Gene, 150
Castner, Joseph C., 101
chairlift, 124–30, 132, 136, 138, 166
Champion International Corpora-
    tion, 167–68
Chapman, Oscar L., 116, 120
Chicago, Milwaukee, and Puget
    Sound Railway Company, 48
Chicago, Milwaukee, and St. Paul.
    See Milwaukee Road
Christine Falls, 36, 65
Civilian Conservation Corps (CCC),
    91, 95–96, 99–102, 107, 109–11
Civil Works Administration (CWA),
    91, 96, 99
Clark, Irving M., 77
Cleveland, Grover, 29
climbing: and campaign for national

National Park Service (NPS)

Tacoma Academy of Science, 11

Tacoma and Eastern Railroad, 35, 48–49. *See also* Puget Sound, Mt. Tacoma, and Eastern Railroad

Tacoma Automobile Club, 32

Tacoma Carriage and Baggage Transfer Company, 33

Tacoma Chamber of Commerce, 11, 53, 97–98, 116

Tacoma Chamber of Commerce and Commercial Club, 40, 62

Taft, William H., 41

Tahoma, 8–9

Tancil, Vernon, 140

T-bar, 108, 127, 130. *See also* chairlift, rope tow, ski lift

Ternes, J. B., 68

Thompson, Erwin N., 140

Thorne, Chester, 32, 65

Timberline Lodge, 115, 124

timber sales, 52–53. *See also* logging

Tipsoo Lakes, 107, 120, 125, 133, 155

Tobin, Daniel J. Jr., 151–53, 159, 169

Toll, Roger W., 77, 170

Tollefson, Thor C., 115–16, 118, 120, 126, 135

Tomlinson, Owen A.: and CCC, 100–102, 105, 110; and concession policy, 115; and master plan, 85–86; and Paradise ice caves, 92–93; and RNPC, 97; and tent cabins at Paradise, 81; and tramway, 83–84; and winter use policy, 107, 122

tourism, 11, 24, 90, 113

tramway, 28, 83–84, 105, 125, 127, 130, 156

transportation service, 3, 73, 76–77, 97

treaty rights (Indian), 55–57, 59

Truman, Harry S., 112, 121

Udall, Stewart L., 135–36

Union Pacific Railroad, 6, 88, 118

United States Geographic Board, 8

University of Puget Sound, 150

University of Washington, 7, 158, 171

unsanitary conditions, 50, 131. *See also* sanitation problem and Public Health Service

U.S. Army, 100–101, 110–11

Vancouver, George, 4–6, 8

vandalism, 10, 22–23, 44

Van Trump, Philemon B., 10, 17, 19, 23–24

Vint, Thomas C., 83, 86–87, 99, 124–26, 132

visitor center (at Paradise), 137–39, 159, 172

Visitor Transportation System. *See* mass transit

visitor use (or visitation, pattern of), 3, 172–73, 176; and crowding, 68, 113, 132, 142, 147; in Great Depression, 90–91; and patronage of RNPC, 61; after World War I, 78

INDEX